Now,
Are You Ready
To Learn Economics?

Now, Are You Ready To Learn Economics?

by Lyndon H. LaRouche, Jr.

EIR News Service, Inc.
Washington, D.C., 2000

LaRouche, Lyndon H., Jr. Now, Are You Ready To Learn Economics?

First printing: November 2000.

Library of Congress Catalog Number: 00-110405
ISBN 0-943235-18-9

Please direct all inquiries to the publisher:
EIR News Service, Inc.
P.O. Box 17390
Washington, D.C. 20041-0390

Cover design: Alan Yue, World Composition Services, Inc.
Cover photo: Hieronymus Bosch (1450–1516), "Hell," detail
of right panel, "The Garden of Earthly Delights" triptych.
(Erich Lessing/ Art Resource, NY)

Printed in the United States of America

EIRBK 2000-2

Contents

Publisher's Preface

AS WE PREPARE THIS edition for press, both the world financial system and the world strategic situation hang by a thread. War, perhaps spreading out from the Middle East, and a spreading New Dark Age loom as what appears to be the unavoidable future of mankind.

It didn't have to come to this. For more than three decades now, American economist and statesman Lyndon LaRouche has put forward the economic science, and the programmatic perspective, which, if adopted, could have prevented such disasters. LaRouche's record of accurate forecasts is unmatchable, especially when combined with the alternatives which he has advanced. Yet both government leaders and American citizens have decided, against their better judgment, to cling to wishful thinking, and to eschew association with LaRouche and his ideas. Opportunity after opportunity was lost, until we reached the present situation—the greatest combined strategic and economic crisis in more than a century, perhaps many centuries.

Nor should anyone think that LaRouche's warnings were just of a general nature. In the fall of 1999, he released a major video presentation, "Storm over Asia," which located the growing conflicts in Central Asia—including the Caucasus, India-Pakistan, and Afghanistan—as stemming directly from the activity of a global financial oligarchy, desperate to try to hang on to power as its system went down the tubes. In the summer of 2000, LaRouche warned once again, as he had numerous times before, that the lack of an economic development perspective in the Middle East, based on water desalination and energy projects, would ensure that that region went up in flames.

The bad news is that the crisis which LaRouche projected would happen, has occurred. The financial crisis is accelerating,

pandemics are taking over huge swaths of the Earth, life expec-
tancies are collapsing, and hallmarks of civilization are disap-
pearing. In the wake of famine and pestilence, has come war.

But there is good news as well. For the collapse of this
rotten financial system provides another, unique opportunity for
those citizens and statesmen who know better, to push the lunatics aside, and take control. Never have institutions such as
the IMF, World Bank, and national central bankers been so
discredited. Never has there been such potential for good ideas,
like the *proven* ideas of LaRouche, to take hold, and provide
the basis for political action. And thinking people still have the
free will to change their fate.

It is with this potential in mind, that *EIR* decided to rush
this current book into print. We are seeking to prepare you,
the citizen-leader and policy-maker, with the ideas required to
rebuild the U.S. and world economy, *after* the ongoing financial
blowout reaches dramatic crisis proportions. The time for you
to study LaRouche, is before the crisis gets worse.

Out of the dozens of major articles Lyndon LaRouche has
written over the past few years, we have chosen three. The first,
most summary in form, is "People First!," a short primer written
by LaRouche at the height of the 1998 financial crisis, when
governments were desperately seeking guidance on what to do.
The second is "Trade Without Currency," a document written
this past summer in direct response to moves by Asian countries,
in particular, to replace the bankrupt IMF system. The third is
almost a book-length document in itself, entitled "The Becoming
Death of Systems Analysis."

It is this last document which readers will find the most
challenging, as it directly takes on, in depth, the axiomatics of
the economic thinking which has driven us into the current
disaster, and counterposes them to the *principles* which must be
followed for the achievement of a lasting prosperity for all nations.

All three documents appeared in *EIR* magazine, and the
first two have already been translated into numerous languages—
among them, Russian, Spanish, German, Italian, French. But,
with the crisis worsening by the day, more must be done.

Face the truth. The major question of this fall 2000 is *not* who gets elected President of the United States. Either Gore or Bush is a total disaster, who will lead civilization to doom, unless an independent force, acting on reason, intervenes to shift U.S. direction. LaRouche is the only voice of reason on the scene. The major question for thinking citizens then—here and abroad—is how they must *change* their thinking about fundamental issues of economy and culture, and put that change into effect *now*. To do that, they must study LaRouche.

To underscore that action is required, we are also printing the latest Call for LaRouche's New Bretton Woods reorganization plan, with a selection of signators.

The total collapse of the financial system, especially the U.S. markets and dollar, is being warned about daily. It could happen any day, any week; it's not worth worrying about when. What is worth doing, is to urgently prepare for what must be done in the face of that collapse. For that, you must read and master this book.

—The Editors of *EIR*
October 23, 2000

Now,
Are You Ready
To Learn Economics?

People First!

October 4, 1998

VERY SOON, THE DOOMED, present international financial system will disintegrate. It can not be managed, or repaired; its doom is certain, and soon. We are already in the final phase of its destruction. This destruction will occur either in a rational way, through merciful, pre-emptive actions by individual governments, or in the most tragic way, spontaneously, and chaotically. Either way, the present financial system is doomed to disappear, very soon.

Under these circumstances, the continued existence of the U.S.A., as of other nations, depends absolutely upon the alacrity with which the government responds with certain required, immediate measures of emergency action.

If the measures specified here are taken, this nation will assuredly survive the crisis, and that most successfully. If the political will to adopt and implement such emergency measures, immediately, is lacking, the nation will be torn apart by the chaos caused by its stubborn refusal to change the present system. If the present posture of clinging to the self-doomed dogmas of "free trade" and "globalization" is not overturned, chaos is already inevitable; in that case, this nation will not survive in a recognizable form.

The following are exemplary required measures.

Reprinted from Executive Intelligence Review, October 16, 1998 (Vol. 25, No. 41).

1.0 General Emergency Policy

When that disintegration of the world's present financial system occurs, the U.S. and other governments, if they are sane, will each consider themselves obliged to take certain, instant, autonomously sovereign, and drastic emergency actions. The immediate purpose of these actions, is to maintain the social stability and general welfare of the nation and its entire population. The rule governing these actions, is: "People first! All the people!"

Using the case of the U.S.A. itself as the example, the case can be stated as follows.

These measures are of four general classes: (a) Emergency measures to ensure immediate and continuing social security, according to the general imperative of the Preamble of the 1789 U.S. Constitution; (b) Emergency measures of general financial and monetary reorganization, measures designed to facilitate the measures designed to ensure general social security; (c) Emergency measures of economic recovery, to maintain and expand the levels of physical-economic output of the national economy, both per capita and per square kilometer; (d) International measures required for this same purpose.

2.0 Emergency Measures of Social Security

2.1. These actions will give absolute priority to the continuity of the essential functions of government itself, but will also give equal priority to maintaining the continuing function of all essential elements of basic economic infrastructure, agricultural operations, manufacturing and closely related operations, and the physical distribution and commerce in those goods and services essential to maintaining the life of persons and households. Enabling action expressed in such legal forms as emergency laws and decrees, will be needed for this purpose.

2.2. These actions must not merely maintain infrastructure, agriculture, manufacturing, household, and related essential physical-economic activity at levels existing prior to the "crash." Immediate steps must be taken, chiefly by initiative of government, to increase the levels of useful output from these categories of activities, this at the expense of forms of services which are not essential to the health of the physical economy and its population. For the case of the U.S.A. itself, these actions will be taken with an eye to the methods of emergency action taken under President Franklin Roosevelt, for the period for World War II.

2.3. Some special, supplementary actions must be taken. These will include a moratorium on financial foreclosures of home-owned residences and closely related, functional essentials of private ownership. This must be complemented by absolute protection of the bank deposits of individuals, up to a specified, modest amount per capita. Similarly, basic health-care programs must be funded to similar effect. The general rule for such and related measures, is to leave the household and small business affairs of the individuals and families at the discretion of the individuals, as much as possible, freeing decisions within this area from the burdensome and complex details otherwise demanded of governmental interference, as much as possible.

3.0 General Financial Reorganization

3.1. The U.S.A., like most nations of the world presently, and most globalized financial institutions, is already hopelessly bankrupt financially. It is not necessary to wait, to see if the bank collapses, to know, already, that this is so. Only desperately wishful fools would deny that to be a fact.

3.2. As in any bankruptcy of a major, once stable economic enterprise, the bankruptcy did not come all at once, but occurred through the cumulative effect of wrongheaded policies, each piled on top of one another, over a long period of time. In the case of the U.S.A. itself, a period of not less than thirty-odd years. Fortunately, the set of principles on which the U.S. economy, in particular, was operating prior to thirty-odd years ago, was predominantly sound in effect. That being the case, we must reorganize the U.S. economy as we would act to bring any essentially sound economic enterprise back to healthful life, by reorganization in bankruptcy.

3.3. The actions to be taken initially, are to eliminate the bad management and the bad policies of practice, and to write off that portion of the total amount of putative present financial obligations, the which must be written off, if the enterprise is to resume the degree of healthy growth it enjoyed status quo ante—prior to thirty-odd years ago.

3.4. In the case of the bankruptcy of the financial system of a sovereign nation-state, there are special rules to be considered, differing from those which might be appropriate to any institution other than a nation-state. Fortunately, in an earlier period the U.S. as a whole was bankrupt, 1787–1789, those implicitly constitutional considerations have already been addressed, principally by U.S. Treasury Secretary Alexander Hamilton's three reports to the U.S. Congress, on the subjects of national credit, a national bank, and manufactures. These rules apply not only as the relevant U.S. precedents, but serve as a model of reference for other sovereign republics.

Although we must give due consideration to debts and assets defined in terms of differing media, the central point of reference for the financial, monetary, and related policies of the U.S. government, especially under conditions such as these, is the sovereign currency of the U.S. government, which can be nothing other than U.S. Currency-Notes issued according to constitutionally prescribed procedures for this. For reasons stated by Secretary Hamilton, that form of currency, and other forms of debt directly incurred as U.S. Debt (rather than other Federal Reserve debt), constitute the primary, absolute obligations of the U.S. government in face of a general financial bankruptcy of the nation, such as that now extant. The "full faith and credit" of the U.S.'s currency and sovereign debt, must be defended, as the premise for the credit-mechanisms employed in coming out of the end of the present international financial system. The role of U.S. currency, on this account, is not limited to the case of the U.S.A.

itself; the special importance of the U.S. dollar is global, still today.

The central principled issue of financial reorganization, is that the defense and deployment of those forms of U.S. sovereign debt, are the financial mechanisms of credit-creation, through which the U.S. real economy shall be revived from its present degenerated, torpid condition.

3.5. With one additional provision, let paper values otherwise, fall as low as they please. "It is only paper, after all." If a bank's net worth is less than zero, we may choose to support its continued functioning, because the sovereign U.S. requires that such a bank exist for the needs of the citizens and economy of that locality. The protection of modest financial and other assets of individuals, households, and certain varieties of enterprises which are defined as essential in physical-economic terms, follows from the same general principle.

3.6. The object is to expand the physical-economic activity and productivity of the economy and of the population as a whole, such that the economy is meeting the needs of the entire population, and also operating above physical-economic break-even levels. To this purpose, U.S. national credit must be supplied, through national-banking methods, radiating through participating private banks, into the relevant enterprises of the nation's government and private sector, as we built up what became the prosperous U.S. economy of the 1950s and early 1960s, from the deep economic-depression levels supplied by Andrew Mellon's policies of the 1920s and early 1930s.

Our nation has done this in the past, has known how to do that in the past, and can apply those lessons to doing the same, or better, once again.

4.0 Economic Recovery Measures

During 1861–1876, again during the economic mobilization of 1914–1917, and during 1933–1945, the U.S. used a combination of large-scale infrastructure-building and science-driver programs in technological progress, with effects whose successes astonished the world of those periods. The leading priorities in organizing a long-term period of successful, global economic reconstruction, are the following.

4.1. Basic economic infrastructure: principally water-management and general sanitation; mass transportation of freight and passengers; power, with emphasis upon increasing energy-flux density and coherence of primary sources; basic urban infrastructure as such; and, national and international mass systems of education, science, and health-care. Large-scale, long-term investment in these improvements in basic economic infrastructure, supply the foundation upon which the potential for real economic growth depends.

4.2. Fostering employment of operatives in basic agricultural and industrial production, with emphasis upon those increases in the productive physical-economic powers of labor which are realized solely through emphasis upon increased rates and levels of per-capita investment in capital-intensive, power-intensive modes of scientific and technological progress.

4.3. Increasing the role of the machine-tool-design sector of production as a percentile of total labor-force employment, and the development of these capabilities to ever higher international standards, and with greater density of efficient delivery into national economies and the localities of those economies.

4.4. Integrating the educational, fundamental research, and machine-tool-design functions of the world's and national economies around science-driver programs, including the aggressive exploration and colonization of nearby portions of our Solar System.

Generations have passed since a very nasty fellow, Harvard Professor William James, wrote of "the moral equivalent" of war. The only true moral equivalent of war, is to mobilize for development of the world's economy, to the benefit of each and all nations of the planet, and to do this in a way we have never mobilized before, except for purposes of war. That, in summary, is the task, the policy which sane governments will adopt now.

On a Basket of Hard Commodities: Trade Without Currency

July 18, 2000

EXCEPTING THE USUAL ROGUES and economics illiterates, influential circles around much of the world are reporting, with ever lessening hesitation, that the presently rotten-overripe, world monetary and financial system, is doomed to an early chain-reaction collapse. Increasingly, among relevant circles outside the U.S.A., world wide, the most notable questions include, how to replace the present global system, and with exactly what?

Consequently, increasingly bold steps in search for a replacement have been taken, in East and South Asia, trends in progress since Malaysia, under the leadership of Prime Minister Mahathir bin Mohamad, has persisted in the clearly successful use of capital and exchange controls. Recent weeks of persisting, desperate, and provocative actions, from U.S. Treasury Secretary Larry Summers and perennial Federal Reserve Chairman Alan Greenspan, have provoked similar discussions currently in progress outside of Asia. These steps point, increasingly, toward the emergence of regional systems of economic cooperation. Such regional efforts, if combined, could serve as building-blocks of

Reprinted from Executive Intelligence Review, August 4, 2000 (Vol. 27, No. 30).

Malaysian Prime Minister Dr. Mahathir bin Mohamad, shown here, has been a leading promoter of moves in Asia to create a replacement for the International Monetary Fund, in the form of an Asian Monetary Fund. So far, those putting together ideas for regional blocs, have tended to propose using "baskets of currencies," to replace the dollar. (Photo: EIRNS/Gonzalez Huertas)

the new world monetary and financial system, once the present International Monetary Fund (IMF) is either sent, mercifully, into bankruptcy-reorganization, or simply disintegrates, soon, of its own accord.

Among those studying the prospect of regional alternatives to the imminently bankrupt IMF, some leading economists have proposed that the precedent, of the former role of the 1945–1966 U.S. gold-reserve dollar in creating a system of fixed exchange rates, might be superseded now by revival of a new system of relatively fixed exchange-rates, which is based upon regional and other "baskets of currencies," instead of the former gold-reserve-based dollar. The presently most publicized proposals in that direction, are those which have come from among the "ASEAN Plus Three" group of nations in Asia, and, secondly, among important circles within continental western Europe.

Similar discussions are in progress among the Organization of the Islamic Conference countries.

In some relevant, leading European circles, attention has been directed to both the IMF Special Drawing Rights (SDRs), and the European Monetary System (EMS) proposal launched jointly by France's President Giscard d'Estaing and Germany's Chancellor Helmut Schmidt, the latter during the late 1970s. It is useful to compare such, and kindred proposals with my own mid-1970s proposal for an International Development Bank (IDB), which attracted vigorously antagonistic attention from sometime U.S. Secretary of State Henry A. Kissinger, and related circles, at that time.

In today's relevant European circles, as elsewhere, it is generally agreed that what President Franklin Roosevelt's U.S. did, to organize a post-World War II monetary system, worked very well, most notably to the benefit of both the U.S. and western Europe. This system prospered until the aftermath of that fateful year, 1963, when Germany's Chancellor Konrad Adenauer was pushed into resigning, U.S. President Kennedy was assassinated, and France's President Charles de Gaulle continued to come under the corrosive pressure of assassination and other attacks, attacks which persisted through the tumultuous cultural and economic paradigm-shift of 1967–1969.[1]

---

1. For those who may have forgotten, the following highlights of the period from the August 22, 1962 assassination attack on President Charles de Gaulle, through the October 18, 1964 rise of the disastrous Harold Wilson as Prime Minister of the United Kingdom, are notable. On October 22, 1962, President John F. Kennedy declared the U.S.-Soviet missiles crisis. The October 28, 1962 establishment of France's Fifth Republic under de Gaulle, is notable. There is the historic January 14, 1963 meeting between de Gaulle and Chancellor Konrad Adenauer. The February 14, 1963 election of Harold Wilson as successor to British Labor Party chief Hugh Gaitskell. A new assassination attack upon President de Gaulle on February 15, 1963. The July 1963 unleashing of that Profumo scandal in Britain, which led to the October 18, 1963 retirement of Prime Minister Harold Macmillan. On April 23, 1963, Chancellor Konrad Adenauer announces his intention to retire in the coming October. On November 22, 1963 President Kennedy is assassinated. This interval, from mid-1962 through the election of Harold

However, it is also emphasized among those who recognize
the urgency of returning to the principles of the pre-1971 types
of international monetary agreements of fixed exchange-rates,
that the U.S. dollar of this year 2000, if compared to the presti-
gious U.S. dollar and economy which still existed while President
Kennedy was alive, is a relatively shabby thing. In addition to
that fact, the fear is, that under either a new U.S. Bush Administration, or a presently unlikely Gore alternative, the worth of
the dollar would sink quickly to incalculable depths. In addition
to those considerations, as relevant circles in Europe and Asia
note, the most conspicuously stubborn current source of resistance to re-establishing a system of fixed exchange-rates, is coming from the U.S.A. itself. *For that latter and other reasons, it
has been mooted that the needed, new monetary and trade system, should use a basket of currencies, as a replacement for the
1945–1965 role of the U.S. gold-reserve-denominated dollar.*

I agree that the model of SDRs could be a leading included
feature of the required economic recovery measures; but, I disagree, although sympathetically, with the suggestion that a basket of currencies could be a successful feature of the urgently
needed reform. Instead of the suggested basket of currencies, I
propose the following two-phased approach to the establishment
of the needed new, global, fixed exchange-rate monetary and
trade system.

I propose, that we structure the discussion of these matters
in the following terms. Let us agree, that, at the present moment,
the agenda for proposed reforms, is organized implicitly around
the notion, that the safe escape from the presently ongoing global
financial and monetary disasters, is likely to occur only in two
distinct, if overlapping, successive stages.

Wilson, is the location of one of the great turning-points in the course of
modern history. The 1968 assassinations of Rev. Martin Luther King and
of Democratic Presidential pre-candidate Robert Kennedy, less than six
years after the Wilson election, and during the approximately half-year
following Wilson's Autumn 1967 unleashing of the first of the series of
monetary crises leading into Nixon's destroying the old Bretton Woods
system, in mid-August 1971, are not to be regarded as the inevitable aftermath of the 1962–1964 interval, but as developments greatly encouraged

That is to emphasize the fact, that, since the tragic blunder adopted by the U.S. Government for the October 1998 Washington, D.C. monetary conference, that government has not only abandoned its earlier options for leading comprehensive monetary reform, but has entered into promoting, most stubbornly, a global financial hyperinflationary spiral, one which has become recently, analogous to that which led into the Weimar Germany commodity-price hyperinflation of March–November 1923.[2] The continued folly of the U.S. monetary and related policies, since the October 1998 Washington conference sessions, aggravated by the conduct and catastrophic outcome of the recent NATO war against Yugoslavia, has ruined much of the U.S.'s former, pre-October 1998 diplomatic potential for playing a constructive leading role in global monetary reform.

Thus, in light of the monstrous degree of degeneration in both U.S. credibility and policy-shaping since October 1998, a feasible reform, if it is to occur at all, were almost certain to come in two successive, regional and global phases.

The first stage, as typified by the ongoing discussion among representatives of the *ASEAN Plus Three* association, is typified by the revival of the 1997 proposal, by Japan's E. Sakakibara, for an *Asian Monetary Fund*. Such a facility is intended, not only as a measure of defense against financial-warfare attacks by hedge

---

by what occurred during that earlier interval.

2. As my associate Richard Freeman has documented the available, pertinent evidence, about the close of July 1923 the German authorities' use of monetary inflation to continue to meet reparations-related payments, produced a phase-shift in the ratio of rates of monetary emission to outstanding financial debt. This unleashed the wild spiral of commodity-price inflation which completed the destruction of the currency itself three months later. The launching of "wall of money" policies adopted jointly by U.S. Federal Reserve Chairman Alan Greenspan and present U.S. Treasury Secretary Larry Summers during the interval October 1998–February 1999, has recently produced a phase-shift between monetary and financial appreciations of the same principled form as the July–August 1923 German case. The recent escalation of inflation in primary commodities, such as petroleum, food, and in real estate, reflects the recent and continuing onset of movement in the direction of a Weimar-style blow-out of both the U.S. dollar and the IMF system with it.

funds and similar speculators. It is also aimed to promote urgently
needed measures of hard-commodity forms of combined trade and
long-term capital improvements among those Asian nations. In
this first stage, we might foresee regional, somewhat overlapping,
groupings of similar outlook appearing, and cooperating among
one another, in various regions of the planet.

The second stage, would be the re-establishment of an effectively global monetary organization, featuring a return to fixed
exchange-rates, to supersede the presently bankrupt IMF system.
This second stage, would be a new monetary system, one assem-
bled on the included initiative of participating regional groups
of nations.

Therefore, examine the issue of "a basket of currencies" in
light of the fact, that the two-phased approach to reform is,
presently, the only visible prospect, if the world still has any
favorable prospect of any kind, during the medium-term decades ahead.

The problem thus defined, is the following.

*As long as the IMF system, and its related attributes exist
in their present form,* the attempt to use a "basket of currencies"
as a substitute for the kind of role performed by the 1945–1963
U.S. dollar, is not a remedy, but a trap. Yet, the world can not
wait until a general monetary reform occurs, to take certain
urgent practical measures of defense against the worst effects of
the presently onrushing global financial and monetary catastrophe. Therefore, at this stage, it has become essential to institute
*preliminary measures which operate entirely outside the supervi-
sion, or other control by the presently doomed, "globalized"
monetary system.*

Hence, today, we need to see monetary reform presently
as a two-step process. The first stage, is the emergence of
regional blocs which operate either outside, or in parallel to
the existing IMF system. The second stage, will be the crucial
role of such regional blocs in constituting a replacement for
the now already hopelessly bankrupt IMF system. In the
interim, measures taken by regional blocs must scrupulously
avoid the ruinous effects which must result, were such measures
to become entangled systemically in the already doomed IMF

system. A prudent man does not remain within a cabin of an already sinking **H.M.S. Titanic.** *The transition must be based upon economic values which exist independently of the present IMF system, and which can assuredly outlive that latter system.*

What Is in That Basket?

In assessing any selection of a basket of currencies, ask the question: "What are any among these currencies actually worth?" A scrupulously crafted answer would be: "Any combination of these currencies would be about as sound an investment as the German Reichsmark was at the beginning of July 1923." In short, the entirety of the present world monetary and financial system, is one gripped by an accelerating rate of financial and monetary hyperinflation in nominal financial assets; it is a system which is presently trapped in a critical boundary-state. We are presently at the verge of general disintegration of the present global system, including most leading currencies, excepting perhaps that of China and a few others, today.

All prudent policies must be designed to protect the credit of national governments from being dragged into the muck in which the present system will be surely buried. In short, the needed advice is: "Don't send good money down the sink-hole with the bad."

The crucial fact upon which all sound economic decisions are now premised, is the evidence which shows that the presently reigning financial and monetary institutions, are so hopelessly and profoundly bankrupt, that the world economy could not be saved without wiping several hundreds of trillions of current U.S.-dollar equivalent from the current, vastly hyperinflated, financial-asset-values account. In other words, outstanding financial claims must be brought implicitly into line with the world's present levels of an estimated hard-commodity valuation of the world's combined domestic product. Without such drastic reductions in nominal financial claims, no economic recovery from this onrushing, biggest and deepest world depression, were possible. As much as the equivalent to $400 trillions in presently extant nominal financial assets of the world at large, will have to be either wiped from the world's accounts, or reduced, by reorganization in bankruptcy, to a mere fraction of their current nominal hard-commodity valuation.

Those claims denoted in such forms as financial derivatives, especially over-the-counter (OTC) derivatives, must simply be wiped from the books, categorically. Claims rooted in so-called "junk bonds" and kindred speculative fancies, must be treated similarly. Much of the international debt created, not by actual purchases, but by synthetic bookkeeping constructions, by administrative mechanisms of a floating-exchange-rate monetary system, must be simply cancelled. Large-scale write-downs in inflated financial value of real estate and other matters must occur. Even much honorable debt, including that actually incurred by sovereign governments, must be reorganized or rescheduled. In general, the total mass of financial claims must be pared down to those rates of aggregated debt-service payments which are consistent with a return to the economic-growth policies prevailing in western Europe and the Americas during the interval 1945–1965.

The principal concerns governing such financial and monetary reorganization, must be to resume and maintain levels of employment, consumption, and production, especially in hard-commodity categories of production and consumption, and to maintain rates of net growth, per capita, and per square kilometer, in hard commodity and related infrastructural qualities, which are consistent with what had been the converging policy-objectives of the governments of the U.S.A., France, and Germany, during the incumbencies of President John F. Kennedy, Charles de Gaulle, and Konrad Adenauer. In other words, the needed reorganization of the presently bankrupt international financial and monetary systems, must amount to a structural reform in composition of categories of employment, investment, and credit-flows, to return to goals and standards which are not inconsistent with the then-current operating objectives of those governments from that time.

Such seemingly drastic and sudden measures are not merely policy options. Such measures are now a precondition for the possibility for continuing anything deserving of the name "modern civilized life."

To those who have not yet thought through the relevant facts, it may seem extravagant to warn, that without such seemingly drastic measures of financial and monetary reorganization, without the kind of reversal of hard-commodity investment and production trends increasingly prevalent today, this planet will soon be plunged into a global dark age, into a downward spiral into sub-Saharan-Africa-like conditions, under which it were likely that world population levels would sink during coming decades, to well below a billion individuals. The alarming, but not exaggerated report of the new level of danger to all nations from global and regional infectious diseases, is to be read by all intelligent governments, and other relevant agencies, as a "marker" reflecting the presently diseased state of the world's economy at large.

This warning will not be considered an extravagant one, by any among those qualified specialists who have studied the physical and immediately related causes for the changes in the potential relative population-density (and life-expectancy levels) of Europe and the Americas since about A.D. 1500. If we consider the cumulative development of infrastructure and productive technology since the mid-Fourteenth-Century New Dark Age, we must recognize that the trends in policy-making under the IMF system since the mid-1960s, have reversed the long-term, net upward demographic trends in the direction of population-levels which had been reached, prior to 1966–1971, which had dominated long swings in European civilization during several preceding centuries. Without reversing sharply the accelerating down-shift in demographically relevant technology of investment and related practice, which has predominated under the IMF system since the mid-1960s, we have recently reached the brink of a global demographic catastrophe.

Such a catastrophe could be averted, even at this late stage, if leading nations of the world were to agree on measures which, in effect, bring the world's economic relations into forms of cooperation comparable to that shared between the U.S.A. and western Europe during the 1945–1965 post-war interval. It were sufficient to return to policies of practice comparable to what we in the U.S.A. and western continental Europe did rather well, if with some ups and downs, during those post-war years. Today, we must add the warning, that such cooperation be based upon a true, essentially global partnership with those nations which have been, until now, the continued victims of the legacy of colonialism, including the neo-colonial practices presently inhering in the common practice of the presently bankrupt IMF system.

The participation of a leading technology-exporting nation, Japan, in the ASEAN Plus Three process, if extended, in fact, into a more general cooperation throughout Eurasia, represents, at least approximately, a "full-set economy" base for high rates of gain in physically defined, per capita, productive powers of labor among all of the partners in such an arrangement. My hope is, that, despite the admittedly lamentable qualities of certain currently predominant preferences for U.S. Presidential pre-candidates, a sane government could emerge in 2001 out of the present, turbulent and mostly disgusting political process ongoing there at this moment, a government which will be a willing, cooperating partner in a global arrangement of the type which the aspirations of the ASEAN Plus Three group imply.

To reach that point in a timely fashion, certain preliminary steps are indispensable. To locate the required measures, we must take into account certain leading lessons from the period preceding the drift into the ruinous, presently bankrupt IMF "floating-exchange-rate" system. We must depart the disastrous changes in policy of the recent thirty-odd years, in preference for lessons to be learned from the successful experience of the 1945–1966 interval.

We are thus, in a condition, in which even many among the world's leading currencies will have to be either simply wiped from the accounts, or put through bankruptcy-reorganization under the authority of a new world system. In this transition, many presently leading currencies are to be, either, systemically reorganized, or, replaced by newly defined currencies and related credit-mechanisms. These currencies can be reorganized or created, so, only by reversing recent trends toward "globalization," by invoking the credit-creating authority of the perfectly sovereign nation-state.

It must be understood, that such reorganization is not the unthinkably radical proposal which some wild-eyed, pro-monetarist hysterics insist it is. As I have said: Either we do this rationally, by will, or the presently onrushing shock-fronts of global financial, economic, political, and social chaos will soon do it for us, whether we choose that outcome, or not.

We have been in similar conditions during the course of the just-concluded Twentieth Century; the present world financial and monetary crisis is deeper, wider, and bigger than anything seen during the Twentieth Century. Also, as in some relevant Twentieth-Century precedents, we shall be obliged to cancel bankrupt currencies from the accounts, replacing those by creating new currencies, new currencies to be established by the sovereign power of nation-state governments.

Admittedly, there is presently, hysterical resistance to any such reform. This is to be seen among politically powerful circles of financier-oligarchical interest, which represent today the same point of view on this matter as those Anglo-Americans, and others, who responded to the outbreak of the 1930s Great Depression, by joining forces to install and consolidate Adolf Hitler in power, during 1933–1934. The relevance of this point is made clear, by contrasting the proposed reform resolved upon by Germany's Friedrich List Gesellschaft in 1931, to the policies of the circles of such representatives of financier-oligarchical interest, as Britain's Montagu Norman, Norman's asset Hjalmar Schacht, New York's Brown Brothers, Harriman, and von Papen.

Today, the policies of the latter class of monetarist opponents of presently needed reforms, today's equivalents of the 1920s and 1930s Normans and Schachts, are represented chiefly, and exactly, by the circles of the Mont Pelerin Society, and such Mont Pelerin Society accomplices as Britain's former Prime Minister Margaret Thatcher, the U.S. Heritage Foundation, and the radical "free trade" fanatics in the U.S. Congress. If these latter, pro-financier-oligarchical forces prevail, as typified, in the U.S.A., by Larry Summers, Alan Greenspan, and the followers of pollster "Dick" Morris today, the world would soon see regimes and conditions worse than those which Europe experienced under Adolf Hitler's reign. *Here, on this point, lies, precisely, the immediate danger to all civilization, as typified by the U.S. Presidential pre-candidacies of Governor George W. Bush and Vice-President Al Gore.*

In this set of circumstances, policy-shapers should study more carefully the more deeply underlying principle behind the approximately twenty-year, 1945–1965, success of the post-World War II, Bretton Woods fixed-exchange-rate system, especially as that system operated in relations among the U.S.A., western Europe, and Japan. In this account, include attention to the fact that the way in which the system was implemented, after President Roosevelt's most untimely death, was vastly inferior to what the result would have been, both morally and economically, had Roosevelt's intentions not been significantly overturned by the successor, Truman Administration. As much of Roosevelt's intentions which were actually adopted, worked to great benefit for both the U.S.A. and western Europe, at least up through the middle of the 1960s. The question now to be addressed, against that background, is: *What are the crucially successful features of that fixed-exchange-rate system, which are fully applicable, as a matter of principle, to the vastly different world conditions of today?*

On the surface, the answer to that challenge for today, is rather elementary, and therefore readily adopted and supported by rational leading political bodies. However, as I shall indicate here, the success of such remedies requires leading roles by experts who also understand certain deeper subtleties of the matter. I explain the distinctions and their implications here.

A Basket of Commodities

In fact, the strength of the 1945–1965 Bretton Woods System, lay in the fact that the standard of value was, *in effect,* a basket of *hard commodities.* The U.S. dollar's strength as a reserve currency, was based upon the assurance that the current obligations against the U.S. dollar would be matched by the combination of an export-surplus plus gold bullion at a standard, fixed price for monetary-reserve gold. The gold-reserve system worked, because it was defended by protectionist and related regulatory measures, both internationally, and within the relevant nations themselves. It was the *physical* strength of the U.S. economy, as measurable per capita, *a strength measured in terms of rates of growth of physical productivity per capita and per square kilometer,* a strength expressed as *periods of high rate of increase in hard-commodity forms of capital formation,* which was crucial for the way in which the U.S. economy performed during the initial two decades of the post-war monetary system. This physical strength, matched with war-torn Europe's needs for both expanded volumes of U.S. agricultural products and machine-tool categories, enabled U.S. credit to stimulate a rate of growth of physical productivity, per capita, in western Europe, a growth from which Europe obtained the means to meet its obligations to the U.S.

In effect, in President Franklin Roosevelt's recovery policies of the 1930s, and in the 1945–1965 Bretton Woods System, the U.S.A. was carrying out the same type of economic-growth policies proposed by Dr. Lautenbach at the 1931 meeting of the Friedrich List Gesellschaft, extending credit to build up the productive powers of its customers, and thus, during 1945–1965, enriching a growing U.S. economy by providing Europe the power to repay the credit extended to it. Thus, Dr. Lautenbach's proposal had been not only congruent with the measures actually taken in the U.S.A. under President Franklin Roosevelt, a Roosevelt legacy which informed the 1945–1965 post-war economic relations between the U.S.A. and western Europe. The point to be stressed, is that the policies of both FDR and Lautenbach, were premised explicitly upon what U.S. Treasury Secretary Alexander Hamilton had defined for the U.S. Congress as the anti-Adam Smith *American System of political-economy,* the same policy represented by the leading Nineteenth-Century economists Friedrich List and Henry C. Carey, and the policies which the Friedrich List Gesellschaft represented in Germany at the time of Dr. Lautenbach's presentation of the proposed policy.

This is essentially the same view expressed by Japan and other current proponents of an ASEAN Plus Three system of cooperation in Asia. Those sectors of the international economy which have the ability to supply nations with the means to increase the latter's productive powers of labor, are to be repaid, according to appropriate medium- to long-term capital funding agreements, out of those gains in per-capita productive powers of labor, which result from the use of the relevant imported technologies.

This had been President Franklin Roosevelt's intention for post-war U.S. aid to nations and peoples he intended should be liberated from the colonialist systems and legacies of Portugal, the Netherlands, the British monarchy, and France. Roosevelt detailed infrastructure-development for Africa as an example of this policy. That policy, as it had been intended by Roosevelt, should become the basis for new forms of cooperation between those sections of the world's economy which have the ability to provide advanced technologies, and less developed regions. This policy-orientation provides the mission-orientation which a new, fixed-exchange-rate, world monetary system must adopt.

A point concerning a fixed-exchange-rate requirement, is to be emphasized, at this juncture. If the discount rate on medium- to long-term extension of international credit exceeds the levels of 1–2% per year *simple interest,* high average rates of hard-commodity capital formation are not possible generally, and, most emphatically, not possible for developing nations as entireties. If the values of relevant currencies are allowed to fluctuate under pressures from financier-oligarchical centers such as London, the general, open-market rate of borrowing-costs must rise accordingly, and must tend to be reflected, even axiomatically, in compounded interest-payment requirements, rather than merely simple interest. In effect, the very existence of a gold-standard system, such as that which London maintained world-wide, until 1931, or, a floating-exchange-rate system, such as that set into motion by President Richard Nixon's decree of August 1971, spells relatively immediate catastrophe for so-called developing nations, and ultimate ruin for the others.[3]

---

3. Typical of the evils fostered by a floating-exchange-rate system, is the swindle by means of which the IMF system looted so-called Latin

In the present situation, where the valuation to be placed on each and every currency of Europe and the Americas, among others, is increasingly in doubt, what constitutes the quality of durable value upon which medium- to long-term, hard-commodity capital formation could be rationally premised? In the celebrated words of Shakespeare's Hamlet: "To be, or not to be: that is the question." When it is, thus, most forcefully demonstrated, that durable forms of economic values, can not be adduced from a quantity of money, where does a measurable valuation of economic activity lie?

Enter, once again, the matter of "a basket of commodities." I mean a "basket of commodities" as that notion implicitly underlies the relative success of the 1945–1965 fixed-exchange-rate monetary system. I mean a "basket of commodities" as U.S. Treasury Secretary Alexander Hamilton's 1791 Report to the U.S. Congress **On The Subject of Manufactures** defined what became known world-wide as *The American System of political-economy.* Just as the success of the 1945–1965 Transatlantic system was premised upon coordinate physical-economic growth in the combined national economies of the U.S.A. and western Europe, so Hamilton, basing himself, via Vattel, on the work of Gottfried Leibniz, based the economic policies of the U.S.A. on the mutual growth of the urban industries and the rural countryside.[4] In short, sound economics premises its measure-

---

America. The London market, which is the center of most of the world's financial speculation, would orchestrate a run against the currency of a nation of South or Central America. Then, the international monetary authorities, would intervene to require a reduction in the value of the targetted currency. Worse, they would then increase the foreign debt of the targetted nation, to compensate the international lenders for the loss in expected debt-service revenues which might otherwise be caused by the forced devaluation. *Thus, since 1971, the nations of South and Central America have, aggregately, paid vastly more debt-payment than they ever actually incurred!*

4. Today, it must be emphasized often, that the U.S. political-economy, and Constitution, echoed the influence of Gottfried Leibniz, and rejected the contrary dogma of John Locke. For example, the use of Leibniz's rebuttal of Locke: "life, liberty, and the pursuit of happiness," in the 1776 Declaration of Independence reflects this, as does Benjamin Franklin's con-

ments of performance upon growth-rates, measured in physical units per capita and per square kilometer, not upon nominal (e.g., financial) prices attached to a list of produced goods.

So, in a situation in which the hard-commodity content among currencies is fluctuating, one has still the option of constructing a synthetic unit of account which is based upon an agreed basket of hard commodities. Thereafter, as currencies fluctuate, it is the currencies, not the commodities, which are given implicitly adjusted values, as based upon the basket of commodities used to define the unit. Such a synthetic unit could serve as the accounting-system of an international credit facility, as, in that sense, the basis for creating a kind of successor to SDRs.

Thus, in the matter of medium- to long-term capital loans for hard-commodity investments, the relevant currencies are priced according to the basket of commodities as a standard. The loan is made in these units, not currency-prices; however, the exporter is credited with that number of synthetic units at the time the product is delivered, and repayments of the loan are determined by the price of the relevant currency, in those units, at the time that specific payment is due.

Thus, in effect, a barter-like system of medium- to long-term lending of hard commodity product, is used to approximate the "gold-reserve plus basket of commodities exported" system which operated in relevant Transatlantic relations during the 1945–1965 interval of a fixed-exchange-rate system.

That is the gist of the matter.

Now, examine the interim use of such a synthetic unit of trading account more closely. Examine the way in which such a unit is to be designed and managed.

It will be obvious to the reader that what is to be said on this account, involves a set of nested approximations of the exact values desired; but, that should not be considered cause for

---

nections to followers of Leibniz in Germany itself, such as Göttingen University's Abraham Kästner. Vattel's influence, on Hamilton and others in the Americas, is reflective of this. (See Robert Trout, "Life, Liberty, and The Pursuit of Happiness," **Fidelio,** Spring 1997.)

reasonable objections. The fact of the matter is, that, contrary to the *Laputa*-like superstitions which certain academic mystics spread to their credulous students at Harvard and Chicago Universities and elsewhere, all prices and related set values in day-to-day economic practice, are never closer to reality, than serving as reasonable approximations; the mythical "right price" exists only in the minds of deluded persons. Contrary to utilitarians such as Jeremy Bentham, there is no asymptotic price-value upon which commodities must tend to converge in a state of "free fall." There are no random numbers in real economic processes, but only the customary charlatans who teach a dogma of random numbers.

The margin of error which may be incurred in adopting an estimated value, such as a standard basket of commodities, should be understood as a reasonable choice made, in effect, by relying upon intelligent management of the relationships by such a qualified agency, and upon an understanding rooted in good faith among the parties to the arrangement.

The Practice and the Theory

The key to establishing a reasonably determined standard unit of account for a basket of commodities, is to reject, from the outset, the reductionist input-output presumption of Britain's Piero Sraffa, for example, that consumption might be represented as a process of production of commodities by commodities. We must examine the way in which combined market-baskets of economic infrastructure (such as public works), combined with household consumption and with technologically progressive, hard-commodity forms of increasingly capital-intensive investments in capital goods of production and physical distribution, increases the relative productive powers of labor, as this is to be measured, in physical product, per capita and per square kilometer. *It is that factor of rate of growth, as expressed in hard-commodity terms, which defines the appropriate notion of assignable economic value.*

So far, so good; but, there is a catch. In some respects, such measurements of growth-rates are relatively obvious; but, therein lies an often overlooked subtlety, to ignore which may have dreadful results. Consider the more obvious kinds of measurements, and then what might appear to some to be the awfully clever subtleties.

The essential calculation to be attempted, in any rational scheme of economic studies, is what is best identified as *the potential relative population-density of the population of the national economy as a whole. The measurement to be derived from this standard, is a measurement of the rate of increase, or decrease of that potential. That measurement defines what should be understood as expressing an underlying notion of economic growth.* The following steps are featured.

Competent study of economic processes begins, not with the production of commodities, but, rather, the production of people. That is to say, with the development of children into becoming, decades later, functioning adult members of the economy as a whole. Indeed, here lies the natural root of the formation of capital.

To structure calculations to this effect, we must define a minimal size of a typical family household, and its included birth and mortality rates. We do this, in order to estimate what is necessary to meet the standard for growth and self-sustained well-being of that population as a whole. One defines the level of technology—e.g., a set of technologies—which allows that population to generate a corresponding net rate of physical-economic growth. We define the relationship between the adult work-force and the total population, as organized in households—that is to say, organized in the way in which viable forms of households produce the emotional and intellectual development which is to be desired in the functioning adult member of society. This establishes a rough standard for purposes of comparison.

One then defines the corresponding structural characteristics of the division of labor in the society as a whole. The first objective, is to estimate the market-baskets of household consumption, infrastructural development (e.g., public works), industrial output, and agricultural output, and to measure these, also, both per capita and per square kilometer of the total territory of the national economy. This defines sets of "market baskets" of the commodities, including professional economic services (e.g., health, education, science) required by each of these broad categories of market-baskets. These categories of consumption, plus waste, are compared with total output of the economy, as measured in the same terms. The obvious comparisons, of *better, less,* or *stagnant,* in rates of increase, follow.

Thus, by applying *a synthetically chosen price* to a household income measured in terms of per capita of labor-force, and also per unit of area, we have a convenient and reasonably reliable method for estimating monetary values. By adding the actual relative free energy generated by production, in addition to costs so determined, we are able to estimate both total output of the economy, and a corresponding, estimated rate of growth. *Insofar as this estimated rate of growth coincides with a corresponding rate of increase of the potential relative population-density, the estimate for rate of growth is sufficiently sound for purposes of accounting and other administrative functions respecting the economy at large.*

Notably, in a rational economy, prices are not set by anarchic free trade, but by human boundary conditions imposed upon the economic process as a whole. These boundaries, by their nature, must be set chiefly by governments.

Typical of such boundary conditions, are so-called "protectionist" measures, such as those former regulations of the economy which have been removed under the influence of the Mont Pelerin Society or kindred fanatics, especially since the January 1969 inauguration of the ill-fated dupe of the Mont Pelerin Society, President Richard Nixon. These protective boundaries were then assaulted, even more savagely, under the 1977–1981 reign of that free-trade and fiscal-austerity fanatic President Jimmy Carter who, with suitable historical irony, launched the chronic indebtedness of the U.S. Government which has plagued the nation since (**Figures 1 and 2**). Similarly, the decline in the percentile of national-income of the lower eighty percentile of family-income brackets, since the 1977 inauguration of President Jimmy Carter, shows a decline in the U.S. popular conditions of life, which corresponds to both the cannibalistic looting of

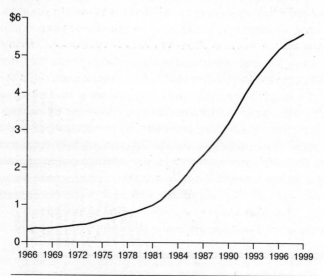

FIGURE 1
U.S. Government Federal Debt Outstanding
(trillions $)

Source: U.S. Office of Management and Budget, *Budget of the United States Government, Fiscal Year 2001, Historical Tables.*

Figures 1 and 2. As these charts show, the rapid rise in the chronic indebtedness of the U.S. government occurred in the wake of the policy blunders of Presidents Richard Nixon and Jimmy Carter.

previous improvements in productive potential, and a corresponding general lowering of the per-capita physical productivity of the labor-force as a whole.

Protectionist measures do tend to increase prices, if only in the short to medium term, as the rabid monetarists never cease in whimpering about this effect. (In the medium to long term, the higher rates of increase of productivity made possible by higher rates of hard-commodity capital formation, result in a secular decline in prices of particular products, while generally improving the quality of those products.) Thus, that increase of

FIGURE 2

U.S. Government Federal Debt Outstanding, Per Capita of Adult Labor Force

(thousands $)

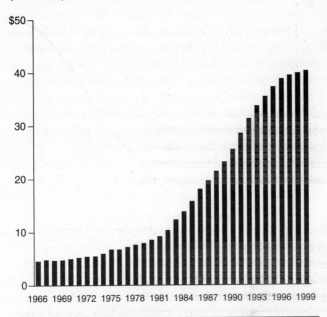

Sources: U.S. Office of Management and Budget, *Budget of the United States Government, Fiscal Year 2001, Historical Tables;* U.S. Department of Labor, Bureau of Labor Statistics, *Employment and Earnings,* June 2000.

prices may be viewed as a rise above a so-called "free trade" level, to a "fair trade" level.

These protectionist, regulatory measures have two indispensable benefits for any economy whose government is sane enough to impose them. First, they provide direct or indirect protection to the income-levels, and therefore to the potential productivity expressed by households of operatives; this, combined with rational taxation policies, ensures that the incurred price, by government and the private sector, of maintaining the desired level of potential relative population-density, is secured.

Second, in so acting, governments create the market for those medium- to long-term public and private capital investments, on which improvement in the potential relative population-density depends.

Promotion of the general welfare, which is an integral part of the fundamental constitutional law of the U.S.A.—if recently a flagrantly violated obligation—demands that those measures which are needed to ensure the improvement of the potential relative population-density of the nation, per capita, and per square kilometer, are taken. This includes public works which no private entrepreneur could undertake as a business proposition; clear, on this account, is the responsibility of the sovereign government for the conditions of life and work of *all of the people* and of *all of the territory of the nation.*

Thus, public policy, so shaped, creates what wild-eyed dupes of the Mont Pelerin Society denounce as a willful, arbitrary intervention by the state, into the affairs of trade. Without those measures which that Society abhors, no modern economy could survive for long. Indeed, three decades-odd of that Society's ideological influence on leading governments, have created a wasteland of the once-successful economies which had grown up in the U.S. and western Europe during the 1945–1965 interval.[5] In this process, the physical-economic values which have been destroyed, since the mid-1960s, include much of the entire net development of modern infrastructure, agriculture, and industry, in Europe and the Americas, during the preceding hundred years, since the middle of the 1860s. Even two World Wars of the Twentieth Century did less net damage to Europe and the Americas than has been done by the "globalizers" and "free

---

5. Typical of charlatans, those U.S. and other influentials who have made a wasteland of once powerful agro-industrial economies, say that this has occurred only because the "old economy" was doomed, anyway. Like the typical charlatan, they point to the vast speculative bubble in physically worthless "New Economy" fluff, as proof that the economy which can no longer afford to pay its social welfare and infrastructural bills, is "really" much a bigger and better "new suit of clothes" for our Emperor.

trade" ideologues during the recent thirty-odd years, since the ruinous first Harold Wilson Labour government came to power in the United Kingdom.

The same question may be posed in a different way. During the recent thirty-odd years, a hitherto successful form of trans-Atlantic monetary system devolved into the present stage of bankruptcy. What were the measurements which were used by policy-shapers to bring about thirty-odd years of such folly? What was so fatally wrong in the assumptions of the institutions which have been most successful, since the mid-1960s, in bringing about this magnificent, global catastrophe?

Those institutions are well-known, readily identified: they are the Mont Pelerin Society and its co-thinkers. The result which that influence has produced, does not reflect merely the accidental result of a sometimes erroneous reading of the dials by the policymakers and managers; the catastrophe which their influence has brought about, is *systemic* in nature. It is the very design of the instruments which have been used to misguide the preponderance of the world's most influential policy-makers and managers, which has brought this epochal calamity upon the planet. It is, thus, the financial accountants and the preponderance of the economists, whose systemically aberrant standards of practice have brought this catastrophe upon us: systemically.

Granted, that the statistics lately reported and interpreted by the U.S. government and others, are, like the insane chatter about "information society" and an actually mythical "New Economy," deliberately, and increasingly falsified, that with the same intensity of desperation otherwise found commonly among those attempting, through fraudulent lures to investors and creditors, to conceal a thoroughly ripened corporate bankruptcy. However, such currently popularized frauds by governments, central bankers, and relevant others, are a symptom of the underlying problem, not the root-cause.

From this standpoint, what has failed is the empiricist system of bookkeeping, often taught under the misleading name of "economics," the system of bookkeeping which came to be associated with such names as Adam Smith, Jeremy Bentham, et al. Here, we go beyond the practical superficialities of a design of a basket of commodities, into the underlying principles, the theory, of the same matter.

The relevant theory is, in summary, as follows. I have stated these points at length, repeatedly, during the five decades since my first consolidation of my original discoveries in the field of physical economy. These need to be said again, until the students have mastered these concepts to the point of knowing the ideas, rather than merely learning the words of the description.

1. In the science of physical economy, as first defined by the relevant 1671–1716 work of Gottfried Leibniz, the specific distinction of the human species from all others, is the fact that only mankind is able to increase its species' potential relative population-density—its power—by an act of will.

   In mankind's increasing power within, and over the universe, the relevant act of will is expressed as the discovery of what is proven to be a universal physical principle. It is through man's accumulation of that knowledge, and man's development of the forms of co-operation through which that knowledge may be applied, that our species is permitted to choose willful changes in our species' behavior, through which our species' power in and over the universe is increased in clearly measurable forms. This measurement is expressed essentially in terms of man's increased ability to exist, per capita and per square kilometer of the territory under control of a society.

2. Insofar as the term "physical science" is used to indicate what today's classrooms accept as a notion of modern mathematical physics, both the existence of living processes and of human beings, are to be regarded as *systemically impossible mathematically*. Since the work of Clausius, Grassmann, Kelvin, Helmholtz, Maxwell, Rayleigh, and Boltzmann, among others, during the course of the Nineteenth Century, it had become conventional to say, that from the standpoint of mathematical

physics so defined, the physical universe is governed by a universal law of entropy. The cause for perpetual embarrassment of the advocates of that statistical dogma was, that neither living processes, nor those processes which set mankind apart from other living processes, obey such a rule of universal entropy. Since living processes and persons are a highly efficient part of the universe, certain doubts respecting the honesty and sanity of the advocates of universal entropy had to be mentioned, even at the risk of seeming impolite, of even triggering the expectable explosion of freakishness from the pompous ass teaching the dogma to the class.

In economics, real profit of an economy as a whole, is expressed as a marginal increase of the potential relative population-density. This marginal gain corresponds to what is usefully termed the *free energy* of the system. Thus, like the living, upward evolving biosphere, the process is characteristically *anti-entropic*. In real economies, the question whether a taken profit is actually a profit to that economy as a whole, finds its answer in comparing nominal profit-rates with the actual free-energy ratio expressed in terms of correlatives of increases of the potential relative population-density. Indeed, most of the profit attributed to the U.S. economy since August 1971, especially since January 1977, has been, in net effect, in the form of pseudo-growth: the burning-up, so to speak, of past investments in basic economic infrastructure, productive capital, and so on, as merely nominal, financial-accounting profit taken out of the real economy, rather than actual free energy added to it.

3. Therefore, chiefly in response to the popularization of the Kelvin-Clausius dogma of statistical thermodynamics, apologists for what is still considered today a conventional view of mathematical physics, adopted the term *negative entropy,* a term sometimes abbreviated as *negentropy.* According to the popularized, statistical approach to such subject-matters, the prevailing assumption is, that: a) universal negentropy does not exist; b) processes which appear, statistically, to exhibit negen-

tropic behavior, are able to do so only by increasing the
rate of entropy in the environment in which they operate.
Ludwig Boltzmann's development of ideas in that direction, and the impact of Boltzmann's influence upon his
students, notably Erwin Schrödinger's pathetic views on
the principles of living organisms, are a notable illustration of the point.

4. Since the 1948–1952 interval, I have rejected these generally accepted mathematics classroom views on entropy
and negative entropy, defining them as reflecting the
influence of what is to be recognized, specifically, as the
social disease of neo-Kantian Romanticism: the denial
of the existence of those consciously apprehensible forms
of cognitive synthesis, upon which discoveries of universal principles depend absolutely.[6] The paradoxes which
show prevailing dogma on entropy/negentropy to be
pathological, compel us to recognize that *the principle*

---

6. My initial focus, from early 1948, was against the use of the term
"negentropy" by Norbert Wiener. That same year, my attention broadened
to include the problematical systemic features of Professor Nicholas
Rashevsky's mathematical biophysics, and also that of Oparin. My views
respecting the relevant systemic characteristics of living processes were,
and remain in the vein of Louis Pasteur and Vladimir Vernadsky. My
preference for Vernadsky's views on biogeochemistry, over the contrary
view of Oparin, Rashevsky, Schrödinger, et al., does not represent the last
word on Vernadsky's own development of this subject; my associate, Dr.
Jonathan Tennenbaum, has been digging out, translating, and assessing
some important later writings by Vernadsky on the principles of both living
and cognitive processes. Notable is a September 1938 paper, whose title
Tennenbaum has translated as **On the Fundamental Material-Energetic
Difference Between Living and Nonliving Natural Bodies in the Biosphere.**
So far, the principal defect in these later writings by Vernadsky, is an
inadequate appreciation of the relevant implications of those discoveries
of Bernhard Riemann which latter contributed greatly to all of my own
work on related issues of the science of physical economy. All of my relevant
work of the 1948–1953 interval, was principally a reflection of my earlier
refutation of I. Kant's attacks on the work of Gottfried Leibniz; hence, my
recognition of the popularized notion of universal entropy as the fruit of
neo-Kantian Romanticism.

of life is a universal physical principle in and of itself, in the sense that the revolutionary work of Carl Gauss's student and follower Riemann defines the notion of a multiply-connected manifold. I have added my own original contribution to the science of physical economy, that *the principle of cognition is also a universal physical principle.* Since, as Vernadsky has presented the case for the biosphere, the anti-entropic principle of living processes, is categorically superior to non-living, statistically entropic processes, and since, as the economic history of scientific discovery shows, characteristically anti-entropic cognitive processes are superior to otherwise merely living processes, these two, respectively distinct universal physical principles, of *life* and *cognition,* must be located in their corresponding place in the body of physical science as a whole.[7]

5. At first glance, the changes in behavior which enable society to increase its potential relative population-density, are a matter of observable changes in the relation-

---

7. I use anti-entropic in the same sense as I define the physical geometry of Riemann as anti-Euclidean, rather than the customary and epistemologically clumsy "non-Euclidean." Such distinctions in terminology are not merely more precise choices than the conventional ones. The lunatic effort to replace living man by devices allegedly exhibiting "artificial intelligence," has no different basis than stubborn, blind faith in defining the physical universe as fully explainable in terms of the hereditary, aprioristic, axiomatic assumptions associated with today's generally accepted, reductionist-deductive schemes of classroom mathematics. It was the Leibnizian legacy of anti-Euclidean physical geometry, as transmitted from Kästner to his student Gauss, to Riemann, which permits us to recognize that it is physics which must govern mathematics, rather than the other way around. The banning, by Riemann, of all *a priori* notions, such as those of space and time, from geometry, and the replacement of such notions by experimentally validated discoveries of universal physical principles, such as life and cognition, has been the breakthrough which opened the door to a saner understanding of the meaning of "physical universe," one in which the existence of those living cognitive beings called people, need no longer be held in doubt.

ship between the demographically defined individual person and nature. Thus, we measure matters in terms of changes in physical values per capita and per square kilometer of surface-area. From this vantage-point, we can estimate the increase in productive powers of labor, as having the form of a change in the characteristic curvature of that Riemannian physical-space-time geometry which represents the current state of scientific and technological development of practice. In this view, the addition of a valid new universal physical principle, changes the characteristic curvature of the physical-economic domain of action. The synthesis of a validated universal physical principle, which occurs only through the sovereign, hypothesis-generating processes of individual cognition, thus becomes the form of human action, by means of which mankind's power in and over the universe is increased.

6. However, closer examination of the matter shows, that we can not limit this function of cognition to the matter of validatable discoveries of universal physical principle. Since notions of universal principle can not be transmitted solely by means of sense-perception, *the ability of society to cooperate in the selection and use of discovered physical principles, depends upon replication of the cognitive act of discovery of a principle by one mind in the mind of another*. This replication, as it occurs in circumstances such as those of Classical humanist forms of education, is known to us as a body of experimentally validated universal principles of Classical artistic forms of composition. Through those forms of art which reference the cognitive processes of mind, rather than mere sense-perception (e.g., sensual forms of pleasure and pain), we foster the forms of insight needed for effective collaboration in producing and promoting the universal physical principles upon which the anti-entropic increase of mankind's potential relative population-density depends. These Classical forms include not only what are

customarily regarded as the combined plastic and non-plastic art forms, but also the development of literate forms of language, the study of history, and of other matters of statecraft, as well.

7. Thus, the manifold of such universal physical and Classical-artistic principles represents the principled medium through which mankind acquires both the physical principles and principles of cooperation on which the increase of our species' potential relative population-density depends.

8. Three crucial points of economic policy are to be derived from the foregoing considerations. A) That the principal human source of economic growth is the education of the young, a span of development which, for the case of the most advanced economies of the mid-1960s, occupies approximately the first quarter-century of the life of increasing portions of the total population of newborn individuals. This means not only a Classical humanist form of scientific and artistic education in schools and universities, but conditions of family and community life which are emotionally and otherwise suited to the promotion of the self-development of the cognitive powers of the young individual. B) Thus, the student's reliving the re-enactment of validated original discoveries of universal physical principle, and the related role of university-centered fundamental research programs as the principal driving force for proliferation of further scientific and technological progress of the economy as a whole. C) The crucial role of the individual private entrepreneur (as distinct from the often *Golem*-like, publicly held stock corporation and holding company), especially those occupied with the kinds of machine-tool practice related to design of proof-of-principle experiments, like the comparable case of the progressive individual farmer, in pushing forward *the suitably impassioned process of technological progress*. A sane form of modern economy demands that the state create the

regulated environment and basic economic infrastructure in which the function of the sovereign cognitive powers of the individual, serves as the cutting edge of technology-driven, increasingly capital-intensive forms of economic progress at large.

Thus, this form of science-technology-education-driven economic growth, is, by its nature, Riemannian in form. The addition of validated new discoveries of universal physical principles, expands the multiply-connected manifold of universal physical principles being applied. That shift in the manifold is expressed, characteristically, by a change in the implied physical-space-time curvature of action within that economy. This shift, in turn, is reflected in the anti-entropic form of increase of the potential relative population-density. It is the rate of change, the rate of increase of productivity so defined, which is the substance of the anti-entropic "free energy" ratio upon which the continued generation of true, rather than fictitious profit depends.

Those eight points summarily identify the setting within which the discussion of real rates of economic growth is to be situated.

The Global Division of Labor

As the cases of China and India underscore the point, most of the world today is imperilled by a shortage of currently usable land-area relative to large concentrations of the world's existing population. The obvious present barriers to improvement of the condition of life of the majority of the world's population, are to increase the ratio of usable to total land-area, to increase the potential population-density of those land areas, and to accelerate the effective rate of scientific and technological progress in the modes of production and household and community life.

To this end, we require the adoption of several rule-of-thumb policy agreements among nations. 1) That the number, scale, and intensity of "volcanoes" from which scientific and technological progress is erupting, must be greatly increased, and the fertility of those sites increased. 2) That, to make possible the assimilation of such scientific and technological progress, the required basic economic infrastructure (e.g., water management, power, transportation, education, health care) must be provided in all of the areas targetted for high rates of gain in productivity and living standard. 3) That the creation of long-term credit for relevant purchases of scientific and technological progress and build-up of needed infrastructure, must be greatly expanded, to enable flows from those places in which the relatively highest rates of technological progress are being generated, into the areas of greatest need and opportunity for such development of land-areas, populations, and productive economy.

This means that related policies must be crafted from the standpoint of looking approximately a quarter-century ahead. This forward span will come to be expressed in the terms of long-term credit advanced for relevant categories of capital improvements. This will represent a desperately needed new chance at life, for a shabby relic of a civilization now at the verge of destroying itself.

Such a program of global reconstruction, will echo the best features of economic cooperation between the U.S.A. and western Europe during the 1945–1965 interval. It must also represent an improved way of thinking about economy, including a sweeping, contemptuous rejection of everything associated with, or resembling the axiomatically irrationalist, *Conservative Revolution* dogma of existentialists such as Schopenhauer, Nietzsche, Martin Heidegger, Friedrich von Hayek, Ludwig von Mises, Norbert Wiener, John von Neumann, Maurice Strong, and the Mont Pelerin Society's ideologues generally. That is to say, we must think of economy in terms of physical economy, rather than placing the emphasis on nominal financial assets, and must view economy as expressing mankind's increasing power within and over the universe we inhabit. It must also express a recognition of the role of the forms of cooperation based upon the cultural principles of cognition, rather than the perverted notion of man as Hobbesian-like, of man as self-degraded into being a mere beast-like creature ruled by pleasure and pain.

There must be a new, deeper, richer conception of the notions of strategy, military and otherwise. The actual cause for warfare in the history of modern European civilization, has been nothing other than the struggle of modern oligarchies to subjugate either one another, or, more generally, to either keep populations in the condition of virtual human cattle, or, as today's Mont Pelerin ideologues do, to return mankind to such a human-cattle-like political and social condition. The insurgency of that treasonous asset of the British monarchy, the Confederacy, to destroy the U.S.A., and to ensure the perpetuation of chattel slavery, is typical of the causes for just wars, such as that led by President Abraham Lincoln, just as Europe's belated agreement to the conditions of the 1648 Treaty of Westphalia, defined the premises in international law for as much civilized life as has actually existed within extended European civilization since that time.

Today, the principal danger to civilization is from that London-centered, global financier oligarchy, which has adopted the proliferating dupes of the Mont Pelerin Society's "free trade" dogma as the instrument for destroying the existence of the sovereign nation-state, reducing the scale and life-expectancies of the majority of the human population, and degrading the survivors chiefly to the status of human cattle, of virtual Nintendo-addicted Yahoos. Those dupes, are in fact fascists, just as much as Adolf Hitler before them. If that oligarchy and its right-wing dupes, were to succeed in imposing their globalization, "free trade," and shareholder-interest ideologies, civilization would soon cease to exist on this planet for a generation or more to come. To defeat that oligarchy in that, its evil, neo-imperial enterprise, would be the only just cause for warfare among nations at this historical juncture. Otherwise, the world has no further, justifiable need of warfare, except in necessary defense of a peaceful order among sovereign nation-states.

The time has come to bring forth on this planet, the rule of man's affairs by a partnership among a community of perfectly sovereign nation-state republics, republics committed to that promotion of the general welfare which is outlined in the opening paragraphs of our 1776 Declaration of Independence, and the Preamble of our Federal Constitution. Among nations so united in a community of principle among perfectly sovereign nation-states, no justified war could occur. The principle, the general welfare of all of the people, and their posterity, of each nation, and the general welfare of each member of the community of such nations, is the only visible means by which a planet-wide state of affairs suitable for human beings can be brought into existence.

In such a community, the jewel of all civilization, is the development of the perfectly sovereign cognitive powers of the individual person. The promotion of the development of that individual, those powers, and the realization of the benefit each might contribute to present and future humanity, must be the conception which motivates all our shaping of economic policies. That must be the case in fact; that must be a shared understanding among the parties.

A basket of commodities, as I have outlined that case here, is thus to be understood as a shared commitment to do good. *The issue of economy is, therefore, not the exact price to be placed on any commodity, but the good will expressed in the way a reasonable estimate of a fair price is adopted.* On that basis, a reasonable price for a unit basket of commodities, will be the right price in practice.

Reality vs. Fiction

The Collapse of the U.S. Economy over the Last 30 Years

The following charts come from the September 2, 2000 address by Lyndon LaRouche to a conference of the Schiller Institute in Northern Virginia.

Collapse Functions

FIGURE 1
A Typical Collapse Function

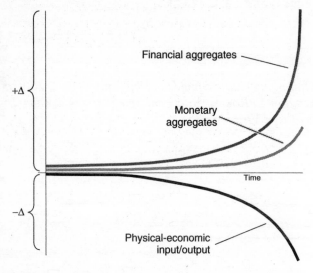

A typical collapse function, showing the interrelated process of increase in financial aggregates, increase in monetary aggregates, and the collapse of physical-economic output and consumption.

FIGURE 2

The Collapse Reaches a Critical Point of Instability

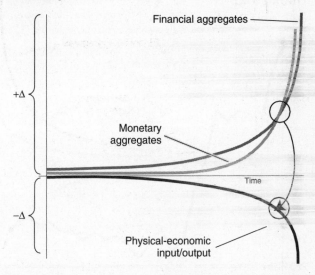

This figure shows the collapse function at the point where the hyperinflationary rise in monetary aggregates overcome the rate of increase in financial aggregates.

U.S. Production Collapses
Over the Last 30 Years

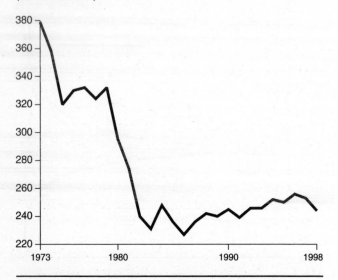

FIGURE 3

Industrial Energy Consumption per Household

(Millions of BTUs)

Sources: U.S. Department of Energy, *Monthly Energy Review*; U.S. Department of Commerce, Bureau of the Census, *Population Surveys*, various years.

These parameters are merely exemplary of the collapse in quality and quantity of industrial production, and the associated clear decline in standard of living for U.S. workers.

FIGURE 4
Number of Paychecks To Purchase New Car

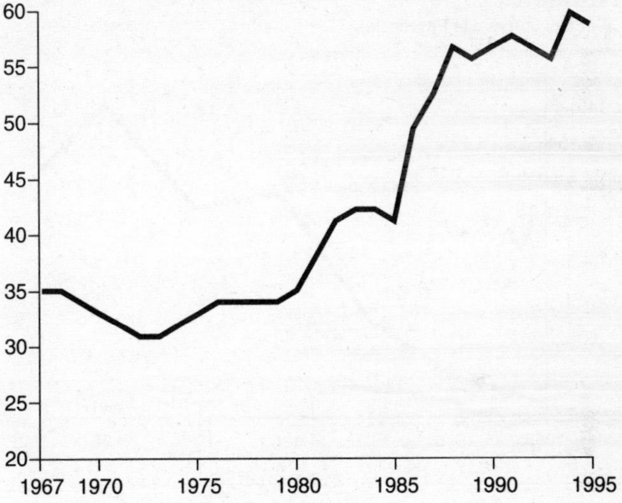

FIGURE 5

Combined Home, Car, Food, and Health Insurance Premium Payments

(Percent of Average Paycheck)

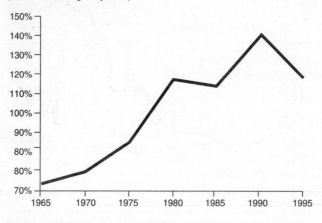

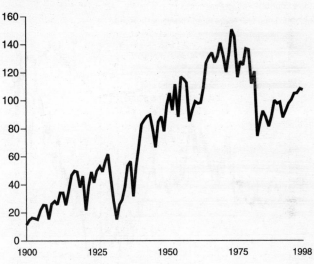

FIGURE 6
U.S. Steel Production
(Millions of Tons)

Source: American Iron and Steel Institute.

Hyperinflation Is Underway

FIGURE 7

Oil Price Skyrocketted in Wake of Big Mergers

Oil price, West Texas crude
($ per Barrel)

millions-line under figure head-Helvetica Reg 7/12

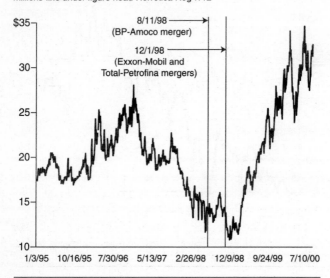

Source: *Wall Street Journal.*

Here you see the oil price increase in the wake of hyperinflationary speculative activity on the markets.

FIGURE 8

Weimar Hyperinflation, Wholesale Price Index (1913 = 1), March-November 1923

Logarithmic scale

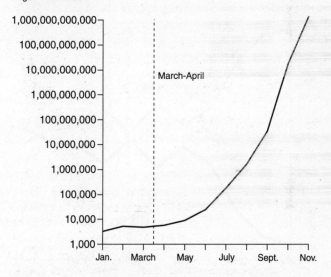

The classical model for hyperinflationary blowout in commodities is the Germany model, which you see above, and which the U.S. economy is headed for.

Volcker's 1979 Interest Rate Hike Had a Lasting Destructive Effect

FIGURE 9

America's Richest 20% Now Make More than the Other 80%

(Percent)

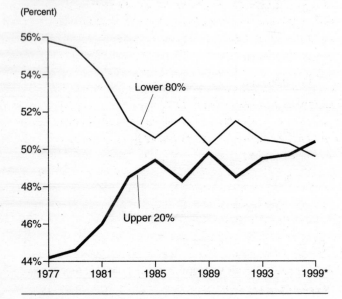

*Projected
Sources: Congressional Budget Office; *EIR*.

See the steep decline in the percentage made by the lower 80% of income brackets after 1979, the year Volcker raised rates through the sky.

FIGURE 10
Prime Interest Rate, Monthly Averages
(Percent)

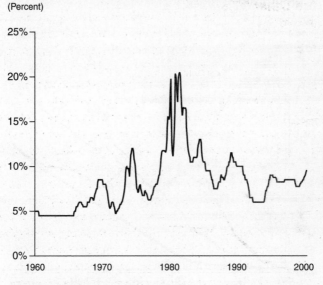

Source: Federal Reserve.

Usurious interest rates killed industries and caused debt to riddle the economy.

What Grew in the U.S. and the World Was Debt

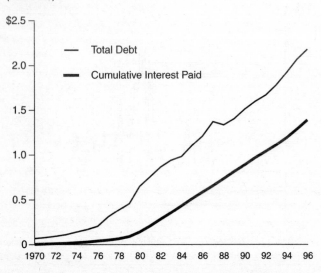

FIGURE 11

Developing Sector Debt Outstanding, and Cumulative

(Trillions $)

Source: World Bank.

FIGURE 12
Rise in Debt for Each $1 Growth in GDP

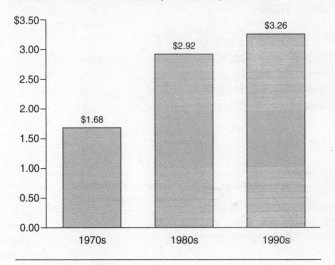

Sources: U.S. Federal Reserve, *EIR*.

Today, Asset Price Inflation, On the Markets, Is Beginning To Go into Commodities

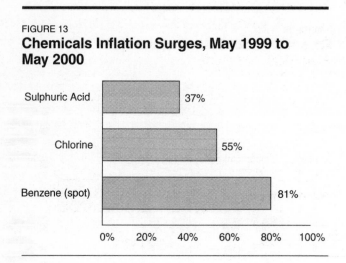

FIGURE 13

Chemicals Inflation Surges, May 1999 to May 2000

FIGURE 14
Plastics Inflation Surges, May 1999 to May 2000

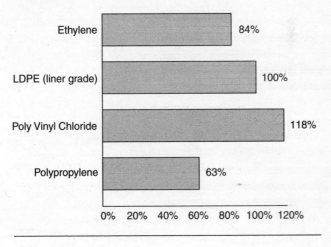

Money Went to Speculation, Not Production

FIGURE 15

Mergers and Acquisitions vs. Manufacturing Expenditures for New Plant and Equipment

(Billions $)

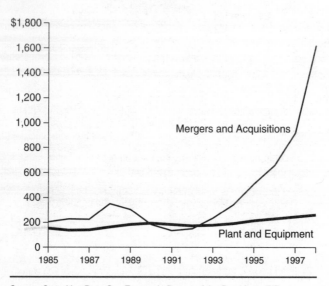

Source: Securities Data Co., Economic Report of the President, *EIR*.

FIGURE 16

U.S. Labor Force, 1970-99; Non-Productive Overhead Grows

(Millions of Workers)

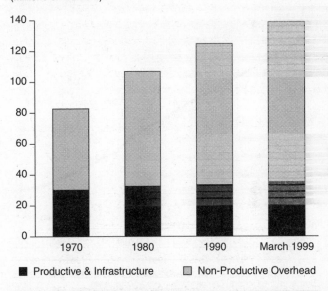

Sources: Bureau of Labor Statistics, Department of Labor; U.S. Department of Education; American Medical Association.

Meanwhile, Vital U.S. Infrastructure Underwent Collapse

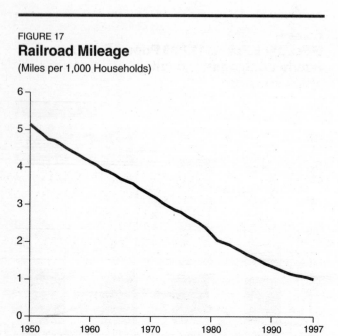

FIGURE 17
Railroad Mileage
(Miles per 1,000 Households)

Sources: Association of American Railroads; U.S. Department of Commerce, Bureau of the Census, *Population Surveys*, various years.

FIGURE 18

Hospital Beds per 1,000 Population Overall, and in Community Hospitals

(Beds per 1,000 People)

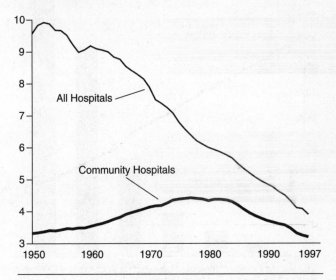

The U.S. Population Increasingly Lives on Debt

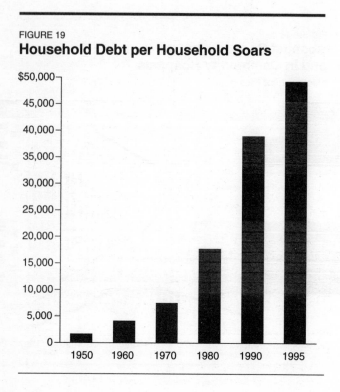

FIGURE 19
Household Debt per Household Soars

FIGURE 20
U.S. Debt per Household

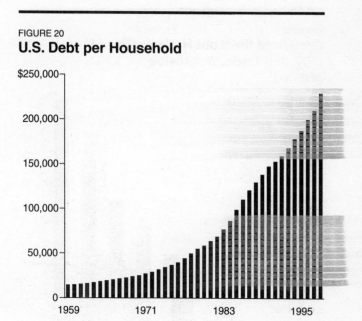

Source: Federal Reserve, *EIR*.

And, the Entire U.S. Economy Is Indebted to the Rest of the World

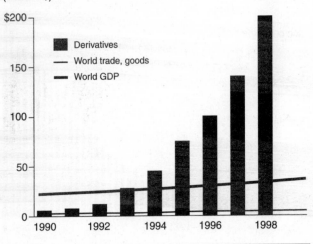

FIGURE 21
Growth of the Bubble: Derivatives Versus GDP and Trade, Worldwide
(Trillions $)

Sources: World Bank, *EIR*.

You see here how money is flowing into speculation (derivatives are likely undercounted massively).

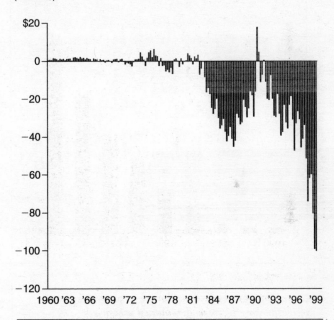

FIGURE 22
U.S. Current Account Balance, 1960-99
(Billions $)

Source: U.S. Department of Commerce.

The Current Account Deficit, shown here, measures the net trade deficit and other obligation the U.S. owes other nations. It is now too much ever to be repaid.

The Eurasian Land-Bridge

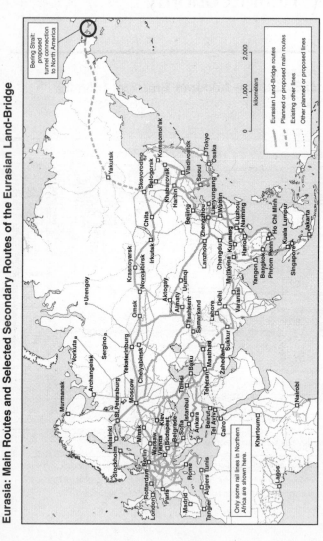

FIGURE 23
Eurasia: Main Routes and Selected Secondary Routes of the Eurasian Land-Bridge

The Eurasian Land-Bridge is the premier world project required for a worldwide economic recovery, which would revive the economy on a global scale.

Financial Aggregates Dwarf
The Real Economy

FIGURE 24
Financial Aggregates Are Ten Times the Gross World Product
(Trillions $)

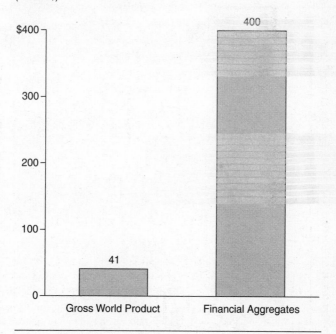

Source: *EIR* Estimates.

NEW ACCOUNTING STANDARDS ARE IMPERATIVE

The Becoming Death of Systems Analysis[1]

March 2, 2000

ON THE DAY ON which, existing money goes out of existence, as in Weimar Germany 1923, but this time more or less worldwide, what do the existing accountants do?

If we are to recover from the social effects of the currently onrushing disintegration of the present world financial and monetary systems, radically new methods of cost accounting will be required for private enterprises, as also for governmental and related kinds of institutions. The previously used, linear, "connect the dots" tactics, of both financial accounting and of systems analysis, must be abandoned, and replaced. A new standard must be adopted, for cost-accounting, budgetary, tariff, taxation policies, national-income estimations, and related practices.

The pivotal question of all competent cost accounting, is: *What causes an increase in the net physical value of the productive powers of labor?* For a moment, put aside calculations made in terms of nominal, that is to say financial, prices. Think solely in terms of *physical contents of market-baskets* of goods and

---

Reprinted from Executive Intelligence Review, March 31, 2000 (Vol. 27, No. 13).

1. The writing of this long-intended report was prompted by my invitation to make a video-webcast, keynote address, by satellite, for the accountants of Lima, Peru. I wish, once again, to thank my hosts for that occasion.

services; measure inputs, as costs (inputs), and as outputs, in those physical terms. Instead of the common practice, of simply comparing ratios of prices of nominal inputs and outputs, seek to define the processes which determine a succession of changes in ratios of physical outputs to physical inputs. As measured in those terms, which increases, or decreases, in specific qualities of expenditure for infrastructure, production and distribution of product, and of which kinds of products, have neither beneficial, nor detrimental impact upon the functionally determined *rate of net physical output,* as the latter may be measured *per capita* of both total labor-force and population, and *per square kilometer* of a nation's, or region's surface-area?

Competent answers to those questions, lie outside the domain of a cost accounting based upon financial analysis, and outside the tyranny of those recently popular, pseudo-scientific hoaxes known as the "systems analysis" of the late John von Neumann and the statistical "information theory" of the late Professor Norbert Wiener. In the circumstances defined by the present crisis, we can no longer tolerate those faulty practices, which have been generally accepted standards of professional and related practice for much too long.

Formerly, this same issue, as expressed in physical terms, had been, for many decades, the most crucial, deeply underlying feature of a systemic conflict frequently erupting, between competent U.S. entrepreneurs and Wall Street's styles in financier management, a conflict reflected in the fierce battles which used to be fought, in happier and better times, between the industrial corporation's relatively competent production management, on the one side, and, on the other side, the usual Wall Street super-cargo squatting in the finance department. Usually, the latter were so obsessed with the proverbial bottom line on this year's balance sheet, that they mustered little patience with discussion of the way in which the productivity of the enterprise was actually, *physically* generated.[2]

---

2. The type of view expressed by Wall Street, was also sometimes expressed by a family-ownership whose relationship to the enterprise had assumed a parasitical character, as merely rentier ownership, the latter of

Germany's Transrapid maglev system could provide the high-speed transportation of the future. It is the kind of technology that fits LaRouche's criterion for all competent cost-accounting: "What causes an increase in the net physical value of the productive powers of labor?" (Photo: Thyssen Henschel)

Many among what had once been formerly successful enter-prises, including national economies, which later, eventually failed, had been led to that latter calamity by continuing the very policies which had ruined them, by such presumptions as the delusion, that pleasing shareholders' gains, as shown on "the bottom line," showed that the recent trends of policy-making in force should be continued. In such cases, the root of the ultimate disaster, is most simply identified as a fallacy of compo-sition: the fallacy of assuming that what might appear to be true

the type more disposed to take the cow's milk, than breed the herd which sustains that flow of milk. The slide of old family ownership unto decadence, and, frequently, takeover by Wall Street-minded so-called chief executive officers, was fostered by the tendency of such follies to arise among decadent elements of family ownership, or as an expression of so-called "shareholder interest" generally.

in reading of *nominal* cost-price ratios in the short term, or in
the small, measures the *physical* result of present policies in the
long term, and in the large. Too often, this fallacy of composition,
this delusion, continued to reign, up to the point that the disaster
struck, disaster caused by just such policy-trends. In short, a
frequent cause of the bankruptcy which occurred in some such
cases, was the cumulative impulse of decadent ownership and
chief executive officers, to increase current short-term profits,
by curtailing those investments, and curtailing payments of those
elements of incurred cost, on which the long-term future of that
enterprise had actually depended. Such were the self-doomed
navigators, who charted a long journey on the presumption that
estimates made for small areas, showed, in effect, that the Earth
is flat. Among those fools, such delusions were often admired
as expressions of "fiscal conservatism."[3]

Today, over the course of the recent quarter-century or so,
the failure, by governments, many leading corporations, and
public opinion, to grasp the nature of those issues, is the cause
for the increasing loss of simple competence of today's managements, among an increasing ration of the leading aerospace and
other manufacturing firms. This includes many among the

----

3. The way in which the U.S. has careened into the present threat
of its national bankruptcy, has been, in significant part, a result of free-
traders' "fiscally conservative" changes in budgetary, trade, tariff, regulatory, and tax policies, during the course of the recent thirty-five years.
The trillions of dollars of unpaid costs for maintaining the nation's basic
economic infrastructure, sharp cut-backs in the highly gainful Kennedy
space program, and the looting of accumulated investment in the productive
physical capital of agriculture, manufacturing, and other categories, has
drawn down the physical-economic productive potential of the nation's
economy to such low levels, that, without a science-driver sort of national
crash program, the U.S. could not regain the early 1970s' levels of physi-
cally-defined, long-term national productivity, in less than one or two
generations. The fact that the U.S. and the London financial centers have
prospered, for a time, through looting the physical wealth of the world
piratically, under a thirty-year reign of a floating-exchange-rate monetary
system, is not proof of success, but only of our folly in tolerating such
arrangements, and, thus, of our ability to reach that present, global state
of affairs, in which a world economy soon comes down around our ears.

world's automotive giants. A presently accelerating, already widespread collapse in both long-term and short-term product-safety factors, is an expression of this. A key factor in promoting the latter trends toward such increasing incompetence, among both corporate managements and governmental budget-management, has been the growing popularity of the fad known as "bench-marking," the substitution of computerized "mathematical modelling" and related "cost reducing" tactics, for the indispensable, science-driven, engineering-based approach to product design and production management.[4]

An hysterical, frankly pagan-religious quality of blind faith in the existence of an "information"-driven economic growth, and related sort of faith in the alleged miracles of "globalization," are expressions of such currently popular forms of economic dementia. The most extreme expression of that growing incompetence of the economic programs of both governments and shareholder interest, is the hyperbolic rate of increase, of the disassociation of nominal shareholder and market-index values from physical economic reality, as my now-widely circulated "triple curve" illustrates that point in the simplest possible, summary way.

As the present world financial and monetary system is now careening toward its inevitable, early disintegration, the old issues between production management and the financial and accounting departments, now assume a qualitatively new importance. These considerations are now crucial, for defining the principles which must guide the urgently needed, global economic recovery, out from under the preceding thirty years of globalized overlordship, by a parasitical, floating-exchange-rate monetary system.

That presently doomed, globalized world financial system, the floating-exchange-rate system of the past three decades, can not be rescued. The Titanic is already doomed; among sane persons, the only tolerable policy is that of bringing the passengers and crew, freed of the grip of the doomed system, into safety.

---

4. The strike ongoing at Boeing, at this moment of writing, expresses exactly these issues, and in the clearest way.

A sudden, relatively convulsive reorganization of the world's finances, monetary systems, and trade-relations, is the only hope to be foreseen among those nations which prefer that their nations survive the sinking of the doomed, present form of the International Monetary Fund's (IMF's), world-dominating, financial and monetary system.

The way in which the nations could actually be pulled safely out of the doomed system, should be obvious, from the lessons of experience, to any reasonably literate person above sixty years of age today.[5] To know which system is to be preferred, we have to compare the way in which Franklin Roosevelt led the U.S.A. out of Wilson's, Coolidge's, and Mellon's Great Depression, and compare the net relative successes of the pre-1966 Bretton Woods, with the catastrophe which has unfolded since August 1971.[6]

We must immediately return to the kind of monetary system which worked fairly well (for the U.S.A. and western Europe, at least) during the 1944–1966 interval, the old, protectionist, fixed-rate, Bretton Woods system. We must scrap all of those post-1971 changes in economic, financial, monetary, and trade policies, which have been introduced since the August 1971 beginnings of the now hopelessly, systemically bankrupt, present world monetary system.[7] This must include an immediate rever-

---

5. In the U.S.A., for example.

6. As I have repeatedly stressed in earlier reports on the subject of a "New Bretton Woods" system, the political feasibility of any sudden choice of emergency remedies for a systemic crisis, has usually depended upon use of precedents recognized from earlier successful actions of that general type. So, the stunning success of the U.S. economy's rise to world leadership as an agro-industrial power, stunned much of the world, including post-1876 Russia, Germany, Japan, and others, into copying crucial features of the Carey-List-Lincoln, anti-free-trade model of the American System of political economy. So, Franklin Roosevelt used both the lessons of the U.S. economic mobilization for World War I, and the protectionist legacy of President Lincoln and Henry C. Carey, to pull the U.S. out of the 1930s Great Depression and through World War II.

7. The term "systemic bankruptcy" is to be used as I use it here, only to describe an entity which is both already incurably bankrupt in its present form, and whose bankruptcy, if not yet officially recognized, is coming about through characteristic, systemic features inhering in the pol-

sal and elimination of all agreements launched in support of so-
called "globalization." That revival of the best features of the
original Bretton Woods system, is not a matter of opinion; it is
a matter of choosing survival over what would be nothing other
than clinging hysterically to a hopelessly failed, and doomed
system. Otherwise, a virtually planet-wide, now imminent new
dark age for humanity, were inevitable for a generation or more
to come.

All of the types of necessary emergency actions needed,
again today, to put a bankrupt world system through an effective
bankruptcy reorganization, were foreseen by President Franklin
Roosevelt and key advisors, up to the point of his most untimely
death. We must presently go beyond the measures which were
actually carried out under the 1944–1964 phases of development
of the old, pre-1971, economic-protectionist period of the Bretton Woods monetary system; but those pre-1964 precedents do
provide a model for the first emergency actions to be taken. To
those actions we must add, very quickly, other actions which
had been intended by that President Roosevelt, but which were
cancelled by the Truman administration almost immediately
after Roosevelt's death.

To appreciate those 1944 designs of intentions for a post-
war monetary system, one must take into account the points
of similarity of the world then, and now. The similarity lies,
essentially, in the fact that, at the time, we had to revive both the
U.S. and European economies from the conditions accumulated
under the exhausting conditions of the post-Versailles Great
Depression and prolonged general war. The world economy
today, especially that inclusive of both Europe and the Americas,
is, systemically, in as ruined a state, or even worse today, if in
a somewhat different form, and from somewhat different causes,
than at the close of World War II. Despite the important differences between the Marshall Plan-led recovery of both the U.S.
and western Europe, and today's circumstances, the framework

---

icy-shaping structures of that entity. In such a case, the posture of reserving
judgment until a bankruptcy is formally conceded to have occurred, is a
childish evasion of truthfulness.

of the needed emergency action establishing a new monetary order, is approximately the same.

However, so that what Roosevelt intended, is accurately understood, some words of caution must be inserted. In reviving the successful features of the pre-1959 form of the old Bretton Woods system today, we must take into account the chief flaws in the changes made in Roosevelt's policy, to which I had referred, above. Take into account the elements of Roosevelt's post-war policies which were summarily discarded, during the indecent, brief interval immediately following his most untimely death.

There were three such chief, categorical errors in post-Roosevelt U.S. policy of practice during the Truman years: First, the failure to shut down the Portuguese, Dutch, British, and French colonial systems and their relics, as Roosevelt had intended should occur immediately, on the ending of the war. Second, the militarily unnecessary, counterproductive, and otherwise foolish and cruel, dropping of two fission bombs on the helpless civilian populations of Japan's Hiroshima and Nagasaki. Third, the failure to launch a forced-draft rate of immediate and rapid conversion of our war-time industrial potential, without losing a step, as Roosevelt had intended.

Despite those terrible errors introduced under President Truman, the immediate need then, as Roosevelt had understood this, was to rebuild a shattered post-war world economy, not only the economy of war-torn western Europe, as the task defined by the leading post-war mission-orientation of the U.S. economy. Thus, those Roosevelt intentions which were put into effect, worked, as far as they were applied. Today, a similar outlook means, that we must implement Roosevelt's own intentions in full, as far as that is appropriate today. Leading developing nations from the so-called developing sector, must be leading partners with the U.S.A., Europe, Japan, and Russia, in establishing and administering the revived form of the newly revived, pre-1968–1972 form of the former, economic-protectionist Bretton Woods system, of cooperation among perfectly sovereign nation-state economies.

Today, such a new monetary system will provide the indispensable policy-framework of opportunity, for a long wave of global real economic growth, as measured in physical terms, per capita and per square kilometer. So far, so good. Then, having given ourselves such an opportunity to take the road to economic recovery, how shall we manage that journey? That situates the task of reformed cost accounting doctrine and practice, as set forth in the following summary of the crucial issues to be considered.

1. Monetary Policy and Cost Accounting

To understand the way in which the needed new world monetary order must be administered, we must begin by defining certain axiomatic principles. For purposes of introducing the argument, I define the meaning of the term "axioms," if but briefly, as in first approximation, in the sense of the definitions, axioms, and postulates of a deductive form of Euclidean classroom geometry. My substitute for such a system of axioms, constitutes the principles of what has become known as the LaRouche-Riemann model of *physical economy*.

In a moment, I shall begin the account of how this discovery occurred, and show how and why the notions of cost accounting being presented here came into being. Yet, before I begin that account, a few words of caution must be presented to the reader.

The subject-matter presented here could not be delivered in a customary textbook-modelled style. The textbook style depends upon early agreement, between writer and reader, on an initial set of axiomatic assumptions. Thereafter, the customary type of report, proceeds from those variously stated and implied assumptions, never leaving them, deriving its conclusions from a series of facts, as the initially stated general assumptions determine the way in which those facts are adapted, to conform to the opening set of assumptions. In this case, the very nature of the subject-matter demands that the writer, in Socratic fashion, tear up sets of what had been the reader's own putatively customary axiomatic assumptions, one set after the other. This obliges both the writer and the reader to share the relevant successive experiences of tearing up customary assumptions which must be uprooted, and presenting the way in which those assumptions are replaced by the generation of the new, alternate, axiomatic and related assumptions, which comprehension of the subject-matter requires.

As I have just said, this task requires a Socratic approach; it also requires that the reader be supplied the means to live through, successively, the relevant discoveries on which comprehension of the final result depends. That is the course followed for this presentation of the subject-matter.

That word of caution stated, I proceed now, by first stating the significance of that term, "LaRouche-Riemann model of physical economy," then showing how that "model" provides an indispensable kind of guidance toward the needed new forms of generalized cost-accounting practices. I begin that now, by introducing the principled conceptions upon which that LaRouche-Riemann model was founded.

My original discoveries in the science of physical economy, which I made during 1948–1952, were prompted by my study and rejection of Norbert Wiener's "information theory." I was prompted to undertake that study, by my recognition of the fact, that Wiener's axiomatic assumption was readily refuted by even the ordinary industrial experience of day-to-day increase in the productive powers of labor, gains generated through scientific and technological progress, in industry. My resulting original discoveries, led me, in late 1952, to recognize a certain special degree of coincidence between those discoveries, and the kinds of *anti-Euclidean* geometry defined by Professor Bernhard Riemann in such locations as his 1854 habilitation dissertation.[8]

---

8. Bernhard Riemann, *Über die Hypothesen, welche der Geometrie zu Grunde liegen,* [On The Hypotheses Which Underlie Geometry] **Bernhard Riemanns Gesammelte Mathematische Werke,** H. Weber, ed. (New York: Dover Publications reprint edition, 1953) pp. 272–286. Sundry English translations exist. The significance of *anti-Euclidean* is that, whereas, so-called non-Euclidean geometries substitute new postulates for those of Euclidean geometry, Riemann, following such predecessors as Benjamin Franklin's one-time Göttingen University host, Abraham Kästner, and Kästner's pupil Carl Gauss, eradicated all of the aprioristic definitions, axioms, and postulates of a common classroom Euclidean geometry, thus establishing a family of hypergeometric, multiply-connected manifolds. The

My own original discoveries in physical economy, had followed the same track I had employed, a decade earlier, in a youthful defense of Leibniz's method against the reductionist method and conclusions of Immanuel Kant's series of *Critiques*. My 1948–1952 attack on Wiener's hoax, had proceeded from my recognition of the fact that Wiener had merely echoed the same fraud as Kant before him, if in a more radically positivist, and vulgar way. Late during 1952, after recognizing that my own original discoveries, could be best restated in a Riemannian form, I redefined the Leibnizian science of physical economy accordingly.

A summary of the relevant features of my attack on Wiener's cultish notion of statistical "information," shows the relevance

---

result of that, was a geometry of physical space-time, in which only experimentally validated universal physical principles, held axiomatic authority. Hence, as Kästner had argued, the result is an *anti-Euclidean* geometry. It should also be noted as bearing upon the following discussion of cost-accounting principles, that since the discoveries of Johannes Kepler and Gottfried Leibniz's discovery of a calculus whose characteristic is regular, but not constant curvature, the assumption that space-time geometry should be defined by a specific curvature, such as spherical or hyperbolic, defines only a formal, non-Euclidean geometry, whereas, as Kepler, Leibniz, Kästner, Gauss, and Riemann emphasized, no one choice of characteristic curvature can be both complete and universal. Riemann's habilitation dissertation made this an explicit principle of a hyper-geometry of multiply-connected, physical-space-time manifolds. I was led to the relevant re-examination of Riemann's dissertation, by a months-long, exciting and yet frustrating study of an English translation, by the dubious Philip Jourdain, of Georg Cantor's 1897 **Contributions to the Founding of the Theory of Transfinite Numbers.** It was only many years later, that I worked through Cantor's most relevant, clear-headed, earlier writings, such as his 1883 **Grundlagen** and 1887–88 **Mitteilungen.** It was at that later time, that I recognized the significance of not only the hateful Leopold Kronecker, but also the mephistophelean theosophist Rudolf Steiner, in driving Cantor to the brink of the episodic insanity suffered during his later years. More careful reading of Riemann's dissertation, late in 1952, led me to recognize the need to regard universal physical and Classical-artistic principles, as equally the axiomatic features of a multiply-connected physical-space-time manifold, respecting the human individual's and species' functional relationship to the universe at large.

of that discovery to cost-accounting methods. In the later re-
finement of that discovery, during 1952, I recognized the appropriateness of applying Riemann's wonderful work to enhance
the application of my own discoveries in the field of economics.[9]

As I have already noted, above, already in 1948, from the
outset, I was encouraged to make the attack on statistical information theory, by my recognition of a crucial vulnerability in
Wiener's fabrication of his hoax; I saw the readiness with which
even the elementary economics of industrial production, refuted
Wiener absolutely. The point was, that society's ability to increase mankind's power over nature, both per capita and per

---

9. Hence, the usage *LaRouche-Riemann Model*. As was emphasized,
above: even prior to my reencounter with Riemann, in 1952, my definition
of validatable universal principles was not limited to physical principles;
it included Classical-artistic principles of composition as well. This view,
of the coherence of universal physical and Classical-artistic principles, as
representing a single domain of *reason,* reflected my adolescent and later
wrestling with the defense of Leibniz from the single central argument of
all of Kant's *Critiques.* It was the need to define a manifold representing
both physical and Classical-artistic principles, which impelled me to adopt
a Riemannian manifold's model, as the needed way to represent my discovery of that combined multiple-connectedness. In the strictest, if seemingly
paradoxical sense, this was a new posthumous discovery made by Riemann
himself, based on my own work of 1948–1952. Applying what I had
adopted as his cognitive state of mind, his cognitive outlook, as ably reflected in his dissertation, the generation of my solution (for the problem of
representing the efficient multiple-connectedness of universal physical and
universal Classical-artistic types of principles), was made intellectually manageable. The significance of that for cost-accounting principles, will be shown
at a later point in this present report. This itself represented a new discovery of
universal principle, made by applying Riemann's thus posthumously-made
discovery to my own paradoxically preceding ones. Hence: LaRouche-Riemann method. As for the legitimacy of attributing such a posthumous discovery to Riemann, one should refer to his own posthumously published philosophical papers, in **Werke,** pp. 507–538, passim. Such is the real meaning of
the principle of time, when time is situated within the domain of persons
still living within the multiply-connected domain of cognitive relations, the
domain of timeless, causally ordered relations among minds dwelling cognitively, like the figures of Raphael Sanzio's **The School of Athens,** in the simultaneity of such an eternity of the past, present, and future.

square kilometer of surface-area, was a reflection of those cognitive powers of the individual human mind which set mankind absolutely apart from, and above the learning capacities of all lower species, the higher apes included among the categorically sub-human types. From the standpoint of production, this unique power of the individual member of the human species, is expressed, most simply, by the individual mind's capacity to generate validatable discoveries of universal physical principles.

This qualitative gain in mankind's per-capita power over nature, is the source of humanity's power to willfully increase its *potential relative population-density,* as no other living species can. These discoveries can not be generated by mere learning, nor by any use of deduction. They can be generated solely by means of that non-deductive, cognitive process, which exists only within the sovereign mental capacities of the human individual, that as a sovereign individual. This is the source of what we recognize as the impact of corresponding, qualitative leaps in the quality of technological progress in agriculture and manufacturing. Typical expressions of this, are revolutionary changes in choice of employed physical principle, in the design of products, and in the processes of production as such.

The function of the human individual's cognition to this effect, is most simply expressed in the form of an axiomatic change in belief, as such a change is typified, in first approximation, by a validated, externally imposed change in the set of definitions, axioms, and postulates of a deductive form of classroom Euclidean geometry, as in a so-called non-Euclidean geometry.

2. Cognition, Science, and Productivity

As we now turn to the body of this report, I shall first state, once again, as I have in various earlier published locations, the essential distinction between mere learning, and its transmission, of which the higher apes, are capable, and the processes of cognition, a capability unique to the human species.

After that, I shall examine the needed principles of cost-accounting in two successive, preliminary steps. First, I examine this in terms of the phase-spatial characteristics of increases in productivity, as these are driven by new applications of universal physical principles; after that, the scope of the presentation is broadened, to take into account the powerful role played by application of ideas in the form of Classical-artistic principles of composition. In the first stage, our focus is upon the functional characteristics of universal physical principles in determining the individual's functional relationship to nature, as per capita and per square kilometer. In the second stage, the emphasis shifts to the determining role of universal principles expressed in such forms as principles of Classical-artistic composition, in governing the social relations through which the individual's relationship to nature is determined. In the latter stage, we take into account the functional, physical-economic role of the costs necessarily incurred in developing the individual mind, and also social relations, to the degree needed to foster both scientific productivity and its efficient, physical-economic application by society.

In summary of the immediate, first series of points to be developed:

The essential, categorical distinction, separating human societies from animal ecologies, is the increase of society's power over nature, per capita and per square kilometer, through cooperation in the fostering and application of discovered universal physical and related principles. The ability to discover and cooperate, in terms defined by such discoveries, is an indispensable source of all willful improvements in the potential relative population-density, and conditions of life of the human species. The generation and sharing of such universal discoveries of principle, is the fruit of a quality unique to human individuals, the power of cognition, as distinct from, and opposed to mere learning, or to mere "sharing of information."

Thus, this faculty and practice of cognition by individuals, defines the absolute separation of the human species from all lower forms of life. Here lies, thus, the only rational definition of *human nature*. Here, in individual cognition, lie all the supposed secrets of humans' behavior, as individuals, as agents of cooperation, and as entire societies. The only rational definition and analysis of political economy, is, therefore, the study of the functional characteristics of those social processes, by means of which the fostering of cognitive propagation and sharing of universal principles, prompts long-term increases in the potential relative population-density of mankind. All conceptions pertaining to these matters, must find their axiomatic roots in the characteristics of such cognitive processes.

Therefore, we now derive the principles of cost accounting, in accord with that. We begin with emphasis upon the generation and nature of universal physical principles.

What is Cognition?

The discoveries of what are later experimentally validated as universal physical principles, are prompted by the demonstration of those qualities of paradoxes, the which are not susceptible of formal solution by means of the deductive and other methods of the philosophical reductionists. Such paradoxes are typified by the ontological paradox of Plato's **Parmenides** dialogue; the impossibility of solving such by deductive methods, is typified by the case of that historical Parmenides, whose method Plato referenced in that dialogue. A successful solution is generated when something occurs, the which is sometimes described as an ignited flash of insight, to produce a validatable *hypothesis* in that person's mind.

The acceptance of that hypothesis by other persons within society, requires that two special conditions be satisfied. First, the same experience of insight must be replicated, independently, within the sovereign cognitive precincts of at least one other individual's mind. Second, that hypothesis, so generated, must be shown to be an existent, efficient principle, by means of experimental demonstration of the efficiency of its willful application to the physical domain as a whole. The latter such experiments belong to the class which Riemann defined as *unique*: it is not sufficient to show experimentally that the prescribed effect might be produced; it must also be demonstrated that that hypothetical universal principle coheres, in a multiply connected way, with all validated other universal physical principles.[10]

_____

10. Crucial illustrations, which I, among my collaborators, have referenced repeatedly in other locations, are typified by the history of the

The crucial point is, that the only way in which we can generate a functionally efficient notion of such a cognitive idea existing in another mind, is the three-step method of sharing such an experience (paradox, hypothesis, validation), as I have just identified this summarily. In such a case, we know three essential things. First, we know, independently of our cognitive processes, the paradox which prompted the generation of a discovery of principle, as the only feasible solution to that paradox. Thirdly, we know the manifest experimental proof of the proposed solution. Thus, by sharing the first and third of those steps, we are able to correlate the specific act of cognition, the second step, in the other mind, with that recallable experience of cognition we experience in our own.

Finally, by comparing that specific, recallable experience,- with a similar but different experience of the same functional type, respecting a different paradox, hypothesis, and proof of principle, we are able to begin to discriminate consciously and willfully among the cognitive experiences specific to each such hypothesis. This ability, so prompted, permits us to recognize each such repeatable cognitive act as a distinct idea within the mind, and to give it a recognizable name, which then identifies that act; that generates the class of what are called *Platonic ideas*. The way in which hypotheses are generated, by Socratic method, in Plato's dialogues, is a now age-old exercise in training the mind to build up a repertoire of nested such Platonic ideas. After Plato, this became the age-old Classical method of cognitive education in globally extended European civilization.

All the outstanding intellects of the Fifteenth Century Golden Renaissance, the associates or students of Nicholas of Cusa, typify minds exhibiting in their practice, the specific meth-

---

derivation of Leibniz's principle of the monad (universal least action) from the preceding discovery of a universal physical principle of least time. Also typical, is the derivation, from Leibniz's methods, of the related principles, refuting Newton and his admirers, for both light and electromagnetism, by the collaborators Fresnel and Ampère. So, Wilhelm Weber, in collaboration with both Carl Gauss and Bernhard Riemann, proved Ampère's principle of angular force, in opposition to the blunders of J. Clerk Maxwell et al.

odologies associated with that method and its associated policies for education of the young. A similar method of discovery of distinct cognitive ideas, is typical of the most enduring contributions of universal and related principle from sources outside extended European civilization. Nonetheless, it is the European experience, and its unique contributions to the development of modern science, technology, and political economy, which is the focal point of reference for this present report.

An hypothesis which has been discovered, shared, and validated in that way, as I have indicated here, represents a *known* universal physical principle of our universe. That use of *known,* as used in that exemplary setting, is, as I shall show, the most crucial issue posed by the fallacies of what are still treated today as commonly accepted, and often potentially fatal errors, errors which are also contained among most currently taught and practiced principles of political-economy and cost accounting.

The most common expression of the fallacy I have implicitly attacked in that way, is the following.

It is common, naive practice, still today, to limit the functional definition of fact, to either mere sense-perceptions, or to the implied superstitions of those putative authorities who are treated as set apart from ordinary witnesses, set apart in the fashion of those putative mystics who, as in Jonathan Swift's allegorical Laputa, are legally classed as experts. In this way, the term knowledge is usually misused, to suggest that, for all ordinary mortals, truth is limited to the domain of the philosophical materialist's simple sense-perception, or to "information" as the hoaxster Norbert Wiener, among other charlatans, has defined statistical "information theory." The two, variously bestial and mystical varieties of superstitious dogmas, implicitly exclude the possibility of the existence of truthful forms of knowledge of the real universe, as Immanuel Kant asserted this denial, categorically, in his *Critiques*.[11]

---

11. Chiefly, in their English translations: **Critique of Pure Reason** (1781–1787), **Critique of Practical Reason** (1788), and **Critique of Judgment** (1790). Kant's view is one of a series of varieties of dogmas, each and all opposed to the notion of cognition in a manner which must be

In what place, then, do validatable universal physical principles exist? How are they to be perceived? How do we reconcile the reductionist's notion of relative truthfulness with the fact, that any validatable hypothesis, nullifies the truthfulness of previously extant, expert opinion, in that degree? Since universal principles can not become known directly through sense-perception, nor known through the quality of expertise whose truthfulness they negate, by what mental faculty are they to be known?

The answer, of course, is: through the faculty of cognition, that faculty of insight found only beyond the bounds of sense-perception, found only within the sovereign precincts of the individual human mind. They are found as I have described the situation, in which the discovery and validation of a universal physical principle is established, through the social relationship between the cognitive processes of two or more individual minds,

---

fairly described as *satanic* in its aims. The mortalism of Padua's neo-Aristotelean Pietro Pomponazzi, is epistemologically consistent with this; the more radical, modern, and literally satanic expression of this, is the empiricism of such followers of the Venetian school of Paolo Sarpi and Antonio Conti, as Francis Bacon, Thomas Hobbes, John Locke, Isaac Newton, Bernard Mandeville, David Hume, François Quesnay, Adam Smith, Jeremy Bentham, Immanuel Kant, the genocidalist Thomas Malthus, John Stuart Mill, and the evil Bertrand Russell. Such among Russell's acolytes as "information theory's" Norbert Wiener and "systems analysis's" John von Neumann, typify this pathology. The frankly satanic "Frankfurt School" circles of Horkheimer, Adorno, and of Hannah Arendt and her Nazi crony Martin Heidegger, were followers of the denial of existence of truth, as such denial was attributed, and otherwise attributable to the *Critiques* of Kant. Also of the same type, are the two most pernicious influences upon the later life of mathematician Georg Cantor, the hateful Leopold Kronecker, and the Machiavellian, one-time theosophist and Lucifer-worshipper, Rudolf Steiner. The common feature of this set of reductionist views, is that their denial of the existence of cognition, rejects thus the quality which defines the member of the human species as made, unlike the animals, in the living image of the Creator of the universe. Their relegation of mankind to the status of human cattle, as Russell, Wiener, and von Neumann do, is exhibited in the explicitly satanic features of their written advocacies respecting society and the human mind. The lunatic notion of artificial intelligence, as proposed by Wiener, von Neumann, et al., is derived axiomatically from their common satanic view.

minds sharing the replication of that same cognitive experience of both discovery and *empirical* validation. Since cognition can not be observed by means of sense-perception, as operations of a strictly formal logic might be displayed in a textbook or on a classroom blackboard, we may "see" the cognitive act in the mind of another individual person, or persons, solely by *the social act* of replication and validation of fruitful forms of insight, those acts which have the form common to successful acts of replication of discoveries of empirically validatable, universal physical principles: principles which are *empirically* validatable *as universal*.

As a matter of contrast: In education, we often experience the case of a student who may achieve a nearly perfect score in the grading of his written or oral examination, and in his grades generally, but who, under different social circumstances, shows that he has learned much, but *knows nothing* of one or more of the matters on which he has been examined. To gain his excellent grades and other awards, he may have either crammed for his examinations, or gobbled up learning with exceptional facility. In that process, he has *merely learned* to pass examinations, not to master the original form of practice of that subject-matter. He does not actually *know* the subject-matter for which he has been drilled, and wrongly certified, by examination, as knowledgeable.

Thus, that graduate, in decision-making and other discussions among his professional peers, often responds, as if ritually, to problematic situations, by means of either arbitrary regurgitations of formulations he has learned to repeat, like an ideologue repeating the political-party line on this or that; he shows, thus, little or no sense of the inappropriateness of that regurgitation to the relatively anomalous challenge at hand. Or, in other manifestations of this type, that person, as a student, may have relied on playful private exercises in which original discoveries of principle were replicated in a cognitive way; however, as that same gifted student had been induced to conform to reductionist methods of argument, as the price of success in securing a terminal degree, or, out of a wont to conform for sake of career opportunities, or in a similar way, the earlier intellectual promise faded;

increasing conformity leads, thus, to an increasing number and variety of non-cognitive dead patches, appearing in more and more of the topical areas of thinking exhibited by such persons.[12]

Today, unfortunately, this saddening state of affairs is often demonstrated in industrial-design, and related practice, for the cases of those design engineers whose practice relies upon so-called mathematical modelling, rather than upon the quality of engineering practice associated with crafting successful proof-of-principle kinds of experimental designs. This deadening of the cognitive powers of the mind, is to be seen respecting their lack of regard both for universal physical principles, and, for the multiple-connectedness of combining two or more of the technologies derived from such principles.[13] The same precaution must be observed in respect to the practices of financial analysis and cost accounting.

Thus, in a competent program of education, efficiently dedicated to the goals of scientific literacy, the emphasis is always upon inducing the student to replicate the relevant cognitive experience of generating and validating universal principles of an implicitly axiomatic quality. This is not accomplished by mere learning, or by substituting simpler experiments in which no axiomatic quality of universal physical principle, is put explicitly at issue for the student's cognitive processes. The most significantly beneficial results, are usually effected, and that quite lawfully, in the instance in which the student is made aware of the fact that he, or she is replicating the original discovery as a personalized, historical event. It is important that the students also conceptualize the validation of the historical act, rather than conjecturing an abstract, ahistorical sort of proof-in-general. Typical of appropriate questions are: "How did Eratosthenes

---

12. Cf. Dr. Lawrence S. Kubie, **The Neurotic Distortion of the Creative Process** (Lawrence: University of Kansas Press, 1958) and "The Fostering of Creative Scientific Productivity," **Daedalus,** Spring 1962.

13. This is a reflection of an included, crucial principle of Riemann's habilitation dissertation. Proof of universal physical principle can not be derived by methods of mathematical formalism. Such matters are the subject of experimental physics. Op. cit., pp. 283–286.

*Construction of the Platonic solids. "Healthy minds of children tend to
see geometry as a matter of the physical world, rather than a purely
formal matter of abstract mathematical, classroom constructions."
(Photo: EIRNS/Stuart Lewis)*

actually measure the length of the great circle of the Earth's
perimeter, and the length of the great-circle arc from Alexandria,
Egypt to Rome, Italy?" "How did Fermat define the principle
of shortest time, in opposition to the notion of shortest path?"

In such an historically specific and personalized, cognitive
approach to the education of students in the rediscovery of
universal physical principles, the student is impelled to replicate
the original acts of discovery and validations of the universal
physical principle, the which are posed to the student in the
form of an ontological paradox. The student is thus induced to
replicate the cognitive act of that original, historically situated
discoverer, thus to live inside that cognitive moment of the discoverer's mind, and to experience that moment as his own cognitive experience, to that degree. All education should be premised
on emphasizing such re-enacted discovery of such principles.

Such were the fruits of the work of truly great teachers, as
distinguished from those showing, customarily, relative compe-

tence in merely describing the relevant subject-matter. These considerations are among the crucial distinctions which qualified cost accountants must take into account, in estimating the necessary costs of fostering the production of creative scientific and related productivity among the generality of future adults of today's society. The issue of cost of both education and related conditions of family-household life, must be situated in terms of that variable quality of resulting cognitive development, or lack of development, in the graduates, as in the policy-shaping of government and private enterprises.

Higher Cognition

However, although we were obliged, here, initially, to present cognition in terms of single acts of discovery of individual *hypotheses* which represent validatable universal principles, the general notion of cognition is found in a higher place, in the notion of *higher hypothesis*.

This distinction is adequately illustrated by the case of a generalized insistence upon the cognitive method of generating, and validating hypotheses of an axiomatic quality, as in classroom and related education. That case is best illustrated, by adopting the view that a child's and adolescent's schooling in matters of science and mathematics, must adopt as its general goal, the rejection of the inductive method, for that of fostering of the Riemannian world-outlook of anti-Euclidean geometry, in the maturing student population. Something approximating this was always manifest in the most creative members of student populations; on that account, early adolescent, or even pre-adolescent, *confrontation with* Euclidean classroom geometry, as opposed to inculcating blind faith in such dogma, was a crucial feature of the education of the secondary pupils.[14]

---

14. A classroom event from my own first-level secondary class in geometry, typifies the point. The teacher posed the question: What is the use of studying geometry? I replied, by pointing out the cutting of holes in structural steel, which I had observed in an earlier visit to the Charlestown, Massachusetts naval base. When I was challenged on my proposing this case, I replied with the obvious answer: "To make them stronger." The notable feature was the angry reaction from among some of the students

Through repeated replications of such original discoveries, as opposed to the process of the acts of merely learning, as by young chimpanzees, the student must replicate some of the cumulative results of those original discoveries. Through continued practice in this way, the student does much more than merely come to know those original discoveries of principle. In this case, such education in matters of universal physical principle, is dominated by a cognitive approach to solving ontological paradoxes. In this setting, the student's progress in education, tends to foster the growing awareness of some higher principle of ordering, a higher principle governing the generation of an unfolding manifold of validatable universal physical principles. It is implicit in the way in which Plato sets forth the paradoxes of his **Parmenides,** this sense of a higher principle of ordering exists, as an underlying, single principle, which subsumes each and all of a manifold of validatable universal physical principles. This shows, that there exists a higher form of hypothesis.

Riemann's notion of a series of multiply-connected manifolds of universal physical principles (a manifold of successive manifolds), which replaces all geometries of an aprioristic form of physics, replacing such as one subsumed by a Euclidean or quasi-Euclidean geometry, is an example of such a higher form of hypothesis, an anti-Euclidean principle of higher hypothesis. In Riemann's Leibnizian approach, each such manifold of a series of manifolds, exists as a distinct idea, an idea distinguished by its specific, experimentally demonstrable, Leibnizian physical *characteristic* of action. This notion of Riemann's is already implied, or, one might say, begged, in Kepler's exposition in his

---

in the classroom. Even fifteen years later, one of those, then a university graduate student in science, brought up the matter in response to his irritation at something which I had just said; he showed that he was still rankled, years later, by his memory of my reply to the teacher's challenge. Healthy minds of children tend to see geometry as a matter of the physical world, rather than a purely formal matter of abstract mathematical, classroom constructions. In my own experience, and what I have observed in the development of other persons, the cultivation of that critical, physical sense of things, is an indispensable feature of the creative development of the young.

The New Astronomy, where Kepler details proof that a common, formalist fallacy underlies the failed astrophysics of Claudius Ptolemy, Copernicus, and Tycho Brahe. The relevant comparison of the successive work of Kepler, Leibniz, and Riemann, suffices to show, that, contrary to scientifically illiterate gossips, there never was a "Copernican revolution" within the historical development of modern Europe.[15] In the domain of physics, this historically shaped emergence of Riemann's revolutionary notion of an implicitly orderable series of multiply-connected manifolds, corresponds to what Plato identifies as a notion of *higher hypothesis*.[16] This notion of higher hypothesis is congruent with *the*

---

15. Through the pre-Roman (e.g., pre-Claudius Ptolemy), Hellenistic period of European civilization, the followers of Plato, and other scientists of that time, had established the so-called "solar hypothesis" on a valid empirical basis. Moreover, during the Fifteenth Century, Cardinal Nicholas of Cusa, the founder of modern experimental physical science, had insisted upon the solar hypothesis. Despite the influence of the Sixteenth-Century Venetian reaction in promoting Claudius Ptolemy's hoax, the students of Cusa, such as Luca Pacioli and Leonardo da Vinci, laid the foundations upon which Kepler explicitly premised his founding of modern, Kepler-Gauss astrophysics.

16. It should be recalled, that Riemann was a product of the developments contributed by the neo-Greek-Classical school in science and art, the which were launched by the three key figures of the mid-Eighteenth Century: Kästner, Gotthold Lessing, and Moses Mendelssohn. It should be recalled, for reasons to be made still clearer at an appropriate place later in this report, that the defense of the combined legacies of Leibniz and Johann Sebastian Bach, was the premise upon which this Classical renaissance in Eighteenth and Nineteenth Centuries' science and artistic composition was premised. The work of the successors Kästner, Gauss, and Riemann, in the development of an anti-Euclidean geometry of physical space-time, was a resumption of the Fifteenth-Century founding of modern physical science by Nicholas of Cusa and such among his followers as Luca Pacioli and Leonardo da Vinci, just as the Seventeenth-Century revolutions in scientific progress were centered around the associates of the anti-empiricists Johannes Kepler and Leibniz. The history of science, and of artistic culture, can not be adequately appreciated, without great emphasis on the role of successive ebbs and flows in the conflicting impulses of pro-Greek Classical renaissances, on the one side, and contrary eruptions of the reactionary Babylonian-Roman, anti-humanistic reactions, on the opposing

Nicolaus Copernicus (left) and Johannes Kepler. There never was a "Copernican revolution"; it was Kepler who proved that a common, formalist fallacy underlies the failed astrophysics of Ptolemy, Copernicus, and Tycho Brahe.

principle of universal change, as Plato illustrates the point in his **Parmenides.** This signifies a principle subsuming the notion of well-ordered, *successive,* validatable changes in the composition of a series of multiply-connected manifolds, as distinct from the hypothesis which defines but one principle to be introduced, as correction, to define but a single new axiomatic mind-set. Call this higher, subsuming ordering principle, a continuing, *ontological* principle of *change.*

Consider the practical significance of that principle of higher hypothesis. Consider the question: What is the practical significance of a student's ability to replicate several individual, validated discoveries of universal physical principle, and to have insight into a qualitatively superior method within the domain

---

side. I employ the term "humanism" here, in the sense of Renaissance Christian humanism, which locates cognition as the redeemable, innate goodness defining man as made in the image of the Creator. The Platonic conception of an anti-Euclidean physical space-time geometry, has been an implicit impulse of these renaissances since no later than the founding of Plato's Academy itself.

of cognition, a method by means of which, an unfolding series of such discoveries can be generated. Consider the question: What is the difference between cognitive knowledge of certain universal physical principles, and an assured capacity and method for generating entire series of original such discoveries?

The crucial question, as directly relevant to economics, is: What is the *causal form of action* which generates a general increase in the relative general productivity of the economy? That action is not simply production, as by labor in and of itself. That action is the expression of a principle of change, a power which generates a principled change in the potential relative population-density of the society. The cause of increased productivity lies in the fruits of cognition, not the simple act of labor as such. *Hence, the functional notion to be employed, can be nothing other than change, as defined by Heraclitus and Plato, as a power-generating change.* The question is not how to make a valid individual discovery of a universal principle; *what is required, is the method for generating an unending series of successive such revolutions. What is required, is the deployment of the principle which assures that latter result.* The question is: how do we shape the economic policies of a society, to ensure that that result is fostered. How do we develop the discoverers, and how do we ensure that the society is disposed and otherwise prepared to assimilate such benefits to the effect of advancing the potential relative population-density of the human species? All that is written hereafter, in this report, should be considered with that statement of this report's assigned mission prominently in mind.

To that latter end, we must approach that challenge by, first, developing a clear conception of the specific distinction which sets the truly cultivated creative-scientific intellect apart from the relatively more pedestrian sort of qualified professional. This is to be found in the implications of this notion of higher hypothesis. Such is the fertility of the creative intellect of an Eratosthenes, a Dante Alighieri, a Brunelleschi, a Nicholas of Cusa, a Leonardo da Vinci, a Kepler, a Leibniz, a Gauss, and a Riemann.

This latter distinction among qualities of scientific thinkers, is not merely a matter of degree. The distinction is, as I have said, qualitative. This point is made explicitly by both Gauss and Riemann, in their replacement of the notion of connectedness among empirically validated axiomatic principles, by the notion of a multiply-connected manifold and its associated characteristic.[17] *This notion of characteristic, together with the associated notion of general principles of curvature, so situated, is a conception of crucial importance for the founding of an urgently needed new set of principles of cost accounting. The equivalence of the notion of higher hypothesis, as summarized here thus far, is crucial for the effective shaping of general, long-range economic policies, both within sovereign nations, and in their choices of long-range cooperation.*

This same notion of higher hypothesis, when so situated within the domain of physical economy, shows the dangerous error embedded axiomatically in the mistaking of sense-experience as such, for a standard of truthfulness. This notion of higher hypothesis, extended from the domain of physical science, to include validatable and universal Classical principles of artistic and related composition, constitutes the domain of *reason*. Cognition, defined in this way, is the cognate of the notion of *reason,* the latter as distinct from mere deductive logic. This distinction is not a merely formal one, but has immediate moral consequences for society, both within the domain of scientific practice, and otherwise. It is in that sense, and only that sense, that the term reason is used hereinafter, by me.

To sum up our discussion thus far. Thus, cognition, as typified by the experience of replicating the argument of Plato's Socratic dialogues, rather than sense-perception, is the only faculty by means of which the individual human mind, and society in general, can actually know the truth in any matter of universal principle.

Here, in this report, our emphasis is upon curing those heretofore commonplace fallacies, the which inhere in the way in which today's customarily taught doctrines of political econ-

---

17. On the uniqueness of Gauss's precedence for Riemann's own discoveries, see the latter's dissertation, pp. 272–276.

omy and cost accounting, especially so-called "standard cost accounting" have been presented. The point to be emphasized, most of all, is that those customary practices falsify the knowable, physically efficient principle of action underlying the apparent connection among the dots of perceived financial-accounting events. It is customarily assumed, that the connection among the dots, is deductive in nature, and therefore linear. There lies the most common folly within today's generally practiced financial analysis.

The axiomatic error characteristic of such customary practices, is twofold. The first error is the assumption that we may define the functional aspects of a political-economic process, by substituting simply defined prices and other quantities, as mere *nouns,* for the *verbs* which a competent functional notion of economic process requires.[18] In other words, the mere "dots" of sense-perception are substituted for that action, which, instead, should be reflected in the proper use of verbs.

The second of those two errors runs as follows. A typical clinical demonstration of the pathological implications of today's widely accepted opinions on matters of political economy and cost accounting, is the delusion that a mere financial gain, such as a financial capital gain, even one premised on the virtual gambler's side-bets called financial derivatives, is a contribution to the nation's prosperity, its estimatable Gross National Product. The delusion, that money as such is wealth, is the specific form of the sometimes fatally ruinous, fatuous delusions common to such cases as the historical tulip and John-Law-style financial bubbles of the Seventeenth and Eighteenth Centuries, the evaporation of money itself in Germany's 1923 hyperinflation, and the mortally cancerous financial bubble which accounts for most of the nominal financial wealth popularly attributed to

---

18. The same point, respecting the dominant function to be assigned to verbs, was made, respecting philology in general, by the great Sanskrit philologist Panini, who was approximately the contemporary of Plato. Most of the intellectual defects in common use of language are reflections of the same pathology, known as *nominalism,* from which empiricism and related mental disorders are derived.

the U.S. and the world today. It was never truly wealth; it was only a wish expressed on paper. So, often, sly merchants have traded wishes for horses.

Physical Science and Productivity

From the outset of my referenced 1948–1952 studies, I adopted the following, somewhat simplified, but appropriate representation, of the functional connection between the discovery of universal physical principles, and the ensuing generation of new technologies of product design and productive practice.

In brief: Of necessity, the appropriate experimental validation of a new scientific hypothesis, must feature, as expressed within the design of that experiment, a direct reflection of the universal principle being tested within the chosen experimental medium. That latter feature of a successful such experiment, is the most appropriate functional definition of a *technology,* as distinguished from that universal physical principle from which that technology is thus derived.

To maintain coherence in this ongoing report, I select, here again, the example of Wilhelm Weber's experimental proof of the Ampère angular force. A study of the experimental apparatus employed for Wilhelm Weber's proof, and measurement, is an excellent choice of example, of the way in which a test of proof of a specific universal physical principle, must include elements of the experimental assembly which correspond to the way in which that principle subsumes one or more implied technologies.[19] The measurement of universal constants, by aid of such apparatus, as in the case of Weber's measurement, is a readily recognized example of this kind of connection.

However, since the relations among physical principles and technologies, must be situated within a valid sort of multiply-connected manifold of the Gauss-Riemann type, we can not limit the notion of technology to so relatively simple a case, as the validation of a single physical principle within a single choice

---

19. This is an especially appropriate case, because of the way in which it situates that angular force, as a principle, within the relevant, multiply-connected phase-space domain.

of experimental medium. A rich plenum of experimental measurements remain to be considered. First, there is the matter of
physical-experimental determination of characteristic curvature
of the domain in which the new principle is situated. Next,
the issue of multiple-connectedness, invades the manufacturer's
department of experimental testing and design, whenever technologies are combined in a new way.[20]

That latter word of caution, represents an extended view
of the same matter addressed in the concluding portion of Riemann's habilitation dissertation. The characteristic curvature of
multiply-connected manifolds, is to be determined by the methods of measurement used for test of principle in physics, not the
methods of a merely formal mathematics. Similarly, the significance of multiple-connectedness haunts the designer, whenever
technologies derived from known principles are combined in a
new way, within a single design. Those combinations of technologies, must be measured as to their effects upon the characteristics of the assembly as a whole. Similarly, when technologies are
generated in new choices of media, and new combinations of
media, this change must also be tested according to Riemann's principle.

Therefore, any cost-conscious corporate management so
reckless, as to imagine it might be permitted to reduce costs by
substituting so-called mathematical modelers, for the type of
design-engineering developed for the tasks of testing new universal physical principles, should be promptly discharged, that out
of consideration for urgent issues of managerial incompetence.

Overzealous cost-cutters must be forewarned, with suitable
penalties attached, against neglecting this matter of principle.

----

20. A notorious case, is the infamous result of an imprudent, excessively cost-conscious use, of an inadequately tested substitution of a change
in composition of an O-ring in a U.S. Space Shuttle launch-configuration.
Reliance on mathematical modelling (e.g., "benchmarking") in the case of
substitution of new materials and sub-assemblies, in a previously tested
design configuration, is always a culpable, if only an ignorant disregard
for elementary standards of competence. The increase in aircraft and automotive design failures, caused by negligent confidence in cost-conscious
mathematical modeling, is typical.

You see here the first Space Shuttle launch, of Nov. 12, 1981. In subsequent years, an excessively cost-conscious approach led to the tragic explosion of the Shuttle Challenger in January 1986, and has plagued the space program ever since. (Photo: NASA)

On principle, neither financial-accounting projections, nor other enterprises in mathematical modelling, have any intrinsic competence, beyond the application of what have already become empirically validated combinations of known principles, technologies, and media of application employed.[21] Indeed, for precisely

---

21. The same precaution is, of course, also applicable to the matter of the physical scale within which the relevant action occurs.

this reason, safety reasons included, empiricists and existentialists should be excluded from positions of supervisory authority
in scientific development, in design of products and productive
processes, and in cost accounting and medium- to long-range
budgeting of large enterprises, national economies, and long-
term economic relations among states.

As I shall indicate at a later point in this report, attention
to these kinds of issues of economic policy, bearing upon the
functions of science and technology, must be shifted from con-
finement to application within the relatively small scale of the
individual firm and locality, to the large, and from the relatively
short-term, of one to several years duration, to the long term
considered in the spatially large. Otherwise, the results will be
akin to the catastrophic consequences for the passengers on a
ship of fools, of relying upon a transoceanic navigator who is
passionately persuaded, by limiting his education to study of
very small areas of space, that the world is flat and the universe
four-square.[22]

That said by way of introduction to the following point,
look at the entire matter of economic policy, in the very large
that is to say, nationally, or globally, and in the long term, a
decade, a generation ahead, or even longer.

Therefore, at this moment we interpolate, and emphasize
the way in which the definition of human nature, as defined by
cognition, assumes the role of the determining consideration in

---

22. Notice should be filed in this location; the caution just supplied
is to be received as including an implicit warning against the folly of
Leonhard Euler's trivial efforts to discredit Leibniz's conception of universal
least action, in Euler's 1761 **Letters to a German Princess.** Euler's trivial
assumption, that the universe is simply linear in the infinitesimally small,
is the root of the principal systemic mathematical follies of such as Lagrange,
LaPlace, Cauchy, Clausius, Grassman, et al. and also the fatal error of
assumption underlying the so-called Kelvin-Clausius "laws" in thermodynamics. The crucial issue, is the false assumption that the proof of physical
principles must be reducible to the form assumed in the algebraic treatment
of the definition of the transcendental, successively, by Euler, Lambert,
Hermite, Lindemann, Felix Klein, et al. This is the devastating fallacy of
axiomatic assumption, upon which both the defective common practice of
cost accounting in general, and systems analysis in general, is premised.

economic analysis and related matters. I situate the connection to be made with a few pertinent background observations.

If the human species were a type of great ape, the human population of this planet would never have exceeded several millions living individuals. Such would have been the ecological state of affairs for such a species under the conditions existing on this planet during any part of a period of approximately the past two millions years to date.

The actually known increases of the potential relative human population-density, consist chiefly of some known historical accounts, dating presently from no earlier than approximately 12,000 years before the present, plus artefacts which date known human existence and activity, to no later than several hundred thousands of years ago.[23] The most notable associated difficulty confronting the paleontologist on this latter account, is to determine whether a relevant relic represents the remains of a human individual, or some higher-ape-like creature. This distinction requires nothing different than evidence which associates that relic with artefacts of clearly human activity.[24] In light of the known ability of higher apes, such as chimpanzees, to learn, and to transmit learning to their offspring, such artefacts, whether as assessed singly, or in combinations, can not be securely identified as products of human activity, unless they are, without doubt, products of human cognition, rather than merely the kinds of transmittable learning associated with the higher apes, for example.

As I have already reported here, the earliest secure such dating known to me, has been identified by relevant scientists as dated to several hundreds of thousands of years ago. The artefacts associated with that site, well crafted throwing spears, reflect the existence of a culture existing in Europe, during what

23. Recent archaeological work in Germany's Hartz Mountains has revealed well-crafted throwing spears, solidly dated to about 400,000 years ago. The implements reflect a technological skill by their makers, that has generally not been credited to humans of this Pleistocene, so-called Lower Paleolithic, period. See Hartmut Thieme, "Lower Paleolithic Hunting Spears from Germany," Nature, Feb. 27, 1997, pp. 807–810; Robin Dennell, "The World's Oldest Spears," Nature, Feb. 27, 1997, pp. 767–768.

24. Brain-cavity size, for example, is not a reliable indicator.

was probably an inter-glacial period, a product of a culture which must be dated even earlier, to many preceding generations. However, precisely because of approximately two millions years of glacial cycles, the repeatedly glaciated regions of the northern hemisphere, are not the likely places in which to locate the settings of the earliest phases of human cultural development and its transmission.[25] Such a broad-brush overview, is sufficient for our consideration here, on the topic of cost accounting, respecting the general state of currently available knowledge respecting the antiquity of human culture.

Such background evidence taken into account, there is no doubt, that the increase of the human species' potential relative population-density since the Fifteenth Century European Renaissance, has been qualitatively greater than in any other known or suspected case prior to that time.[26] The figure for population

---

25. For that and other reasons, the most important area of potential continuity of cultures prior to the currently waning interglacial warming phase, is the emergence and persistence of transoceanic cultures, notably those known trans-Atlantic and trans-Pacific maritime language-cultures which overlap the earliest portion of current history. Only wildly ideological presumption supports the "history began at Sumer," and related dogmas, such as the "hydraulic society" myths. The fact is, that a maritime culture of the "black-headed people," a Dravidian-language-group, founded Sumer, and colonized the Semites of that locality. It was the collapse of Sumer, which led into the Semitic copy of that Dravidian maritime colony's culture. An analogous pre-history, from Egyptian accounts, traced the origins of Egypt to a similar maritime culture's intervention, resulting in a Mosaic Hebrew culture, that of an Egypt-typical set of cleanliness rules, directly opposite to those of the Mesopotamian Semitic sect. See later note, on Moses and monotheism, below.

26. The only approximation of similar progress in Europe earlier, is that of the development of pre-Roman, Classical Greek culture, the culture on which the Golden Renaissance was premised. The triumph of Rome, from about the beginning of the Second Century B.C., was, overall, a cultural and demographic disaster. Indeed, the Romantic legacy left behind from the collapse of decadent pagan Rome, has been not only the curse of Europe ever since, but the principal factor in every moral and related setback to modern Europe's civilization, since the A.D. 1511–1513 triumph of Venice over the League of Cambrai.

growth shown here, [**Figure 1**] has the double significance, that it has been used repeatedly, as a statement of fact, by each of two diametrically opposing factions, both the pro-Malthusian and the anti-Malthusians. I use it here to illustrate the correlation between the emergence of the institution of the sovereign nation-state, during the Fifteenth Century Golden Renaissance, and the emergence of the indicated long-range trend of increase of potential relative population-density. Those who promote drastic reductions in the human population, the modern Malthusians, such as U.S. Vice-President Al Gore, for example, use it as evidence to show the urgency of eradicating the modern sovereign nation-state. The latter propose to arrest technological progress, reduce sharply the life-expectancy of selected portions of the human population, as savagely as Adolf Hitler attempted, and to destroy the sovereign nation-state, in favor of a return to the kind of world government which existed under both the Roman Empire and European feudalism.[27]

---

27. Al Gore, Jr., **Earth in the Balance: Ecology and the Human Spirit** (New York: Houghton Mifflin, 1992). The school of neo-Malthusian of Canada's Maurice Strong, to which has Al Gore attached himself since the early 1970s, demands reductions as high as 80% more, of current world levels. Even far lesser reductions could not be effected except by emulating the genocidal methods of Adolf Hitler, et al. In the modern history of European civilization, Nazism was but one variety of those oligarchical, Romantic currents of oligarchism modelled upon the cultural model of the Roman Empire, and Babylon before it. All seek a return to the Roman imperial model of a society under a single, global "rule of law," a rule of law merely typified by the Code of Diocletian. Gore is a representative of one of those currents, a variety of fascist current typified by the so-called "Nashville Agrarian," neo-Confederacy legacy of Robert Penn Warren, William Yandell Elliot, et al. Lest there be indignant protests against that use of the term "fascist," the reader should be cautioned, that, in modern European history, it signifies radical expressions of those social and political movements which are to be identified with the modern Conservative Revolution, those radical movements based on an oligarchical lackey's type of impulses, as by the would-be Caesars, Napoleon Bonaparte and Adolf Hitler, for example, to reinstate the Roman tradition in law, in opposition to the modern nation-state's law of the general welfare. Like Ku Klux Klan enthusiast Woodrow Wilson, the "Nashville Agrarians" meet the requirements for such classification of radical Romantic conservatism, as "southern fried fascism," exactly.

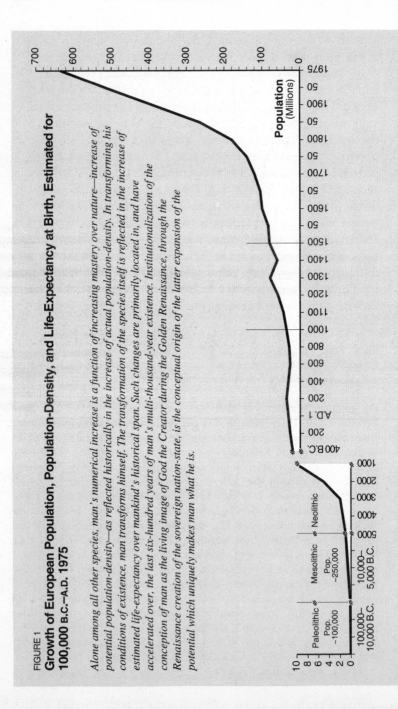

FIGURE 1
Growth of European Population, Population-Density, and Life-Expectancy at Birth, Estimated for 100,000 B.C.–A.D. 1975

Alone among all other species, man's numerical increase is a function of increasing mastery over nature—increase of potential population-density—as reflected historically in the increase of actual population-density. In transforming his conditions of existence, man transforms himself. The transformation of the species itself is reflected in the increase of estimated life-expectancy over mankind's historical span. Such changes are primarily located in, and have accelerated over, the last six-hundred years of man's multi-thousand-year existence. Institutionalization of the conception of man as the living image of God the Creator during the Golden Renaissance, through the Renaissance creation of the sovereign nation-state, is the conceptual origin of the latter expansion of the potential which uniquely makes man what he is.

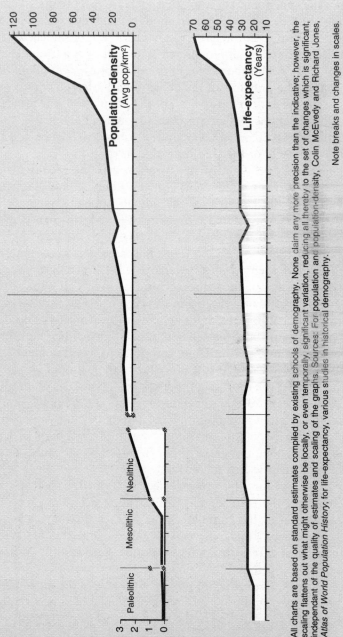

Population-density
(Avg pop/km²)

Paleolithic   Mesolithic   Neolithic

Life-expectancy
(Years)

All charts are based on standard estimates compiled by existing schools of demography. None claim any more precision than the indicative; however, the scaling flattens out what might otherwise be locally, or even temporally, significant variation, reducing all thereby to the set of changes which is significant, independant of the quality of estimates and scaling of the graphs. Sources: For population and population-density, Colin McEvedy and Richard Jones, *Atlas of World Population History*; for life-expectancy, various studies in historical demography.

Note breaks and changes in scales.

The functional basis for that increase in potential relative population-density, as brought about by globally extended modern European cultural progress, was the establishment of the modern, sovereign form of nation-state. This was a form of state organized around that same Fifteenth Century *commonwealth* principle, the principle of the obligation of government, to promote the general welfare for all of the population, the principle of a true republic, which was later adopted in the opening paragraphs of the U.S. 1776 Declaration of Independence and the 1789 Preamble of the U.S. Federal Constitution.

Prior to the Golden Renaissance, and the resulting new form of sovereign state under France's Louis XI and England's Henry VII, the majority of the human population, under all governments, was treated as human cattle, virtually owned, used, or culled, by choice of either a ruling oligarchy, or by an imperial power, such as the Caesars, which had been chosen to represent and regulate such a ruling oligarchy. It is the demographic and related benefits of that modern form of sovereign nation-state republic, which are reflected in the Figure shown here.

That commonwealth, or republican principle, as President Abraham Lincoln defined our republic (but neither Presidents Theodore Roosevelt nor Woodrow Wilson), was the immediate and principled cause for the doubling of the national income of France under the short reign of Louis XI. It was as a by-product of those measures taken in France, then, and England shortly after that, that the conditions of life, national income, and potential relative population-density of European population, have enjoyed the long-term rate of improvement experienced, in net effect, during the half-millennium since.

The fact that this improvement continued, as a long-term trend, until the turn for the worse, thirty years ago, with the introduction of the cumulatively disastrous floating-exchange-rate monetary system, reflects the combined impact, and interdependency of several fruits of the nation-state institution itself. These fruits included the political and social reforms in aid of the general welfare, the promotion of the role of the state in both economic-protectionist measures and building of basic economic infrastructure according to the requirements of the general welfare, and the related promotion of education in physical science, technology, and Classical culture. That interdependency of these cited influences, that under the indispensable role of the institution of the sovereign nation-state, defines the point of birth of modern political economy.

At this point in this report, our attention is focussed upon the functional role performed, to this *physical-economic* effect, by promotion of scientific and technological progress. The interrelated role of the latter with social and political reforms in the practice of political economy, we shall examine at a later point in this report. At this point, our attention is focussed on the causal (functional) relationship between discovery and validation of universal physical principles and increase of potential relative population-density.

The listing of the immediately preceding considerations brings us, to the way in which the most specific distinction of the individual person, the universal principle of cognition, defines the characteristic features of both mankind's functional determination of increases of its potential relative population-density in general, and the underlying principles of a modern political economy, in particular. To situate this phase of the report, I return your attention, briefly, to my work from the 1948–1952 interval, focussing on a work being done circa 1948. In the effort to sort out the tumult which my undertaking against statistical information theory, had generated within me then, I compared the problem of defining the impact of technological progress, with the seemingly analogous problems of defining living processes, other than in the customary clinical way, as the axiomatic issue of the functional nature of life itself was addressed in Professor Nicolas Rashevsky's two texts on mathematical biophysics.[28]

---

28. Nicolas Rashevsky, **Mathematical Biophysics: Physicomathematical Foundations of Biology** (Chicago: University of Chicago Press, 1938), and --, **Mathematical Biology of Social Behavior** (Chicago: University of Chicago Press, 1951). Rashevsky's work complements that of such followers of the Mendeleyev tradition in chemistry as Oparin and Vernadsky. The latters' bearing on the same matter received much attention from me during that same general period of work. Vernadsky is the figure whose

As to the matter of physical principle, it was then already clear to me, that increase of potential relative population-density, must be defined as a function of the application of additional, validated universal physical principles. It was also clear, that the role of the new technologies derived from validation of such universal principles, were a subsidiary function of the demographic function, a function driven primarily by the unfolding of new physical principles. However, it also became clear to me, and increasingly so, over the course of the years 1948–1951, that, for elementary epistemological reasons, the kind of mathematics employed so cleverly by Rashevsky et al., could not describe such a demographic function. Had Rashevsky's approach been premised on an epistemologically sound conception, of the crucial, axiomatically categorical distinction of living from non-living processes, the problem would have remained, that the categorically axiomatic uniqueness of human cognitive processes, among living species, was clearly the root of the stubborn difference between the cognitive nature of the human individual, and the qualitatively inferior quality of all other *living* species.

Therefore, it was made clear to me then, that the possibility of uncovering the specific quality of superiority of the human individual, to that of any other species, could not be found in any formal-mathematical modelling; it could be located only in an empirical approach to the *event-experience* of cognition itself. I have described the elementary expression of that event-experience (paradox, cognition, validation) above.

The most direct way to get at "the structure" of the interior of that kind of event-experience, was to note the equivalence between the role of metaphor in the composition of Classical poetry, and the re-enactment of a validatable, cognitive generation of universal physical principle. For various reasons, the most reliable way of defining this aspect of Classical poetry, was to

work on this topic I find most agreeable, epistemologically. Indeed, the founding of the Fusion Energy Foundation was a direct outgrowth of a letter on the subject of an epistemological view rooted in issues of an hylozoic standpoint in Riemannian biophysics, a letter which I issued to my associates during Spring 1973.

focus upon certain song-settings of Classical poetry. The strictly defined metaphor of Classical poetry, has the same characteristic features as the ontological paradox of Plato's **Parmenides,** and, also, the prompting of a validatable discovery of a universal physical principle.

The meaning of such a poem, can never be located in the mere grammatical ordering of the words themselves; it depends upon the correct, polyphonic rendering of the poem's utterance, the quality of polyphonic rendering typical of the song-settings of Classical, and also folk poetry and song. Such are the methods of motivic thorough-composition, as typified by the methods shown in the span of Classical composition, from Wolfgang Mozart's **Das Veilchen** through the **Four Serious Songs** of Johannes Brahms. Such song-treatments of Classical poetry, come nearest to making implicitly clear the idea of the poem itself,[29] and the appropriate literate form of prosody essential to enabling the individual hearer to replicate the cognitive idea of the poem in his or her own cognitive experience. Civilized people do not recite poetry; they sing it. The best musicians never sing the mere notes, and the best actors never recite the mere words; they sing the music heard in the cognitive processes of the mind. They sing, to convey that music heard in the cognitive processes of their own mind, into the mind of the audiences. As the great Classical poet, John Keats, wrote: That music of the mind, that sweetest sound, so composed, so performed, subsumes the appearance of the mere notes—the mere "dots" of sense-perception.

The cognitively witting scientific thinker, recognizes a connection between the emotional function of such sung Classical prosody, and the passion of concentration required to generate a validatable discovery of a universal physical principle. This is the same passion which Plato identifies as *agapē*, the passion for

---

29. This was the common standpoint, on setting of poetry to music, of Friedrich Schiller, Ludwig van Beethoven, and Franz Schubert, in explicitly stated opposition, on this issue, to Goethe and to the composer Reichardt. The same issue was the point of the disagreement between Goethe and Mozart on the subject of Mozart's song settings.

truth and justice, and the same notion of *agapē*, elaborated by the Christian Apostle Paul's **I Corinthians** 13. Without that specific quality of passion, common to scientific discovery and the expression of the same quality of passion in such artistic forms as great Classical song-prosody, valid replication of a validatable universal physical principle, were not possible.

This quality of passion can not be expressed in nouns; it is associated with the verb, but, that only in the case that the use of the verb corresponds to *a form of action* which results in a change in state of some stated or implied object, subject, or both. This includes all literate uses of the verb "to be," those which express the notion of *becoming*.[30]

This notion of the proper role of the verb in rigorous use of language, is determining in both Classical artistic composition and physical science, as the philologist Panini stressed this point. The strict, correct usage of the term "non-linear" in physical science, is also associated with that employment of the verb in literate forms of language and Classical artistic composition in general: something—my self or some other agency—is acting to change the universe from what it was during an antecedent moment. This same notion is the pivotal feature of competent forms of cost accounting and economic forecasting. This view of the role of the verb, is crucial for grasping the Riemannian non-linearity of the form of action which generates those transformations which link one dot to another, as in cost accounting and economic forecasting.[31]

---

30. For example, the corresponding usage of "I am" would be better expressed by the use of "I am making myself so" (or, "becoming more myself," or "becoming less like myself") as an implied synonym for "I am."

31. The term "non-linear" is used here in the sense of regular, but non-constant curvature. That notion is defined by the work to this effect by Kepler, Leibniz, Gauss, Riemann, et al. It coincides, in physical-mathematical practice, with the Leibniz-Gauss-Riemann notion of a *characteristic* curvature of the relevant physical space-time, as this distinctive *characteristic of action,* of specific manifolds, is to be associated with the notion of a well-ordered series of Riemannian multiply-connected manifolds. Like the notions of curvature defined by Nicholas of Cusa, as in his **De docta ignorantia,** as opposed to the algebraic, formalist standpoint of Euler,

The fundamental principle of the science of physical economy, is *the anti-entropic effect of the efficient application of an expanding, Riemannian, multiply-connected manifold of universal physical principles, expressed as an increase in the general potential relative population-density of society.*[32]

In the history of science, this use of the term *anti-entropy,* or negative entropy, in the science of physical economy, was borrowed from biology. It signifies the principled difference between the axiomatic type of behavior exhibited by developing living organizations, as contrasted with non-living ones of very similar, or closely related, organic chemical composition.

The demonstration of that fundamental principle of physical economy, implicitly generates the following, most important ontological paradox of all physical science.

The fact, that the universe submits consistently, in that way, to such application of advancing discovery and application of all validatable universal physical principle, and not otherwise, shows, in first approximation: *that the universe is implicitly predisposed, as if by pre-design, to submit to mankind's will, on this account, whenever mankind acts on behalf of those discoveries of universal physical principle.* Since the effect of this cooperative social application of the sovereign power of individual cognition, is to increase mankind's power in and over the universe—per

---

Lambert, Lagrange, Laplace, Cauchy, Hermite, Lindemann, Felix Klein, et al.

32. The use of the term *anti-entropic,* rather than "negative entropy," has been made necessary by the popularization of the way in which the term *entropy* is used, increasingly, during the post-1946 decades, that under the pernicious influence of the radical Malthusians, and the spreading cult of information theory. The pathological use of the term entropy, dates from the formulation, by transparent fallacy of composition of evidence, of the dubious "laws of thermodynamics," by Clausius, Grassmann, Kelvin, et al. The Twentieth-Century abuse of Ludwig Boltzmann's work, by Wiener's abuse of "negative entropy," and congruent charlatanry by von Neumann et al., during the past six-odd decades, has spilled back into broad areas of academic and related professional uses, from the incestuously intertwined, post-war cults of "information theory," "systems analysis," and "artificial intelligence."

capita, and per square kilometer of the Earth's surface, that connection shows, that the characteristics of the underlying laws of the universe, and the characteristics expressed by the processes of cognition, are congruent. That is to say: *the underlying law of the universe, is expressed by the same principle of higher hypothesis which is expressed by the generalized processes of well ordered individual cognition.*

This expresses a unique quality of experimental evidence of a universal principle. The implications of that principle may be read, either as the secularist version 1) the universe generated the emergence of a species, mankind, which could manage, and become a cause for the continuing, *noetic* self-development of that universe; or, in other words, the Biblical view, 2) that the Creator of the universe made men and women of such a human nature as in His own image.[33]

The corollary of this, is that these considerations define a corresponding, implied body of *natural law,* truthfully knowable by means of cognition, which is the highest body of man-made law, superior in authority to all man-made constitutions, or other man-made law. On this account, the fundamental principle of constitutional law, is, that the only source of legitimate authority of government, is the state's unshirkable duty and unique power, to promote the general welfare of all the living and their posterity.

----

33. My distinction between those two views, here, should not be read as implying either aprioristic arbitrariness, or paganistic anthropomorphism, respecting the Christian concept of the *cognitive personality* of the God of Moses' **Genesis** 1. The personality of the Christian Apostles' Mosaic God, is of a being who pervades efficiently the simultaneity of eternity, the implicitly knowable personality of that Platonic *Good* which subsumes the principle of higher hypothesis. As Cusa demonstrated from the records of the Greek Orthodox authorities, the Augustinian insertion of *filioque* explicitly within the Nicene Creed, has this implication. The contrary view, of God as having set a lawful, thereafter fixed Creation and its laws into initial motion, is, as Philo of Alexandria and many other theologians have shown, an impossible ontological paradox. Nonetheless, as I am in the process of exposing this fact now, the expression of that issue within the scope of the principal issues of this present point of our report here, is that exactly such an impossible ontological paradox, is demonstrably the usual, pathological standpoint of the view and practice of physical science today.

So, for example, the first three paragraphs of the 1776 U.S. Declaration of Independence, and the corresponding 1789 Preamble of the U.S. Federal Constitution, are the sole ultimate authority in law for the U.S.A.

Not only are those latter conceptions epistemologically legitimate ones. Without taking these explicitly into account, there will never be a competent conception of the proper meaning of the term "physical science," nor of the underlying, fundamental principles of political economy, either. Therefore, let us briefly draw out the practical implications of what I have just emphasized.

The prevalent, false portrayal of physical science, as expressed, wittingly or not, in today's typical university and its textbooks, is a reflection of the imposition of the same aprioristic notion commonly underlying both the mortalist, neo-Aristotelean doctrine of Padua's notorious Pietro Pomponazzi, and the so-called empiricist, Voltairean, or Enlightenment tradition of Venice's Paolo Sarpi and Antonio Conti. This is the aprioristic view expressed as the central principle of Thomas Hobbes;[34] John Locke and Isaac Newton;[35] Bernard Mandeville's pro-satanic *The Fable of the Bees*;[36] François Quesnay's pro-feudalist,

---

34. Hobbes was a student of Paolo Sarpi's house-lackey Galileo Galilei.

35. As Leibniz emphasized this, respecting the aprioristic reliance of Newton's mechanistic doctrines on the notion of "God's Clock," in the Leibniz-Newton-Clarke exchange. Note also, that the language, "life, liberty, and the pursuit of happiness," in the 1776 U.S. Declaration of Independence, was taken directly from Leibniz's posthumously published attack on John Locke. On the latter, see the report of Phil Valenti, "The Anti-Newtonian Roots of the American Revolution," EIR, Dec. 1, 1995.

36. The Fable of the Bees, or Private Vices, Public Benefits, 1714. This same pro-satanic doctrine of Mandeville, was anointed, and explicitly so, by Friedrich von Hayek, as the kernel of the religious faith of the doctrine of "freedom" adopted by both the British Mont Pelerin Society and its Washington, D.C. subsidiary, the Heritage Foundation. This adoration of the necessity of universal immoral licentiousness, is the notion of "democracy" espoused and practiced by Project Democracy, since the founding of the National Endowment for Democracy, in 1982. The shameful support for legalization of narco-terrorist drug-trafficking, from Colom-

mystical dogma of laissez-faire;[37] Adam Smith's axiomatically irrational doctrine of "free trade;"[38] and British Foreign Office head Jeremy Bentham's 1789 *An Introduction to the Principles*

---

bia, into the U.S.A., by Secretary Madeleine Albright's State Department, is consistent with Mandeville's, Jeremy Bentham's, and George Soros' dogmas.

37. Quesnay, like Newton and Voltaire, was a follower of the doctrines of both Sarpi and Conti. He argued, that the feudal title to estates made the fruit of production an epiphenomenon of that title, and thus the sole "shareholder value," Lockean "property," of the landlord, for which that shareholder owed nothing to the work performed by the serfs, or any other agency in society. This mystical dogma of *laissez-faire,* is among the numerous plagiarisms of France's Physiocrats by Lord Shelburne's lackey, Adam Smith.

38. Smith, like Immanuel Kant, originally a follower of the so-called "Scottish moral philosophy" of David Hume, was picked up by the British East India Company's Lord Shelburne, no later than 1763, and assigned, by Shelburne, to develop a policy used for the double purpose of destroying both the economy of France, and the industrial development of the monarchy's English-speaking colonies. Shelburne's protégé Smith spent much of the interval 1763–1776 in France, plagiarizing much from the writings of Physiocrats such as Quesnay and Turgot. Later, during an interval of 1782–83, while Shelburne was Britain's Prime Minister, Shelburne inserted agreement to the Mandeville-Quesnay-Turgot-Smith dogma of "free trade" into the preliminaries of the peace-treaty between the warring France and United Kingdom. The continued prosecution of these "free trade" negotiations, was marked by the role of a Swiss banker from Lausanne, the infinitely picaresque rogue, Jacques Necker, a close confederate of Shelburne's circles, and sometime Finance Minister and also Prime Minister of France. Necker's wife, had been involved, prior to her marriage, in a protracted Romantic liaison with Shelburne's lackey Edward Gibbon, of **Decline and Fall of the Roman Empire** notability. Necker's daughter, Germaine, was the notorious Madame de Staël of Kant foe, and poet Heinrich Heine's attack upon the corrupting influence of Romanticism in Germany. All were intimately associated with the network of salons which had been established by Antonio Conti, as typified by the circles of Voltaire et al. in France, Switzerland, and Germany. These were also the salon circles of Shelburne in France, since his education there. It was Necker who brought about the bankrupting of the French monarchy, from the inside, and who served as the dirty Duke of Orleans' confederate in launching the celebrated incident of July 14, 1789, as part of Necker's own campaign for appointment as Prime Minister,

of Morals and Legislation.[39] Notably, this array of rabid, hedonistic irrationalists, represents the continued building of the foundation of the ruinous British doctrine of political-economy, to the present day. This is also the most important of the anti-Renaissance influences which, by no mere coincidence, have continued to pollute the teaching and practice of physical science, from the time of Padua's Pietro Pomponazzi, to the present.

Consider a frequent expression of that same crucial element of irrationalism, in the behavior of even today's otherwise gifted science professional. Observe the incidence of those cases, in which one among them protests against my view. In my experience, a typical such professional, may either profess, that he has no professional responsibility to understand economics, or, much worse, he gives his implicit political support to the dogmas of such figures as the Mont Pelerin Society's Friedrich von Hayek and Milton Friedman, or even Vice-President Al Gore's lunatic political-economic "algorerythms." *Physician, heal thyself:* such are typical of the conceptual aberrations prevalent among today's science professionals. Recognizing the nature of such behavior among some specialists in physical science, sometimes even oth-

---

which began the unleashing of the initial bloody phase of the Jacobin Terror in France.

39. The aprioristic so-called hedonistic principle, or "felicific calculus," on which the utilitarian dogma of Bentham, John Stuart Mill, et al. was premised axiomatically. Bentham was made the first head of the British Foreign Office, beginning 1782, by the intervention of the same Lord Shelburne who was also the patron of Adam Smith, Edward Gibbon, and many others of the same stripe. As head of the Foreign Office, Bentham was the personal controller and trainer of the infamous Danton and the Swiss recruit Marat, each of whom Bentham personally trained, and deployed from London, to Paris, to lead the model escalation of the Jacobin Terror in France. This was the same Bentham whom Simon Bolívar later denounced as the author of the worst evils inserted into the Hispanic Americas. Bentham was also the creator of the infamous Lord Palmerston. It was the same Bentham who, as he had trained and deployed Marat and Danton, had a key role in orchestrating the Duke of Wellington's use of the decadent Fouché, to put the pathetic British puppet, King Louis XVIII, rather than Presidential candidate and republican patriot Lazare Carnot, into power in France.

erwise outstanding such figures, should evoke compassion for the related conceptual shortcomings found among so many of today's accountants and financial analysts, who, typically, lack a competent education in the basics of science.

The simplest approach to understanding the source of such aberrations among scientists, is to trace the problem to the increasing popularization of mathematical models, both in classrooms, and in the daily practice of today's scientists and engineers. The outlook so induced in the mind of the victim, is a certain, induced habit of thinking about the physical universe, a practice which implies, that universal physical laws pre-existed, prior to mankind, in the form of the mathematical models widely adopted, *ex cathedra,* today.

For example, as what appears to have been typical of him, Bertrand Russell carried this pathological view of science to a point even beyond its deductive limits, during an utterance of the late 1920s. He asserted the coming end of scientific progress. He argued, that the available, untapped hoard of such universal mathematical-physical laws, represents nothing but a rapidly vanishing residue of what had been, from the start of Creation, a fixed set of such discoverable mathematical laws.[40] Many scientists might disagree with Russell's argument, as to the quantity of discoveries still available to be made. After the rampant decay of university education, during the course of the recent decades, relatively few remain, who would be able to identify correctly the precise nature of the systemic fraud implicit in Russell's argument.

The point here is, that *it is only in that view of economic*

---

40. Since Russell insisted that he, as a titled British imperial oligarch from the Palmerston and John Stuart Mill era, bitterly resented the United States and agro-industrial, science-driven economy, one must ask oneself whether Russell's desire to see the backside of God in this matter, were not the determining element of wishfulness in his argument of that time. Nonetheless, there is no doubt that Russell's view of scientific creativity was, like that of his sycophant John von Neumann, of the mechanistic sort. His view of scientific discovery accords with the impossible ontological paradox of a Creator who had created a fixed universe with permanently fixed laws, thus rendering Himself, as the mephisthophelean Russell seems to have wished, impotent to perform any further action upon that universe.

The aberrations among scientists are typified by the case of the pathological Bertrand Russell, who asserted the coming end of scientific progress, since once the fixed set of mathematical laws was discovered, there would be nothing left to explore.

processes supplied by a science of physical economy, that the proof of the validity, and nature of universal physical principles, could be securely established. To test each principle individually to that purpose, would represent a fallacy of composition. The test, to be rigorous, must be defined in terms of larger, multiply-connected aggregations, as phase-spaces. The designer of such tests, must think, on a broad scale, in terms of long waves, of general scientific and physical economic progress. Such waves must be correlated with the growth of per-capita and per-square-kilometer productivity over significant periods. Study such patterns, under conditions within periods both of stagnation in, and during bursts of investment in scientific and technological progress in agriculture, manufacturing, and basic economic infrastructure-building in the public sector.

To illustrate that, study the manner in which Benjamin Franklin's great-grandson, Philadelphia's and West Point Military Academy's Alexander Dallas Bache, played a key role, in bringing the impact of the scientific work of the circles of Germany's Gauss and Alexander von Humboldt into the United States. Think of Bache's role, in terms of such outcomes as the "Thomas Edison phenomenon," the rapid electrification in the U.S. and Emil Rathenau's Germany. See this leading to an explosive upsurge in U.S. industrial productivity, during the early Twentieth Century. That result is typical of appropriate economic demonstrations, of the efficacy of scientific discovery, as demonstrated by the increase, as under France's Louis XI, of the potential relative population-density of the human species.

In these, as all related matters, the test of truthfulness in expressed opinion, is a test of the efficacy of the powers of that anti-empiricist faculty, Socratic cognition, as typified in variety by Plato's **Meno, Theaetetus,** and **Timaeus,** in producing validatable discoveries of universal principle. In the final analysis, the only valid test, on which the truthful authority of all opinion depends, is the willful increase of mankind's power in and over the universe, as measurable per capita, for the entire population, and as measurable per square kilometer of the Earth's surface-area. It is upon that standard, as defined by the science of physical economy, that the validity of any presumed universal physical principle, depends.

Thus, stating the matter in these appropriate terms, so the authority of the putatively trained scientific professionals must be measured. So, their competence must ultimately be judged. They are all, whether they wish to acknowledge this fact, or not, subject to that standard of a science of physical economy. Indeed, the authority of all opinion depends upon that same test of man's power to increase his power in and over the universe. That physical-economic, *cognitive* standard, is the ultimate scientific measure of truth in all matters, including the domain of mathematical physical science. So, a professional, in any profession, is to be judged, primarily, as a human being. Otherwise, science itself might be left to roam perilously, unguided, like a Bertrand Russell or John von Neumann, near the outer rim of Jonathan Swift's floating island of Laputa.

To summarize the argument made, up to this point, we have the following.

Consider the case of those pitiable illiterates, such as the licentiously liberal doctrinaires of the ultra-Conservative, Mandevillian Heritage Foundation, who insisted upon a separation of "pure" from "applied" science. Their argument, typified by the case of Heritage's since-deceased Lt.-Gen. (ret.) Daniel Graham, was that the process of discovery and validation of new physical principles, such as the discovery of principles of nuclear fission and fusion, of space exploration, and so on, was the work of impractical, "ivory tower" academics. It thus appeared to escape his attention, that none of these discoveries would have been effected without governmental funding. On these premises, Graham proposed, that instead of investing in discovery and development of validatable new physical principles, government development programs should be limited to what would be in fact technologically obsolete new assemblies, composed of technologies already gathering dust on the shelves of Wall Street-owned private military contractors. He made this the theme of a virulent attack on the proposal, and upon me, personally, for what became the Strategic Defense Initiative (SDI), during 1982, before it was adopted; immediately after its adoption, he led in the preponderantly successful campaign, to exclude all those viable lines of fundamental research, which might compete with off-the-shelf approaches to the technologies of Wall Street-controlled military vendors.

The case of the Heritage Foundation's Graham, although a lurid one, the more clearly and simply illustrates the general problem. As if in loving memory of the Roman Emperor Diocletian and his Code, the advocates of such distinctions between pure and applied science, are arguing against any direct or indirect, putative subsidies of scientific progress, by government, either in the form of direct grants of government funds, or indirectly, through taxation policies and other forms of regulatory measures. Theirs is that sick mentality which fosters rabid cuts in taxation on purely speculative, and therefore parasitical forms of financial capital gains, while refusing to consider a President John Kennedy-style of investment tax-credit, which has been shown, repeatedly in our national history, the best suited to promote the kinds of capital investment fostering the increase of scientific progress, and of its productive and related applications.

Pose the view directly contrary to that of the Heritage Foundation and its like. Does science have a moral responsibility for promoting, both the discovery and economic realization of those advances in technology, which flow, as products, from the discovery and validation of universal physical principles? Does government not have a profound, unshirkable responsibility, under the general welfare principle, for promoting both such scientific progress, and its realization as the fostering of improvements in the potential relative population-density of present and future generations? Is this not an integral part of the axiomatic prerequisites, something akin to the Hippocratic Oath among physicians, for the role of government in qualifying a professional as a scientist according to the constitutional principle of the general welfare? Is it not, therefore, clearly, the case, that a nominal scientist who views himself and his work as a kind of "ivory tower" practice, is not morally qualified to be considered as a scientist, not fit to be considered as implicitly morally trustworthy as a true expert, in his proclamations? Are we not obliged to end the trend toward replacing competent scientists, by Heritage's reign of money-grubbing yahoos? Are not all qualified scientists to be held morally accountable, not only to promote no unnecessary harm, but also not to neglect the duty of promoting benefits for the general welfare, including the promotion of the increase of the potential relative population-density of the human species as a whole?

More important than the case of the individual scientist, or relevant policy-shapers in industry, education, and government, is the need to define the responsibility of government itself accordingly, especially its economic policies. As accountability for efficient promotion of the general welfare is the only legitimate premise for even the very existence of a sovereign nation-state, this policy respecting the function of scientific progress, is a matter of a test of the government's moral fitness to exist. Since the functions of accounting and financial analysis impinge upon the policy-shaping of government in this respect, those professions must adopt a congruent standard of truthfulness respecting the profferred product of their professions.

On this account, the referenced policies of the Heritage Foundation and its Daniel Graham, represented implicitly culpable fraud and negligence. Indeed, that liberal school of empiricist political-economy and related policy-shaping, is less of a profession, than an infectious disease preying upon humanity, that in the same manner the economists associated with the British East India Company's Haileybury School, authored such genocidal atrocities as the organized famines which the British Empire deployed to regulate the population of Nineteenth and also early Twentieth Centuries India. "Free trade" for everyone? Or, better said, perhaps, rendering "*Vogelfrei*" those deemed "useless eaters," as Wall Street's approach to looting of health-care and related entitlements, increases the morbidity rates of entire strata within the U.S. population itself.[41]

'Non-linear': What Does it Mean?

I shall now indicate the reasons why the results of any application of what have been, heretofore, generally accepted

---

41. **Vogelfrei:** German slang-expression for a soul freed from the body. Hence, also frequently used during the Nazi period for such topics as the release of deceased victims of Hitler's "useless eaters" policy. The comparison to the demographic policies, foreign and domestic, of Wall Street's neo-Malthusians, and others, is more than fair. Compare the explicit apologies for such genocidal measures, by then U.S. National Security Advisor Henry A. Kissinger's **NSSM–200**. See also Sergei Glazyev, **Geno-**

methods of financial accounting, to cost accounting and to cost-accounting-related, functional forms of financial analysis and forecasting, must be judged intrinsically incompetent, *by definition*. The practical side of that matter to be addressed in this location, is: *how are these incompetencies to be recognized, and what general remedies must be adopted to remove them?*

At this point, we shall limit our attention, to emphasizing those features of the case which must become obligatory knowledge among cost-accounting professionals. This signifies that, in this location, we cling as closely as possible to the bare axiomatic issues of the matter. Therefore, our approximately bare-bones account of the matter runs as follows.

The more general of these incompetencies, is simply the use, and reliance upon today's generally accepted statistical methods, for interpreting the array of financial and related events. The incompetence of the extension of such financial accounting practices, to cost accounting and functional financial analysis and forecasting, is most readily located simply in the fact that the methods of financial accounting and related analysis rely upon the implicit assumption of a child's game of "connect the dots." The essence of the incompetence at issue, is approximately the same as in the case of Sarpi lackey Galileo's use of nothing other than the same childish notion of "connect the dots," to define what become known as the basis for his, like Isaac Newton's, fraudulent claims to have discovered a universal principle of gravitation and other action.[42] The crude notion of

---

cide: Russia and The New World Order, Rachel Douglas, trans. (Washington, D.C.: EIR News Service, 1999).

42. The discovery of a principle of universal gravitation, was made originally by Johannes Kepler. The fulsome statement of that discovery is to be found in Kepler's **The New Astronomy**. Through Kepler's work with Galileo's father, the musician Vincenzo, on matters of tuning, Kepler became acquainted with Galileo and conducted a correspondence with him, a correspondence which Galileo mined for certain plagiarisms. The first notable attempt to replicate Kepler's already known original discovery of universal gravitation, is that popularly attributed to Isaac Newton. The work attributed to Newton, attempts to degrade what is copied directly from Kepler's **New Astronomy**, into the now familiar, bowdlerized "three

"action at a distance," as attributable to Galileo, typifies the axiomatic incompetence of the employment of common statistical methods in financial accounting and related practice. It is the intrinsic absurdity of that assumption of "action at a distance," which is the kernel of our treatment of the issue of "non-linearity."

It was consistent with the homicidal enforcement of the reductionist dogmas of Pomponazzi, Sarpi, et al., during the interval of the anti-Renaissance, Conservative reaction and its religious wars, 1513–1648, that only a few souls dared to speak publicly, of any suggested composition of the universe contrary to what would be still considered today as standard classroom Euclidean geometry's definitions, axioms, and postulates.

After Kepler, the first crucial attack on the kind of axiomatic linearization associated with Galileo, was by Pierre de Fermat, in his physical demonstration that the refraction of light was governed by a principle of *least time,* rather than shortest (linear) path. However, for a time, this was treated as a demonstrable anomaly (a paradox), within the framework of a physical universe assumed to be, axiomatically, one defined as consistent with "Euclidean," *a priori* presumptions of limitless linear extension of space and time. The deeper implications of Fermat's discovery began to be made clear during the middle of the Seven-

---

laws;" however, the effort of Newton to linearize the relations of gravity, results in the fatal error of the "three body" paradox. The most significant of the actual derivations of Kepler's original work, is Leibniz's original development of the calculus, based upon the specific problems of astrophysics which Kepler had left to be addressed by future mathematicians. Despite the now-popularized bowdlerization of the infinitesimal of the Leibniz calculus, by Newton devotee Augustin Cauchy, that characteristic is not reducible to a linear form, but reflects, typically, an elementarily non-constant curvature, as a matter of principle. This addresses the specific problem of normalization of astronomical observations, which was posed to future mathematicians by Kepler. The first general solution of this problem of normalization for solar orbits was provided at the beginning of the Nineteenth Century, by Carl Gauss's discovery of asteroid orbits corresponding to the values which Kepler had estimated for a missing planet locatable between the orbits of Mars and Jupiter.

teenth Century, through the intersection of a leading student of Kepler's work, Blaise Pascal, with the collaboration which began in Paris, between 1672 and 1676, between Christiaan Huyghens and Gottfried Leibniz.

The demonstration of both an isochronic and least time characteristic, for gravitation and refraction of light, by the combined work of Huyghens,[43] Leibniz, Römer,[44] and Jean Bernouilli,[45] provided the experimental proof of the universal physical principle, that action in physical space-time did not conform to those linearized notions of time, space, and matter associated with Galileo, Descartes, and Newton. The demonstration, by Huyghens, and also his followers, that the pathway of gravitational action could be shown to be not straight-line, but a curved pathway, which was isochronic, and, also, relatively,[46] of least time, and, that this was also true for refraction of light, was experimental proof that physical space-time is not Euclidean, and that action in that physical space-time is not elementarily linear, not Cartesian, not Newtonian.

Thus, the first implication of Fermat's discovery of an experimental principle of least time, was his introduction of a devastating paradox within the pre-existing, Euclidean domain of *a priori* physical space-time. The cognitive generation, by Fermat, of an hypothesis of least time, begged the development of experimental tests whose included obligation must be, to begin to define a universal notion of physical space-time in which the recognition of a newly discovered universal physical principle, would define a domain freed of the paradox posed by Fermat's discovery. Huyghen's work in developing his pendulum clock, and his generalization of those results, led to the introduction of the isochronic principle, and least time, into the physical

---

43. Christiaan Huyghens, **The Pendulum Clock or Geometrical Demonstrations Concerning the Motion of Pendula as Applied to Clocks**, Richard J. Blackwell, trans. (Ames: Iowa State University, 1986), and —, **Treatise on Light** (1677) (New York: Dover Publications, Inc.: 1962).

44. ibid.

45. ibid. also **Acta Eruditorum,** May 1697.

46. The cycloid is an approximation.

space-time of constrained falling bodies. Related work on determining the characteristics of the speed and refraction of light, by Römer, Huyghens, Leibniz, and Jean Bernouilli, situated Leibniz's superseding of simple least time, by a more general principle of least action. This provided the setting in which the future refutation of the Newtonian dogma on light and electromagnetism, was accomplished by the collaborators Fresnel, Arago, and Ampère. The work by Leibniz's follower Kästner, contributed crucially to the setting of the development of anti-Euclidean geometries, successively, by Gauss and Riemann.

There are many lessons to be adduced from that and related elements of the history of the development of the Gauss-Riemann notions of anti-Euclidean hypergeometry. The lesson to be emphasized here, is not those events, but rather that subsuming process of development, which the pattern of those unfolding discoveries expresses. In science, it is not the individual discovery which is the essence of the matter; it is, rather, the adducing of the process which subsumes a series of successive discoveries of principle, as in the historical series which I have just outlined. It is in that process, that the true, categorical meaning of "non-linear" is to be situated.

The practical point of this, for cost-accounting practice, is that the ordering of those events which we might perceive as sequential "dots" in a time-series, is not an axiomatically linear order. Therefore, the series of such data is not necessarily ordered in a way which can be competently approximated by linear approximations, such as deductive methods. The same applies to the data-field in which the series of choices is located. Therefore, the use of statistical methods of financial accounting, to construct what is represented, thus, as a functional (e.g., "cause-effect") analysis of such a series, is an intrinsically incompetent form of *general practice,* on principle. Under certain special circumstances, such crude approximations may be harmless; but, as a matter of general practice, they are intrinsically incompetent, recklessly so.

Consider the implications of what I have just said, in the following terms of reference. These are the terms to which we shall return, repeatedly in the later, successive phase of this report. Let us zoom in upon some of the relevant problems to be addressed in the production of products. These illustrations will provide the framework, in which to situate the issues of non-linearity in practical terms of production and related practice.

Choose any relatively simple case, in which a combination of materials is brought together in such a fashion, that a transformation occurs in that combination, with the result we recognize as *production.* The transformation may be mechanical, chemical, etc., in nature. In the analysis of production, we focus upon the immediate relationship between the individual functioning as an operative, such as a farmer or a factory workman, and the quality of physical transformation which depends upon the active role of that operative, in respect to the process for which he is responsible. In other words, the operative is performing some necessary, controlling function in relationship to the physical transformation occurring at that point in the productive process. Such transformations, are to be represented by intrinsically non-linear orderings.

At a later point in this report, when I shall return our attention to that relationship, we shall focus upon the internal features of the operative's role as such. For the moment, now, take the necessary role of the operative in the productive process as a given fact; that said, focus on the physical transformation, as this is occurring in the process which the operative is controlling in some way.

In any such physical transformation, the function described by that localized productive function, involves primarily, three crucial kinds of distinguishing elements: physical principles, and also specific technologies, as the latter are subsumed by both these principles, and, thirdly, the choices of physical media in which the transformation is occurring.

Once we have identified those categorical features of the ongoing transformation, we must take into account the scale on which the relevant features of the transformation are occurring. The relevant scales include, for example, the astrophysical, the molecular, the atomic, the nuclear, and the sub-nuclear, and include accounting for both the wave-length and "energy-flux density" of the relevant actions. The qualities of action to be considered, include the functional distinction which deeply underlies the functionally determining differences between a living process and one which has just ceased to be living. In respect to human behavior bearing on the productive process, the qualities of action to be considered, include the functionally determining, principled, *physical* distinction between animal learning and human cognition. In all of these matters, there are qualitative distinctions peculiar to specific ranges within the respective domains of astrophysics, macrophysics, and microphysics. The relevant "local laws" of physical processes may change, as we pass from one such range to another.

In all such matters, the specific way in which the connections among the relevant "dots" of the transformation are ordered, may change in characteristic local curvature, from one case to another. Thus, the determination of the way in which the transformation proceeds, from one observed "dot" of that process, to the next, may rarely correspond, in fact, to a simply linear connection of a Euclidean or Cartesian type. In the practice of cost accounting and forecasting, it is essential to recognize this principle of non-linearity, and to be guided thus in knowing when linear approximations may be tolerable, or not. The importance of making that distinction is magnified, sometimes perilously, by any effort to forecast long-range consequences from short-term apparent changes, or the observer's failure to look behind the superficial indications of a lack of apparent changes in trends.[47] In such cases, it were prudent to have re-enacted Gauss's laborious discovery of the asteroid orbits from several relative momentary observations, a labor which, as viewed in retrospect by Gauss himself, provides an excellent demonstration of the long-term significance of recognizing characteristic expressions of non-linearity, even in the relatively very small.

Mathematical knowledge of the characteristic types of

------

47. Typical of such observer's negligence, is today's rather popular delusion, the fallacy of composition of evidence represented by seeing only the rising trend in certain classes of nominal financial assets, and thus failing to take into account the explicitly contrary evidence which is summarized by my "Triple Curve."

changes which may be applicable to the task of connecting the dots, has increased in known ways over the recent millennia. The known methods for estimating π, for example, have changed from those on record as used by the ancient Egyptians, for example: from series of fractions, to the irrational magnitudes mistakenly adopted by Archimedes for the quadrature of the circle, to the proof of the existence of the transcendental nature of π by Nicholas of Cusa, as in his work founding modern experimental physical science, **De docta ignorantia.**

The corresponding definitions of each class of numbers which might be employed to trace the determining pathway between two observed dots, rational, irrational, and transcendental, or higher orders of the transfinite, are supplied in two distinct ways: arithmetic-algebraic, or geometric.

The model distinction among number types, is that originally provided by a leading follower of Plato, the so-called "sieve" of the famous ancient astrophysicist Eratosthenes. This sieve was updated by mathematician Georg Cantor, to include higher orders, such as the transcendental and higher transfinite. As Plato's **Meno, Theaetetus,** and **Timaeus** illustrate the point, the method of Plato's Academy, including Eratosthenes, was essentially the geometric method. Cusa discovered the correct definition of the transcendental, by geometric methods, during the middle of the Fifteenth Century. The more elaborate, inferior proof of the distinctness of the transcendental, is that formalist one developed centuries after Cusa's original discovery, by Euler, Lambert, Hermite, and Lindemann. However, the issue, which method, algebraic or geometric, is superior, is actually governing, was settled in principle, in favor of the geometric, by the successive work of Gauss and Riemann in the domain of number theory. Riemann's treatment of the prime number domain, correcting the initial attempts by Euler, and continuing that of Lejeune Dirichlet, is exemplary.[48]

A modest few remarks on the history of this matter, are of crucial significance at this point.

---

48. *Über die Anzahl der Primzahlen unter einer gegebenen Grösse,* **Werke,** pp. 145–155.

Even beginning at the simplest level of classroom instruction, the paradoxes arising in the effort to define simple agreement between multiplication and division, for example: the theory of numbers becomes increasingly a thicket of paradoxes, thus assuring employment for both many number theorists, and also any supercomputer which might otherwise sit idle. The question this fact poses, is: "What does all this really mean?"

The case of Gauss's youthful dissertation, his **Disquisitiones arithmeticae,** published in 1801, exhibits the mind of a master of number theory whose method of thinking was essentially geometric.[49] The geometer's view of the density of paradoxes which appear in the number domain, demystifies arithmetic, and aids us in appreciating the geometric standpoint of physical space-time, as the location where the significance of such number-theoretical paradoxes is to be uncovered, as such masters of number theory as Gauss and Riemann illustrate the point.

That is to say, that numerical operations should be understood to be reflections of some corresponding physical operations, the latter to be comprehended from a geometrical standpoint. One outstanding example of this, the origins of ancient astrophysics, expressed in terms of relatively simple, but relevant illustrations, up through the discoveries of Eratosthenes, will suffice for our purposes here.

The characteristic features of ancient Vedic astronomy, as studied by Europeans, from Kepler on,[50] include the great equi-

---

49. Every secondary pupil should have worked through much of this masterpiece. Encountering this, later in my life, filled me with regret at the amount of avoidable agonies I might have avoided having to work through by other means, had I become familiar with this during my school years. The reprint of the original Latin edition (Leipzig: 1801) is extant as Vol. I of the **Werke** (Hildesheim-New York: Georg Olms Verlag, 1981). Sundry translations into modern languages are available, including the English Arthur Clarke, trans. (New Haven: Yale, 1966), and the German, **Untersuchungen Über Höhere Arithmetik,** H. Maser, trans. (New York: Chelsea reprint edition, 1981).

50. See Bal Gangadhar Tilak, **Orion** and **The Arctic Home in the Vedas.** As noted by Mahatma Gandhi and others, Tilak's work contributed a crucial part, in freeing India's intellectual leaders from the sense of cultural

noctial and other millennial or longer cycles, which correspond to a language reflecting prolonged earlier association with a transoceanic form of ancient maritime culture. Harvard Professor Barry Fell's solving the mystery of the Egyptian discovery of the Pacific coast of South America, using the methods of celestial navigation developed by Eratosthenes, has similar implications, to which I shall make reference here.[51] The fact, that the founders of what became known to historical times as ancient Greece and Cyrenaica, established maritime colonies of the type of the legendary, transoceanic Peoples of the Sea, is highly relevant to our illustration here.

Look up to the stars. What do you observe? Chiefly, nothing but regular, zodiacal, angular, apparently circular motion. Such observations assume qualitatively more significance, when they are made, for purposes of navigation, by members of a transoceanic maritime culture, especially when those travels carry the party in question from the northern into the southern hemisphere. The position of Egypt on our planet, with its long history of astronomical work, is notable on this latter account.

For purposes of reference, consider the specific case of Captain Rati and navigator Maui, two Egyptians of Cyrenaican extraction, recording their voyage in the writing of an ancient Cyrenaican language. They, using the astrophysics of Eratosthenes for this purpose, led a flotilla of large wooden Egyptian ships typical of that time, for an attempted west-east circumnavi-

---

inferiority to Britain, the which had been induced by the British Empire. Thus, this work of Tilak contributed significantly to changing the character of India's National Indian Congress, making possible a more effective effort to secure sovereignty for the people of the subcontinent.

51. Barry Fell's writings on Eratosthenes, celestial navigation, and his decipherment of inscriptions describing a Third Century B.C. voyage to America, appear in the early issues of the Epigraphic Society Occasional Publications. See also, Lyndon H. LaRouche, Jr., "On Eratosthenes, Maui's Voyage of Discovery, and Reviving the Principle of Discovery Today," 21st Century Science & Technology, Spring 1999. Fell's son Julian discusses his father's knowledge of astronomy and celestial navigation in a biographical article, "Barry Fell, Epigrapher: Biography of a Renaissance Man," in the Winter 1999–2000 issue of 21st Century Science & Technology.

gation of the planet [**Figure 2**]. The eastward voyage of that flotilla was halted, by encounter with the Pacific coast of South America, and probably, as navigational logic and some other evidence indicates, also parts of Central America, too. They gave up the effort to continue the eastward journey, after going south to seek a passage around South America, returning to a cave located near today's Santiago, Chile, to record their discovery of the continent, and to claim it for Egypt's Pharaoh.[52]

At that time, prior to the devastating cultural decline hitting the Mediterranean region with pagan Rome's rise to dominance,[53] not only the size of the Earthball, but also the Earth's orbitting of the Sun, had become well known. The measurement of the circumference of the Earth by the Platonic Academy's Cyrenaican, Eratosthenes, was part of the science which, according to the record of navigator Maui, guided Egypt's flotilla eastward, through the Indian Ocean and across the Pacific. Notably, the accomplishments of Eratosthenes reflected a direction of Classical-Greek, Egypt-linked scientific progress since Pythagoras and Thales. Notably, ancient Egypt's accounts attributed the founding of Egypt to colonization by an ancient maritime culture. My point here, is to prompt the reader to think of the notion of non-linearity, from the geometric standpoint of the legacy of

---

52. In addition to the references cited in note 51, see Marjorie Mazel Hecht, "The Decipherment and Discovery of a Voyage to America in 232 B.C.," **21st Century Science & Technology,** Winter 1998–99; Karl Stolp (1888), "Indian Inscriptions from the Cordilleras in Chile," **21st Century Science & Technology,** Winter 1998–99; Marjorie Mazel Hecht, "Eratosthenes' Instruments Guided Maui's 3rd Century B.C. Voyage," **21st Century Science & Technology,** Spring 1999; and Sentiel Rommel, Ph.D., "Maui's Tanawa: A Torquetum of 232 B.C.," **21st Century Science & Technology,** Spring 1999.

53. This precipitous cultural ruin of Mediterranean civilization began as a transformation induced during the period 218–146 B.C., the period from the beginning of the Second Punic War, through the crushing of the Achaean League. Typical was the murder of Archimedes by Roman soldiers in 212 B.C. Without that cultural debasement, far below the level of earlier Greek and Hellenistic culture, the fraud of Claudius Ptolemy, for example, would not have been tolerated.

ECONOMICS

FIGURE 2
Probable route of the Egyptian journey in 232 B.C.

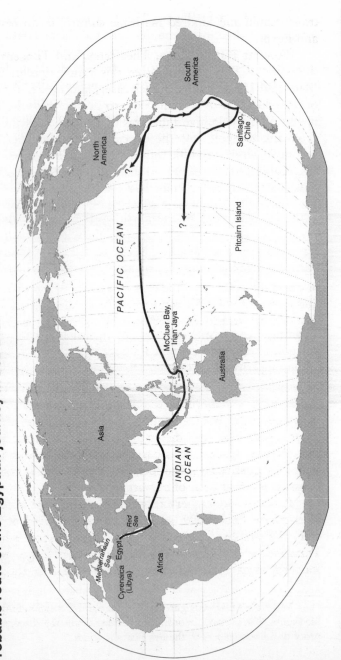

transoceanic and kindred maritime culture, in ancient Greece and Egypt.

Look at Plato's **Meno, Theaetetus,** and **Timaeus,** as also the work of Eratosthenes, from this vantage-point. Read the **Meno** and **Theaetetus** as, in each case, Plato's use of the example of the education of a young boy, to demonstrate the necessity of use of the cognitive functions of the mind, as the basis in geometric thinking, for the education of young persons into becoming future scientific thinkers.[54] The **Timaeus** has a different, higher quality of aim, in its address to the same essential topic, the principles of cognition.

To know, rather than merely learn, the significance of the appearance of the subject of the five regular solids in the **Timaeus,** think of the view of the universe by one who knew, at that time, that the Earth is a planet of approximately spherical shape, as the Greeks of Plato's time knew this. Look at the subject-matter of those solids through the eyes of ancient navigators. Look at that matter on the scale represented by transoceanic navigation. Explore the paradoxes, as shown by comparing a global map with Mercator's projection, which the evidence of that navigation poses to simple sense-perception. Then, it is more readily clear, that the five Platonic solids have the immediate significance of being characteristic of the projection of a specific choice of curved form of astrophysical space-time, as opposed to the arbitrary conceit, of bodies floating within a homogeneously four-square space-time. In other words, the characteristic action of that physical space-time is curved, not linear, not to be determined by quadrature. The fact that it is curved is certain; the question is, what kind of curvature?

Return to our earlier exposition of the concept of cognition, of cognitive *knowledge,* as distinct from the kind of learning from the simple experience of direct, naive sense-perception. Transoceanic navigation requires true knowledge, not mere learning, as navigator Maui recorded his praise of the scientific

---

54. Plato's fictional figures were often named, meaningfully, for real-life figures. Theaetetus, according to accounts, was the discoverer of the proof of the uniqueness of the five Platonic solids.

achievements of Eratosthenes, midway en route to the Pacific coast of South America.[55] Here lies the significance of the transcendental, as Cusa is the first known to have discovered it, that from the geometric standpoint of Plato and Eratosthenes. Here lies the crucial role of Cusa in that work of Paolo dal Pozzo Toscanelli, which gave Columbus the map reflecting the discoveries by Eratosthenes, and supplied the strategic impetus used for the rediscovery of the Americas.

Plato uses this demonstration of the five solids, relative to the characteristic differences between living and non-living processes, to expose a more general, deeper principle, the principle reflected in the very title of Cusa's **De docta ignorantia,** the universally cognitive nature of knowledge, that as opposed to mere learning. This is the principle which was re-established in European science by Cusa, Pacioli, and Leonardo, and, through them, occupied a central place in the founding of both modern astrophysics and also a comprehensive form of mathematical physics, by Kepler.

To be fair, entire chunks taken from this work of Plato and his Academy, are reflected in the latter part of the **Thirteen Books of Euclid.** As I have stressed earlier here, and, repeatedly, in other locations, the evil of classroom Euclidean geometry lies not in the work of Euclid, but in the imposition upon the mind of the young, of the *a priori* notion of infinitely extended (to both the large and small) linearity of space and time, the same aprioristic folly which foolish Leonhard Euler and his fellow-ideologues adopted, in defense of Newton's follies, against Leibniz.

Apply such considerations to the real-life problems confronting the hardy entrepreneur in his management of a technologically progressive manufacturing enterprise. Like Gauss's choice of approach to the problem of defining the asteroid orbits,

---

55. Maui's inscriptions on the wall of one of the "Caves of the Navigators" in New Guinea (now Irian Jaya), include his demonstration of Eratosthenes' measurement of the size of the Earth. These were photographed in 1937 by Josef Röder of the Frobenius Institute in Frankfurt, Germany, but they were not deciphered until 1974, by Barry Fell.

that entrepreneur must make long-ranging investment decisions, on the basis of the relatively few crucial experimental measurements available. The differences are small, but the longer-term implications may be enormous.

So, the characteristic curvature which, in physical reality, connects the dots of cost accounting's observations, can not be safely presumed to be linear. In important cases, it is not. In crucial cases, failure to recognize that principle, has proven disastrous. We must now wait to complete the immediately foregoing discussion of this matter, at the appropriate later point, after we have first addressed the prerequisites respecting the role of culture in cost accounting. Then, after that, we shall complete the discussion under the heading of budgetary and cost-accounting principles.

3. Culture as a Cost of Productivity

As summarized in the opening portion of the preceding section of this report, the possibility of cooperation in applying validated discoveries of universal physical principle, among persons considered pair-wise, or the members of society in general, depends upon what I presented there, as the three-step prerequisites for sharing such knowledge among two or more persons.

I also stressed there, that to achieve the same quality of knowledge of past time's discoveries of universal physical principles, the student, or other living member of society, must replicate the original enactment of that discovery, in accord with the same three-step prerequisites required for sharing such knowledge directly with a living acquaintance.

I stressed there, that, in this way, the accumulation of a living person's actual knowledge of such principles, produces in that person's mind, an array of images of both those earlier, and contemporary discoverers of such validated universal principles, an array typified by the example of Raphael Sanzio's celebrated **The School of Athens.** Such persons from the past, although deceased, have, nonetheless, spoken directly to the living individual child's, or adult's mind, through the transparent medium of time, through that medium of communication called cognition.

Those persons from our past, constitute an assembly of conscience, a court of living personalities, seated, at our beckoning,
within the simultaneity of eternity. So, at our calling, they are
constituted as a great council, before whom we must defend and
judge the truthfulness of all among our own opinions, including
new hypotheses. Only among those about us, who are sterile
formalists, virtual Yahoos, or outrightly malevolent persons, is
this not so.

Some, or all of such members of that great council of truthfulness, may be in error in appearing to oppose my opinion, but they
must be countered on that issue in a certain, specific way, a way
which compels that council of immortals to judge whether or not
that proposition is truthful, even if it contradict what they had
believed before. To saints of such distinction, from such a council,
a devout person might justly, and fruitfully pray for guidance. So,
aided by such resident immortals, conscience disciplines true
statesmen, scientists, and poets, in the art of being truthful, in opinion, and in the submission of practice to uncompromising service
of cognitively defined universal principle.[56]

---

56. Contrast my use of "conscience," here, with Shakespeare's in-
sightful treatment of the contrary mind-set of Hamlet, in the famous Act
III soliloquy: "Thus, conscience doth make cowards of us all." It is the
swashbuckling swordsman's, Hamlet's, lack of a truthful conscience, by
which he is self-doomed to the outcome of the final scene of that tragedy.
Hear that in the setting of the relevant excerpt in which the statement
is made:
". . . that dread of something after death
The undiscover'd country, from whose bourn
No traveller returns, puzzles the will,
And makes us rather bear those ills we have
Than fly to others we know not of?
Thus conscience doth make cowards of us all;
And thus the native hue of resolution
Is sicklied o'er with the pale cast of thought;
And enterprises of great pith and moment,
With this regard, their currents turn awry,
And lose the name of action. . . ."
It is the lack of a true conscience, as I have described it, which is the root
of swashbuckling swordsman Hamlet's fatal cowardice.

Within the mind whose individual cognitive powers have been cultivated to such effect, that great council of truthfulness, is the living essence of the unfolding of past, present, and future scientific knowledge. All of us who have acquired cultivated minds, have such a council readily at hand, our old friends such as Plato, Eratosthenes, Cusa, Leonardo, Kepler, Leibniz, and so on, many of whom one knows by a familiar name, who are called from the past, to express cognitive moments from their living personality, within us, in some present moment.

That same council, is also the only true choice of place where the greatest compositions of Classical art, are composed and justly performed afresh. There dwell some of the greatest Classical poets, musicians, dramatists, painters, architects, and sculptors, and other masters of true metaphor, of the past. The subject of great Classical artistic compositions, is always, essentially, a celebration of those powers of communication through which we, as individuals, are able to share the ongoing development of our individual cognitive powers. The subject of art, is the rudimentary expression of this sharing of truthfulness, as that is also expressed by the three-step method of validating a discovered, universal physical principle.

Truthfulness is not von Hayek's cafeteria, not some "greasy spoon," from whose steam-table, or salad bar, one might select liberally one's choice of dish. The attempt to separate scientific from artistic truthfulness, as the irrationalist Immanuel Kant does, is the mark of an intrinsically immoral personality.[57] Truth

---

Similarly, it is, therefore, no less than fair to say, that any university in today's globally extended European civilization, which subscribes to a policy, under which students are not obliged to study the Classical forms of scientific and artistic composition of "dead white European males (DWEMs)," is fairly described as a virtual "Hell hole," steeped in untruthfulness and related expressions of immorality.

57. For example, in Germany, the neo-Kantian dogma, decreeing an absolute separation of *Geisteswissenschaft* from *Naturwissenschaft,* of G.W.F. Hegel's Romantic crony, Professor Karl Savigny. The less elegant version of Kant's and Savigny's immoral dogma, is the doctrine of "art for art's sake." The crudest form of expression of this same moral degeneracy, is the Yahoo bordello called "popular culture."

rules one's choice of what each of us is morally permitted to select. This is true in science, in economics, in statecraft generally, and in the composition, selection, and public performance of artistic compositions.

Such a commitment to truthfulness, respecting both science and art, is the only mode in which anyone among us might become his, or her true self. Unfortunately, few, especially nowadays, succeed in becoming their own true self. Yet, seeking that Socratic pathway to truthfulness in opinion and practice, is the only course which does not lead the deceased individual, ultimately, as failed, or even evil souls, into waiting before the great council seated in the simultaneity of eternity, to await judgment on their prospective relegation to the rubbish-bin of true history.

In successful approaches to these Classical forms of artistic composition, the underlying subject-matter is the same cognitive social relationships, the which are the substance of the sharing of the discovery and validation of solutions to well-defined scientific paradoxes. In Classical artistic composition, we speak of metaphor, or dissonance, terms whose proper use in the domain of artistic composition, identifies the same function, named ontological paradox, in the domain of physical science and epistemology generally.

On this account, we include under the heading of Classical artistic composition, the transformation of a relatively brutish form of spoken or written language, into a medium which is well suited to the processes of communicating cognitive conceptions of both relations among persons, and of mankind with nature. The work of Dante Alighieri, is an outstanding example of such work; yet, all great Classical poets, as Shelley wrote of this, in his **In Defence of Poetry,** do the same. On the same account, we include under Classical artistic composition, the study of the unfolding of history according to the development, or retrogressions in the evolution of the common manifold of both universal physical principles and Classical-artistic forms of principles. Statecraft is properly the subject of such a Classical-artistic approach to the comprehension of history.

A system of education of the young, which meets that com-

A children's violin orchestra in Leesburg, Virginia. A humanist education "is the only form of education which is in agreement with the development of those cognitive powers which are the essence of human nature." (Photo: EIRNS/Stuart Lewis)

bined use of the term *Classical,* is rightly distinguished as a system of Classical humanist education. This is rightly termed "humanist," because it is the only form of education which is in agreement with the development of those cognitive powers which are the essence of human nature.

Such a policy respecting the education of the young, typifies those expenditures which society must incur, to foster that ongoing development of the entire population, upon which the fostering of continuing cognitive development, and of the productive powers of labor, within all of that population, depends absolutely. Such costs of explicit and implied education, including the conditions of family and community social life necessary for the household of that pre-school child and later student, provide us a point of reference, which aids us in defining those costs which must be met if the fostering and productive realization of scientific and technological progress is to be sustained. Culture,

so defined and otherwise implied, is a prime cost of that increase
of productivity, upon which the viability of the modern sovereign
nation-state economy depends absolutely.

To assess the true costs of maintaining and generating increase of physical productivity of labor per capita, and per square
kilometer, we must consider not only the physical costs of production and distribution as such. We must be able to supply a
reasonable assessment of the costs of sustaining the development
of the cognitive powers, of both the productively employed labor
force, and the supporting population behind it.

Turn first to those cultural costs which today's lunatic popular opinion tends to consider of the least relevance, if any, to
fostering the physical productive powers of labor.

To that end, examine the accelerating rate of moral degeneracy of the U.S. population generally, during the recent thirty to
thirty-five years. By degeneracy, I mean the decadent slide of
U.S. popular culture into life-styles mimicking the self-doomed,
ancient pagan Rome from the period of Rome's Civil Wars and
the subsequent reign of the Caesars. I mean a slide into a culture
which mimics that Roman tradition of "bread and circuses," in
the manner with which we are familiar from observation of our
fellow-man, and his life-style, especially his choice of entertainment, today. The yardstick we adopt for that summation, is the
role of the sense of personal identity in showing us, once again,
today, how the decadent Roman force of *vox populi*—signifying,
literally, the voice of the predators—ensured the collapse of
Roman culture from below.

Personal Identity and Productivity

The most simple fact of mortal life, is that each of us is
born, and will die. That prospect of mortality prompts the person
to think of his or her life in one of two ways.

To the degree that the cultivation of the cognitive powers
of the developing individual predominates, in defining the sense
of personal mortal identity of the individual, that individual
locates his or her personal mortal identity in the transmission
of distinctly human qualities of the person, the transmitting of

shared cognitive experiences, from predecessors, and to successors. An individual with that sense of cognitive identity, has an enduring reason to live, a meaning of life which death can not interrupt. That is the connection, the defense of the meaning of life, in service of which he or she is prepared to die. This approximates the cognition-driven social relations I have summarily described above.

On the opposite side, together with Shakespeare's tragic Hamlet, we have the empiricist's sense of identity, that we associate with Hobbes, or the modern existentialist. As a Nazi philosopher, the existentialist Martin Heidegger, expressed it, the individual senses a quality of being thrown into a society against his will. Heidegger's follower Jean-Paul Sartre, and such associates as Hannah Arendt, expressed philosophical world- outlooks close to that of the Nietzschean Nazi Heidegger. Such were the Romans marching into the Colosseum, to cheer for gladiatorial spectacles, chariot races, or Christians being crucified, or torn apart by Nero's lions. Such was the Romantic's tradition expressed by Adolf Hitler's plebiscites: "Hail! Caesar!"

In short, the method is the man, and the man is his method. The primary distinctions in method, are the cognitive versus the hedonistic. The former is the premise for a human sense of identity, the latter the premise of the beast-man type, such as a Hobbes, Adam Smith, Jeremy Bentham, Immanuel Kant, satanic Friedrich Nietzsche, Bertrand Russell, John von Neumann, Karl Jaspers, Adorno, Arendt, Heidegger, Sartre, or Frantz Fanon.

The contrast between those two poles of choice, in what is called art or recreation, expresses precisely those contrasting tendencies in choices of preferences for adopted sense of personal identity.

One expression of such contrasts, is the opposition of the Classical musical current of Bach, Haydn, Mozart, Beethoven, Schubert, Schumann, Brahms et al., to their Romantic opponents, such as Rameau, Liszt, Berlioz, Wagner, and poor and tiresome Anton Bruckner. Those expressions are reflections of the continued opposition of the Greek Classical legacy in art to the Romantic, as the Classical is to be contrasted with the decadent preferences of the Roman pagan tradition. The art preferred by the first, locates the sense of identity in cognition; the latter, in the hedonist's tintinnabulations of the senses, the empiricist's and existentialist's disdain for truth, as expressed in preferences rooted in desire for sensual effects.[58]

There is a third sort of art, the pathological form which reflects an irrationalist's wish for the power of magic: symbolic art, as a pathology related to symbolic "reasoning," or, more elegantly, "symbol-mindedness."[59] The latter are extensions of the Romantic's yearning for sensual effects, but emphasize the existentialists' violent yearning for an ecstatic sense of magical power lodged in the unreal.

Apart from such distinctions among such qualities of culti-

---

58. Typical of decadent musicians and their audiences, on this account, is the irrationalist doctrine of "instrumental music." Classical musical composition, as from Bach through Brahms, is premised upon the Florentine *bel canto* training of the human singing voice. All Classical composition for, and authentic performance using man-made instruments, is based upon developing the capability of those instruments to mimic the registral and coloration qualities of the six primary species of human singing voice; all Classical composition is polyphonic, in the sense of Bach's system of well-tempered polyphony, and the tuning which agrees with the *bel canto*-trained human singing voice. Modern Romanticism's perverted approach to performance of Classical compositions, was an outgrowth of the mangling of the compositions, to eliminate the control of performance from the standpoint of those methods of polyphonic motivic thorough-composition which are premised upon the preceding revolutionary developments in *bel canto*-keyed polyphony. Typical of the frauds employed to bring this change about, was the misinterpretation of the Classical composer Frederic Chopin as a pro-Liszt sort of composer at the keyboard, and the matching general, hedonistic doctrine of so-called "instrumental music."

59. Typical, in today's world, are such existentialist, emotionally infantile depravities as "Dungeons & Dragons," the cult-series titled **The Lord of the Rings,** and homicidal-training exercises for the young, typified by electronic parodies of Samurai fantasies, such as Nintendo and Pokémon. The wave of "new violence" by children, such as the Littleton massacre, typifies the current lunacies of that sort. Such techniques of mass-brainwashing of young children (from about three years of age and up) and adolescents, as by mass-drugging of children with drugs out of Aldous Huxley's **Brave New World,** such as Ritalin, are coherent with the use of low-frequency brain-wave entraining and "non-linear spiking" in both video

vated art-forms, we have, close to the Romantics, the lustily boorish traditions of *vox populi,* the simply hedonistic recreations preferred by the common Yahoos of society, typified by those kindred popular traditions, gambling and prostitution, and by today's increasingly degraded popular television entertainments, and mass-spectator bodily-contact sports.

These distinctions between the cognitive sense of identity and the hedonistic, also show in the workplace. In descriptive terms, the cognitive sense of personal identity impels one to turn the workplace into a place of useful creative innovations. The cognitive personality, even when engaged in the relatively crudest form of repetitive manual labor, is thinking about improving the product and workplace. If successful in that attempt, such a personality says that he enjoys his work. The Yahoo, by contrast, would prefer to smash his tools, were it not that he needed the wages.

That is a simplified portrayal of the matter, but brevity is preserved through such simplifications, without misrepresenting anything essential respecting the point at hand.[60] The most important among the points I am stressing in this way, is that *the improvement of productivity depends largely upon the moral character of the individual member of society. By "moral character," I mean, in this case, the distinction between mere learning and cognition.* Cognitive development of the personality, as distinct from mere learning of formal competence in specific techniques, fosters a compulsion to know and to improve products and practices.

---

games and children-oriented television broadcasting of the Nintendo-Samurai varieties.

60. I work about 10–12 hours a day, sometimes longer, that usually seven days a week. Admittedly, my work has exceptional importance attached to it, but even when I was engaged in manual labor, a long time ago, it was the same with me. I always found a cognitive interest in what I did, and was often reluctant to interrupt the ongoing work-day, on that account. This was typical among high-grade operatives, skilled, or other, among my generation, and older. The suggestion-boxes of enlightened manufacturing firms, reflected a considerable amount of cognitive reflection about the work occurring among the operatives.

It is not education, as such, which promotes relatively high rates of technological progress. It is the impulsion supplied by cognitive ferment within the individual. We might refer to this as the impulse for enjoyment of the pleasures of progress through cognitive innovation. It is not mere learning which fosters high rates of technological progress and related improvements in productivity; it is the fostering of the kind of sense of personal mortal identity associated with the sharing of cognitive experiences, which bestirs within the population a restive disposition to make improvements, simply because they are useful improvements.

A scientist may require a certain income, that as conditions required to free him from concern for matters other than his profession; the motivation of scientific work is not material rewards, but progress for its own sake. Whenever we witness a capable scientific professional obsessed with material rewards, we are witnessing threatened, if not actual death of that person's capacity for competent scientific judgment.

The operative who says of his employment, "I make a decent wage, which I need, of course, but I am happy about the fact that I can support my family by doing what I like to do," is typical of the quality to which I refer. We saw the same principle expressed in the production miracles which the U.S. accomplished during the first several years of World War II. The sense of personal identity involved, was key in the quality as well as quantity of the resulting changes. The same human factor is to be seen in science-driver forms of so-called "crash programs," such as the Manhattan Project and the ascending phase, until the setbacks of 1966–67, of the Kennedy Manned Moon Landing program, which produced technological economic spin-offs for the U.S. economy more than a dozen times greater than the outlay for that program. It is the kind of motivation for change which springs from the aroused cognitive sense of personal identity of the operative, which, in the longer run, is crucial in fostering higher rates of gain in per-capita rates of national physical-economic productivity.

That said, the matter to be examined so situated, how shall we define the factors of cost associated with the desired rates of increase of physical-economic productivity per capita?

Cognition as a Cost of Labor

Typically, for the case of a modern industrial-manufacturing complex, the core of the production process itself, apart from infrastructure and distribution, is composed of three functionally interdependent, categorical elements of that portion of the total division of labor: 1) *Scientific research and testing,* both of physical principles and of the technologies derived from them; 2) *Design engineering and machine-tool development and testing;*[61] 3) *Production operatives.* Typically, these three, paradigmatic elements of the composition of the productive sector of the labor-force, reflect a parallel composition of social functions in family household life, and also in the community within which family life is situated. The preponderance of the circumstances determining the potential relative productivity of all members of the total labor-force, is situated in the latter circumstances of family-household and community life.

As a model bench-mark for our discussion at this point of this topic, we limit our attention to three types of U.S. communities: *urban-industrial-commercial, rural,* and *suburban.* Keep in mind, as a useful rule-of-thumb, that contrast among urban designs, which is typified by such comparisons as the high-rise characteristics of cities such as the island of Manhattan, and the spectacle, suggesting a toppled skyscraper, of the traditional, sprawling London of yore. A space below, we shall compare the three general categories of communities in terms of their relative potential economic, and also cultural efficiencies. We shall examine these with a view to outlining the requirements of these types, which must be considered, in defining the market-basket of physical-economic costs required, to produce and sustain a certain typical quality of productive potential in the labor-force as a whole.

For purposes of first approximation, it is fairly said, that the labor-force available for employment, corresponds to a potential productivity inhering in the cultural development of the total

---

61. This applies to each of the first two categories here, whether that function is performed in-house, or in the form of purchased services.

labor-force. This labor-force, is, in turn, a reflection of and "output" of, the ongoing process of development of those family households and communities of which the entire population is composed. The realization of that potential, requires the provision of the matching conditions of production itself. The object of production is, in first approximation, to combine the potential inhering in the labor-force, with the conditions of production and distribution needed to permit realizing the potential represented by the labor-force. In the second approximation, we must correct the first approximation, to take into account the generation of *increased* potential productivity in the labor-force itself, and, also, to match that with relevant kinds and rates of improvements in the conditions provided by relevant, task-oriented, new qualities of investment in the productive employment of that improved labor-force.

In that, the resort to unavoidable approximations, will not represent a defect in the corresponding cost-accounting practice. *What is crucial, is not the merely formal-mathematical precision with which we might estimate the relevant quantities; crucial, is the way we think about the way in which we are estimating.*

We are implicitly returned, thus, back to the topic of the higher hypothesis. Once again, for pedagogical reasons, we shall address the questions we have just implied, in three steps. We shall look at a cross-section of the relationship between current potential of the labor force, and realized levels of productivity in the population as a whole. Second, we shall consider a stepwise "model," as represented by a series of upgrades in both population potential and realized productivity. Third, we shall pose the challenge, of defining that principle of change, which subsumes a *functionally defined* continuing progress of the type approximated by the second "mode," *a progress subsumed functionally by a single, continuing principle, a principle cohering with the notion of higher hypothesis.*[62]

---

62. This notion of an action coheres with the derivative, as a *characteristic*, in Leibniz's development of the calculus. This coheres, for example, with Leibniz's principle of universal least action, and with the core of a posthumously published work of his, called **The Monadology**. This was

However, we must precede those steps with a focus upon certain among the crucial internal features of the pair-wise, cognitive relationship among individuals sharing the *ongoing action* of discovering, or rediscovering, a single, validatable hypothesis. That focus enables us to show the most elementary expression of the relevant type of social relationship upon which the increase of the productive potentials, of both population and the economy as a whole, depends. That also shows the interior of the most elementary interval of an expressing of a principle of culture. In respect to both economy and culture, the crucial verb is, *to know, the act of knowing:* the ability to prompt and to observe the inducing of the replication of the relevant act of discovering in the mind of another, as by the three-step principle of knowing cognition, as introduced here earlier. That action, which includes that of Classical-artistic composition, is the elementary term of all the relevant functions to be considered here.

That verb "to know," the act of knowing, corresponds not to something in the form of the sense-perception of an object, nor merely to operations of deduction from sense-certainty; it corresponds, not to an *act,* but to *an ongoing action,* an expressed principle of change, an *action* which defines knowledge, defines social relations, defines science, defines culture, defines society, and defines economy.[63] *To know,* is to recognize an *idea* through the *process of replication of its discovery,* a discovery which is to be made in the same manner as in the three-step process used for defining a discovery of a universal principle, as I have

---

the central issue of the attack on Leibniz by Antonio Conti's agent, Dr. Samuel Clarke, and was the point at issue in the fraud of "least action" perpetrated by Conti, posthumously, by his salons' Maupertuis and Euler. This same notion of characteristic, is—I repeat once again—fairly approximated by the notion of ordered change in the *characteristic of action,* in a well-ordered series of Riemannian manifolds of physical space-time.

63. The term "culture," is not freely applicable, in the same sense, to both human beings and to animals. Animals, as pets, when very young, may make attachments to human beings, to such effect that, in the argument of Nicholas of Cusa, the lower species may *participate in* the higher species. To speak of such animals as "socialized," is appropriate; to attribute social relations, in the human sense, to wild beasts, is an act of maudlin fantasy.

underscored that connection earlier in this report.[64] Such ideas,
define all expressions characteristic of human nature: the faculty
of seeing with the higher faculty, the mind's eye of cognition,
as distinct from mere "information," distinct from what are
merely statistical constructions from memories of sense-perception as such. All functional notions pertaining to human cognitive
potential, to increase of productive powers of labor, and so forth,
are of the character of such Platonic ideas: *ideas* of *continuing
change,* generated, and recognized through the cognitive processes of the individual, as those processes become subjects of
cooperation and culture, through the pair-wise function I have
defined here.

Here, earlier, we supplied, if in but summary, elementary
definitions, the notion of the generation of the *ideas* of universal
physical principle and technology. Now, to address the issues
introduced at this point, we must locate the origins and eco-
nomic-functional significance of principles of a Classical-artistic
form. To that purpose, the notion of "Classical," as used respecting both science and artistic composition, signifies ideas which
correspond to acts of cooperation, *per se,* among the cognitive
processes of participating persons. This includes, in the case of
a single, momentarily isolated person, the disposition to participate functionally in such forms of cooperation.

The subject of Classical art is mankind, *human nature.*
The form in which that subject, human nature, is addressed, is
Classical artistic composition, whose elementary subject is the

---

64. *Idea* is used in this report only in the sense of Platonic idea, a
conception which has been generated by cognition, rather than as constructed, as deductively, for example, from memories of sense-perception.
The action referenced here, corresponds to a non-linear interval of continuing change, as expressed within the interval of a pair-wise sharing of a
validated discovery of universal principle prompted by an ontological paradox. The term "non-linear," in this employment, signifies a case of regular,
non-constant curvature, the kind of Leibnizian *characteristic* signified, as
higher hypothesizing, by the evolution of the characteristic in a well-ordered
series of Riemannian manifolds. The latter characteristic, is expressed as
the rate of change of the *characteristic* potential relative productivity of
the relevant physical, economic-development process.

pair-wise action of cognition itself. In the case of validated universal physical principles, as considered earlier, we were examining the generation of those ideas through which mankind's per-capita power in and over nature is increased. Now, as we turn to the related matter of the universal principles of a Classical form of culture, we are looking at the individual's power in and over nature, in terms of the principles of culture, the culture upon which we depend for our ability to cooperate in ways essential to realizing mankind's increase of potential power over nature. Thus, we see physical science rightly, as a subsidiary feature of what is best represented by the principles of a Classical form of culture. *We see physical science, now, as an attribute of human nature.* In turn, all Classical culture's development, is subsumed by two interdependent subjects: the action of cognition itself, and the way in which human cooperation should be organized, through acts of pair-wise cognitive action.

The subject-matter through which the cultural aspects of cognition and cognitive relations are addressed, is always the demonstration of ambiguities of a general type, usually known as *irony,* including a special quality of irony called *metaphor.*[65]

-----

65. For example, in J.S. Bach's domain of well-tempered polyphony, as expressed, since the early 1780s, by the motivic thorough-composition of Joseph Haydn, Wolfgang Mozart, Ludwig von Beethoven, Johannes Brahms, et al., the kernel of musical composition is two distinct voices, elaborating an entire, unfolding composition, on the basis of the interplay of counterposed voices, and the use of a core cluster of intervals in both an initially stated form, and a contrasting inversion: as in the opening measures of J.S. Bach's **A Musical Offering.** This is already irony in the sense of ontological ambiguity. The pivot of the entire composition so unfolding, is a conflict in tonality, derived lawfully from those simpler ironies of well-tempered counterpoint, but expressing a clash of ironies equivalent to an ontological paradox in physical science. Thus, it is physical reality, as represented by the natural (i.e., *bel canto*) composition of the natural-determined division of the human singing-voice, among soprano, tenor, etc., which imposes naturally generated ironies and paradoxes upon the formalist's musical scale. Three examples of this, of musical paradoxes as metaphors, are perhaps sufficient at this point. The first example, is the opening measures of Mozart's Köchel 475 C-minor keyboard Fantasy, in which, as this appears, in contrast to the suffixed K. 457 sonata, boldly

Metaphors are *truthful falsehoods* of the type and form corresponding to ontological paradoxes.[66] The resolution of the paradox (i.e., metaphor) is accomplished solely through introducing a new, validatable principle, just as in a Riemannian manifold of universal physical principles. This latter discovery, situated with respect to that defining of that metaphor, becomes the unifying subject of the artistic composition as a whole.[67]

The most ancient of the explicitly known cases in which a trace of the later development of the forms of modern European civilization's Classical composition is well defined, is ancient Classical poetry. By tradition, such poetry was always sung,

---

stated, at the outset, Mozart situates the F# from the opening of Bach's **A Musical Offering,** as the metaphor which defines the composition as a whole, unifying idea. Secondly, Beethoven's Opus 132 string quartet "In The Lydian Mode," carries that same discovery of Mozart explicitly to a higher dimensionality. Thirdly, Beethoven addresses this lesson from Mozart in a striking way, in two of his later piano sonatas. The first such example, is to be found in a crucial development within the second movement of his Opus 106, a passage occurring in measures 70–86. A similar event occurs in measures 30–49 of the Coda of the Opus 111. In the latter, Beethoven quotes from Mozart's K. 475 explicitly. To the same effect, it is beyond doubt, that the deceased Beethoven, from his place in the simultaneity of eternity, performing in his own mind the score of Brahms' Fourth Symphony—especially that Fourth Symphony—would recognize that the living Brahms had become possible, because Beethoven, and Bach and Mozart before them both, had lived.

66. That is to say, they are contradictions, truthfully expressing a conflict between reality and a referenced, pre-existing mind-set, a conflict which is forced, intentionally, by the author or composer, upon the attention of victims of the latter mind-set. The falsehood lies in the minds of those victims, who see the metaphor as being false to their prejudices; the truthfulness is the contribution of the composing artist, as John Keats emphasizes in his famous **Ode on a Grecian Urn.**

67. Franz Schubert's song-setting from Shakespeare, as **An Sylvia,** offers an exception which proves the rule. In German, the result is problematic; one should recall that the German text usually associated with that musical score, was written after Schubert set Shakespeare's English poem. Sung in the English text used by Schubert, that is, according to the relevant English vocalizations, the appropriate tempo and other matters fall nicely into place

rather than "recited." It was sung according to the same principles of vocalization adduced, in particular, for Italian Florentine
bel canto by Leonardo da Vinci; it bears, thus, the trace of the
familiar strophic form from the historic period of Indo-European
Classical poetry. Apart from the Italian tradition of Dante Alighieri, Petrarch, and Leonardo da Vinci, the best models of this
from modern times, after Shakespeare, are the German Classical
poetry, and its Classical song settings, from Goethe and Schiller
through Heinrich Heine, and the English productions of Keats
and Shelley. The best modern renderings of the Negro Spiritual,
since the collaboration of Harry Burleigh and Antonin Dvorak,
are treated as strophic, sung poetry, according to the same principles of rendering of traditional folk-song by Haydn, Mozart,
Beethoven, and Brahms.[68]

On this matter, note, that often, when the repeats of a
Mozart or Beethoven sonata or quartet are played as simply
repeats, the principle of strophic poetry is cruelly violated by
the performers. To the degree the composer has indicated this,
the notes are those which the composer has indicated in the
score; but, it was the composer's intent, that they be performed
in a manner contrary to the artistic blindness of the minds exhibited by far too many among the usual performers. The composer's rendering of the repeat, is that it should be varied in such
a way, as to function as a cognitively adducible progression in
development, differing from that during the previous hearing
of that repeated strophe. In reality, what is repeated, is sung
differently, as in apposition to the preceding statement of the
same, or similar strophe.[69] In Classical composition, and its ap-

---

68. Brahms' counsel on the rendering of traditional folk-song, is
reflected in Gustav Jenner, **Johannes Brahms als Mensch, Lehrer und
Kunstler: Studien und Erlebnisse** (Marburg am Rhein: N.G. Elwert'sche
Verlagsbuchhandlung, 1930). See, **A Manual On the Rudiments of Tuning
and Registration,** John Sigerson and Kathy Wolfe, eds. (Washington, D.C.:
Schiller Institute, 1992). Brahms' counsel was employed by Dvorak during
the latter's work on the Negro Spiritual, in collaboration with Burleigh,
in the U.S.A.

69. The principle is the same as for the opening of Hamlet's Third
Act soliloquy; there must be a change in coloration, in the succession of

propriate performance, the appropriate change in the repeated strophe, is governed by the principle, that the procession of strophes, is always arrayed ironically in performance, *such that the composition as a whole is an integrated process of cognitive development, from outset to conclusion.*

The individual performance is heard in the intention of the qualified performer, as an expression (in the small) of a cognitive simultaneity of eternity, each moment of action within, subsumed by an idea which encompasses the entirety of the development. That unifying idea of the development, is the idea of the composition and its performance as a seamless entirety.[70] The name of that composition, then becomes the name of that idea, with the same significance for a person who knows that idea, in the guise of a personalized name, as is given, similarly, to the idea of a discovery of universal physical principle. This is so required, explicitly, by *the method of motivic thorough-composition,* used from Mozart and Haydn, through Brahms. Thus, so intended and so performed, the ironical procession of the strophes, moves the emergence of the anticipated metaphor into position, up to the point the attack by the metaphor strikes.

This aspect of the common features of Classical poetry and musical compositions, is ironically underscored by the metaphor of comparing the principles of composition of the non-plastic media, such as poetry and song, with the development of Classical plastic composition, from the Greek sculptures of Scopas and Praxiteles through the paintings of Leonardo da Vinci and Raphael Sanzio, as also typified by Rembrandt's celebrated portrait of blind Homer looking insightfully into the unseeing stare of Aristotle. The element of meaningful "off balance" of the Classical Greek sculpture, is to be contrasted to the archaic

---

"To be, or" and the apposited "not to be." The "to be" of "not to be," must be darkened, either by a register-shift, or otherwise. The literacy of the delivery of the entire soliloquy, and the clarity of the tragic principle of the entire play, depends implicitly upon that distinction within the utterance of that pivotal line. This paradox defines the tragic principle of the drama in its entirety; it expresses the *characteristic action* within the tragedy.

70. The conductor Wilhelm Furtwängler is famous for his practice of what he sometimes identified as "performing between the notes."

Egyptian and Greek, just as Leonardo da Vinci brings the same underlying principle into exposition, full force, with his Milan **The Last Supper.** In the related case of Raphael's **The School of Athens,** there are three principal metaphors: 1) A portrayal of a cognitive simultaneity of eternity among most of the figures; 2) The metaphor of Plato versus Aristotle; and, 3) as, according to one qualified observer, also probably the contrast of the Classical painter, Raphael, with what is suspected to be his opponent, the Romantic Michelangelo, as the gloomy figure of sensuality, lurking, like a foretaste of Caravaggio, in the foreground.

The principle of metaphor is made explicit, in the greatest Classical tragedies, such as those of Aeschylus, Sophocles, Shakespeare, and Schiller. Here, the subject is explicitly, political morality in the domain of statecraft. Yet, in all great works of Classical artistic composition, the pair-wise cognitive relationship between composer and performer, on the one side, and audience on the other, pervades to similar effect. What is lodged here, is *the principles of cognitive communication, always expressed in terms of developing the mind of all, thus to find the means by which to cooperate in service of reason.* The principles so situated, are principles of the same quality of universality as are universal physical principles.

These Classical-artistic principles, as an integral feature of development of the population's powers of communication, are to be integrated into the culture of a people, by means including that of assigning them a dominant place in education of the population generally, where these principles are to be employed to develop the cognitively determined character of the family household, community, and population generally. The included purpose is, to free the people from the pathetically ironical condition of a promising, trained engineer, who became, by or after his graduation, a crippled personality in his social life, a more or less brutish Yahoo, more or less a Hobbesian, or a Mandeville, in his voting patterns, and other ways.

It is through this role of the cognitive experiencing of the discovery, and rediscovery of universal principles of science and Classical-artistic composition, in the family household, in the community, and in the population at large, that the productive

Retired physicist Dr. Robert Moon (now deceased) is shown here teaching children at a summer camp in 1986. Retired persons "are among the indispensable assets for reaching and maintaining a standard of culture" which is required, LaRouche argues. (Photo: EIRNS/Philip Ulanowsky)

potential of the population's labor-force is generated, sustained, and increased. Without the fostering of that Classical approach to science and Classical-artistic composition, the potential productivity of the members of the family household, community, and general population, must tend to be poor, stunted, and tending toward that brutish character which has been increasingly characteristic of the maturing post-war additions to the populations of the Americas and Europe However, presuming that we are committed to reverse the recent descent into decadence in those latter parts of the world, the principles which I recommend here, become imperative. In that case, *those conditions of life which are necessary to sustain that general cognitive development, are to be considered as an essential part of the costs of sustaining and enhancing that potential productivity.*

That correlation between costs of cognition and potential productivity, is to be recognized as located, in its germ-form, in the internal characteristics of the pair-wise *action* of knowing. The comprehension of that correlation, lies in focussing upon the cognitive characteristics specific to Classical-artistic composition.

From the standpoint of the enlightened industrial entrepreneur or farmer, the objects of both public primary and secondary education, and of family life, are, to develop new citizens, who shall represent the general level of potential productivity required for carrying scientific and technological progress of the entire society to new heights. The goal of higher education, whether public or private, is to produce the professionals, who will both lead in bringing about that development of the young, and become the pioneers in both scientific and technological, and also Classical-artistic forms of progress. The goals require not only certain forms of education and related cultural development in the family household, and the functions, such as educational institutions, of the community and the nation. Such cultural development also requires certain physical and other environmental conditions of family household and community life. Taken all together, these represent what must become understood by that common term "standard of living."

In defining a required standard of living within the household and community, the first consideration is physical, a matter of simple demographics. That signifies, that to continue the required devotion, for virtually all among the young, to education through higher education, means, today, the goal of a universally typical school-leaving age of between twenty-two and twenty-five years. That were impossible in a society in which the typical life expectancy were between thirty and forty years, or even fifty years. A modern European standard of Classical culture, and associated level of minimal standard of physical economic equality, could not be developed, or sustained, without a typical life-expectancy of not less than seventy- to eighty-odd, or more, years. The cognitive functions of the so-called retired persons, are among the indispensable assets for reaching and maintaining such a standard of culture, for achieving a comparable physical standard of consumption, without actual or virtually colonialist looting of other, large parts of the world.

That means, cohering standards of public and other sanitation, health-care, nutrition, safety, and so on. The related requirements per capita are not to be defined as a list of items of bills of consumption as such. The required bill of consumption of goods and services, is *whatever is necessary to achieve certain combined cognitive and demographic standards. A standard of living is not defined by simply comparing bills of consumption; rather, a required bill of consumption, is whatever satisfies a family household and community's requirement of a certain demographic and cognitive standard.* Whatever is required to satisfy that combined demographic and cognitive standard, is the required bill of consumption.[71] We must eradicate the assumption of the North American variety of "cargo cultists," who delude themselves that delivering a certain market-basket to a point on the demographic landscape, means that that delivery will automatically secrete certain targetted results, as defined in terms of demographics and potential productivity. It is the achievement and maintenance of certain standards of cognitive development, as such, which must be the primary measure.

Take the case of comparisons of levels of cognitive development among those among today's adult "Baby Boomers," between the ages of thirty-five and fifty-five, as compared with those of a comparable level of formal education from the preceding generations. In most of these cases, the quality of family household life and cognitive development, has been increasingly of a poorer quality, especially since the 1966–1976 interval, than prevailed among the preceding generation, during the post-Depression years preceding the assassination of President John F. Kennedy, and the successive ousters of President Charles de Gaulle in France, of Chancellors Konrad Adenauer and Ludwig Erhard in Germany, and the assassination of Enrico Mattei in

---

71. The importance of this is heavily underscored when we address the task of building up the standard of living and potential productivity in Africa, Asia generally, and so on. It is the demographic characteristics and cognitive development, which are the basis for setting standards of family household and community life, not necessarily carbon copies of currently imputed requirements for the U.S.A. or western Europe.

Italy. Similarly, although the quantity of education, per capita, increased during the U.S.A.'s two post-war decades, the cognitive quality of the result, per school-year of increased levels of education, and per student attending, decreased even then. During the interval 1966–1976 and following, the decline in cognitive quality, relative to school-leaving age, accelerated.

Those among the morally and intellectually better quality of those graduates, from among those now in the thirty-five to fifty-five age-interval, may recall their outstanding secondary teachers and university professors; remembering those teachers and professors, they are pained to be confronted by the collapse of vocabulary, and deterioration in both rigor and other quality of formulation of argument, among university graduates, over the course of the past half-century. This difference is a reflection of that downward trend; but, that shrinkage is relatively mild, compared with the correlated, precipitous loss of relative cognitive potential, over the course of the 1966–2000 interval. Over the course of the recent decade, the rate of collapse, as measured in these terms, has been increasingly precipitous, and catastrophic.

It has been fairly said, by an increasing ration of knowledgeable Europeans viewing the Year 2000 U.S. election-campaign so far, that in today's Wall Street-dominated U.S.A., families fairly representative of cartoonist Charles Addams' unpleasant characters, with their Bozo-like qualities, are considered the only leading pre-candidates for "First Family" status. More and more among leading European observers, seeing Wall Street and its financial bubble, say of today's U.S.A.: the *lunatics have taken over the asylum!* It is the quality of the combined demographic and cognitive results, which measures the quality of the sausage produced, not the sheer quantity of meat, fat, grains, seasonings, and sawdust, combined, packed into the intake of the sausage-machine.

The classroom, considered together with whatever passes for its textbooks, provides a useful illustration of the point. The mass drugging of pupils, from very young ages, with Ritalin and the like, combined with the aversive social-theory dogmas brutally enforced in the classroom, and the brutal hostility expressed toward the student who dares to exhibit cognitive play-fulness, were better viewed as a malicious dumbing-down of young minds, than education as we used to know it, prior to the past thirty-five years mass-indoctrination with an Orwellian cultural-paradigm down-shift.

The Family Household and Community Life

In the infant and child, the healthy development of the young individual's cognitive potentials, is principally associated with a phenomenon observable as *happy play*. This notion of play, is that identified as *Spieltrieb* by Friedrich Schiller.[72] We recognize something akin to this form of happiness, in a young dog and colt, for example; but, with human beings, such expressions are associated with a quality unique to human beings. That quality is cognition, as I have presented the rudiments of the notion of cognition here. As the young person emerges from infancy, the most significant form of such happy cognitive play, is the game of "Why?"

In the healthily maturing child and adolescent, the role of this quality of happy playfulness, is shifted, more and more, into emphasis on awareness of the role of Socratic play, as the only way in which *systemically truthful answers* can be found to the perennial question, "Why?" With such a mode of growing maturity in the use of this play-principle of cognition, the quali-ties of the prospective scientist, creative Classical artist, and great statesman, may begin to appear in that personality. Sometimes, we hide the true meaning of such maturity from ourselves, when we mystify such developed qualities of cognition, by a hand-waving reference to some mysteriously arbitrary donation of "genius."

However, especially during the past decade, in today's U.S. classroom, the expression of this healthy state of playfulness, is

---

72. Friedrich Schiller, "On the Aesthetical Education of Man, in a Series of Letters," in **Friedrich Schiller, Poet of Freedom**, Vol. I, William F. Wertz, Jr., trans. (New York: New Benjamin Franklin House, 1985), pp. 223–298. Schiller first references the *Spieltriebe*, or *play drive*, in the Fourteenth Letter, p. 256.

brutally suppressed, in various ways. Typical means for doing this, are Ritalin dosages, and forms of the types such as Makarenko-like behavioral modification,[73] in the classroom. Typical is, the wickedly motivated, induced use of the 911 telephone dial-code, to assist the efforts to foster a break in the relations between the parents and their children. The increasing role of the National Training Laboratories' decades-old, radiating influence within teacher associations, compounded by the "new violence" of conditioning of even pre-school-age children by Nintendo-like games, and the related sorts of publicly broadcast children's TV cartoon fare, is part of the virtually Pavlovian decortication of what is becoming a destroyed minority, perhaps even soon a majority, of the present generation of children and adolescents. The presently accelerating upsurge of the "new violence," as merely typified by the recently celebrated Littleton horror, is a typical production of this Nintendo-style cognitive decortication of our children, or grandchildren. This destruction has been

---

73. In the young Soviet Union, Maxim Gorki follower A.S. Makarenko launched a program to transform masses of children without parental care, into a kind of asocial type used by the Soviet political police, the Cheka, the forerunner of the later KGB. Gorki's association with satanic cults, is documented to approximately 1906–1913, as a fellow-traveller of the explicitly pro-satanic, Theosophist movement of Bertrand Russell associate Aleister Crowley et al.; during that time, Gorki conducted an international salon in the grotto of that Theosophist center, the Isle of Capri (the Mithra-cult location dedicated to worship of the Emperor Tiberius as the anti-Christ). This tainted and inherently destructive model of education, was spread throughout Europe, and also into the U.S.A, by the followers of dictator Bela Kun's cultural minister, Georg Lukacs, and his former Budapest associates, such as later Hollywood film-maker Korda, Bertrand Russell's lackey Leo Szilard, et al. Lukacs' and kindred influences were spread widely among the leading, pro-satanic figures of the so-called Frankfurt School and its cronies, such as Horkheimer, Benjamin, Adorno, Hannah Arendt, Nazi philosopher Martin Heidegger, et al. An overlapping dogma of Bertrand Russell, and such among his cronies cronies as Aleister Crowley and H.G. Wells, in deploying such satanic figures as Aldous and Julian Huxley, Karl Korsch, Margaret Mead, Gregory Bateson, et al., typifies the hand behind the deployment of the Frankfurt School degenerates into the U.S.A.

entirely intentional on the part of the institutions responsible for pushing this satanic subversion into the recently redefined norms of individual and family intellectual and emotional life.[74]

Granted, all of these recent changes in standards of education and family relations, must be promptly, and radically reversed, if this nation is to survive for as long as even the relatively short-term ahead. However, while it would be a commendable reform in itself, to return to the standards of decency from the time of Franklin Roosevelt's revival of the U.S. and its public morality, from the Great Depression caused by the policies of Teddy Roosevelt, Woodrow Wilson, and the "flapper era" of Calvin Coolidge and Andrew Mellon, that return, by itself, would not be sufficient. Nor would it be sufficient, merely to uproot the kinds of evils to which I have just referred. This time, we require nothing less than an axiomatically new standard of policy-shaping, one premised upon the affirmation of the lately much-forsaken cognitive principle itself.

The place at which to begin our focus on education of the cognitive potential, is in the matter of relations within the family household itself. This provides the benchmark, with respect to which to correlate the effects of relations within the household, with relevant effects of relations within the school setting, and within the immediate community otherwise. From the beginning,

---

74. See the exposition of the explicitly subversive doctrine of the so-called "authoritarian personality," by the circles of Theodor Adorno, Hannah Arendt, et al., as set forth in T.W. Adorno et al., *The Authoritarian Personality* (New York: Harper, 1950). This doctrine, those authors openly represented, as an intention to destroy the intellectual tradition of the U.S. Declaration of Independence, Constitution, and Abraham Lincoln heritage. That doctrine has been promoted, to this day, as the hard-core dogma of the continuing "Age of Aquarius" cult, the Russell-Huxley-like utopian scheme, which took over the shaping of what has become the "New Era" policy of the thirty-five to fifty-five generation in today's U.S. Typical of the mechanisms deployed to spread that filth, is the role of the Wall Street-linked American Family Foundation (AFF), it the sponsor of the now-defunct Cult Awareness Network (CAN), the latter notable for such obscenities as its key contributing role in orchestrating the creation of the notorious Waco, Texas massacre.

within the household, we must bear in mind the distinctions among cities, towns, rural settings, and suburbia, on these accounts, as we shall examine that matter below.

Within the family household, we require a situation in which the relations among the family household's members, are defined by emphasis on preference, in respect of importance and other authority, of reason—i.e., cognition—over learning. This signifies, in first approximation, the repeated exercise of the principle of pair-wise cognitive sharing, of the original and replicated discovery and validation of universal principles, and their approximation, in preference over mere deduction and learning. In higher approximation, this means an emphasis upon the historical social relations which correspond, in approximation, to the cognitive relations among the successive generations of grandparents, parents, and their young. The latter set of across-generational relations, is the location of both an intimation of the principle of higher hypothesis, and of the developing child's own individual sense of personal identity, an identity rooted in a transparent principle of reason. On all accounts, including the cognitive interplay among siblings, but especially among grandparents, parents, and children, the family household whose internal and external social relations are so ordered, is not only the foundation of cultural and economic progress, but provides the indispensable foundations for sanity itself.

This locates the so-called "nuclear" family household, as properly but an expression of the extended family. This signifies the integration of adopted members of that immediate and extended family, as fully members in good and equal standing. However, the healthy functioning of that extended and immediate family, as an institution for progress and sanity, is conditional upon the efficient supremacy of cognition, over mere learning and other acquired prejudices.

On this account, the indispensable costs of production of a viable quality of labor-force, include the costs of sustaining such extended- and immediate-family institutions as functioning institutions with such qualities. Thus, the costs which must be incurred to sustain such principled conceptions of the extended and immediate family, as a necessary institution, dedicated to such cognition-centered functions, represent an incurred, un-shirkable obligation, to promote the general welfare, an obligation incumbent upon the economy and nation as a whole.

In considering the nature of the family as an institution, the principle of individual privacy, is, ironically, a characteristic feature of the cognitive principle of socialization. An original discovery, or a replicated discovery of any universal principle, occurs within the absolutely sovereign bounds of the individual cognitive powers. *The characteristic feature of all such discovery, is extended, uninterrupted periods of concentration. The most efficient way to prevent the efficient moral and intellectual development of the young individual in society, is to apply, wittingly or otherwise, a regimen which has the effect, of preventing frequent resort by the individual to cognitive moments of individual, private concentration.*

It is in such arts of privacy, that many an individual who would be otherwise destroyed, both morally and intellectually, by aversive family and general social circumstances, may defeat those oppressive forms of excessively socialized conditions of life, thus, to come, in the course of time, to achieve even greatness of character and intellect. The sane family, or educational institution, is careful to foster such necessary forms and degrees of personal privacy. *This notion of cognitive privacy, is the only rational basis for the existence of the privileges of private entrepreneurship in a well-ordered sovereign republic.* The same provision should be a concern for the employer desirous of the benefits of fostering of fruitful innovation among employees.

The denial of efficient access to such cognitively oriented uses of personal privacy, is most cruelly visible in the implications of pure and simple economic poverty in the local community and family household, as also in the disruption of the family as an institution. A society which does not defend the notion of the extended and immediate family household, as I have summarized the case for that here, is a society in which the production of intellectually and morally defective new individuals, will tend to be typical. An economy which imposes the denial of access to efficient privacy, even simply by the nature of physical-economic circumstances extant, will suffer a relative impairment of the cognitive potential, on that account.

The composition of the structure of the living week, and living day, of the individual and family household, is of extremely significant, if not absolute relevance to this. An increase in the number of working hours of the day and week, is often not only tolerable, but even desirable, *if* the nature of the relevant paid (or, unpaid) work is intensely cognitive in characteristic quality. The requirement of leisure, is essentially a requirement for exercise of cognitive activity, relative to, in contrast to merely learned behavior. *The more one's cognitive self-development, the more truly human, and the more useful one becomes, to society as a whole, one's family members, and oneself.*

As a matter of principle, the more hazardous among common family situations, is, obviously enough, the plight of the "nuclear family," especially the single-parent household, under conditions of an extended work-day and -week, and extended daily losses of time required for commuting. This same kind of risk tends to become acute, under conditions of relative poverty, and especially so in those neighborhoods and wider communities in which the opportunities for individual privacy and cognitive play, especially that by children, are minimized by pervasively aversive circumstances.

Two general categories of actually incurred costs of family household life, locate the non-disposable factors of cost to be considered: the costs incurred on account of the necessary physical conditions of life of the family household represented by the individual members of the labor-force, and the costs incurred on account of the cultural quality of cognitive sense of personal identity, which must be fostered in each member of that household and relevant community. These are the incurred costs which the nation must develop the means to pay, even if it can not find such means at the present moment, as necessary costs of maintaining the increasing productive powers of labor expressed by the nation's labor-force.

These cultural factors feature the historical sense of personal identity, and what may be fairly described as the Riemannian

scientific-cultural potential, as represented by the cognitive en-
richment of the state of mind of both the individual as an individual, and as a characteristic of the minds of, and cognitive ordering
of relations among the individual members of the corresponding
community, or nation. The required physical costs to be honored
in practice, are those which bear upon the physical conditions
necessary for promotion of that cultural development, both
within the family household as such, and in the relevant community.

Accordingly, the span of time over which the determination
of incurred costs must be made, requires a study of causal relations, a study which is to be constructed upon the premise of
the span of not less than a generation. Today, in modern economy, that signifies approximately a quarter-century into the future: the expected first twenty-five years of life, and development
to economic maturity, of a new-born infant. Determinations of
cost which are based on other, shorter-cycle models, such as
comparative annual performance, represent an implicitly fraudulent fallacy of composition of the relevant evidence. This is the
case for the physical economy of the family household, and also
of the economy as a whole.

That represents a statement of principle, of the manner in
which the non-disposable costs of maintaining the labor-force
are to be decided.

Cities, Towns, and Suburbia

In brief, the proper physical-economic function of a city or
town, is that of *a machine for living*. Its functional characteristics
as an institution, for better or for worse, are properly to be
adduced from the standpoint of that cognitive definition of human nature which I have stated, and otherwise implied thus far.

Cities so examined, when they and their development, or
decline, are studied as expressions of mankind's relationship
to the entirety of the surface-area of this planet, are the most
characteristic feature of the appearance and future development—either for better, or for worse—of all civilizations. In
ancient and modern European civilization, that corresponding

*The development of cities, with the proper functional relationship to
both seas and countryside, was a major achievement of modern
European civilization. Here we see the Italian city of Florence, adorned
by Brunelleschi's famous dome.*

functional relationship among cities, their characteristics, and
their functional relationship, mediated through towns, to both
the seas and countryside, is the medium through which the individual personalities of a society, participate in a nation's, even
the entirety of mankind's relationship to nature, even, yearning
upwards, to the stellar universe as a whole.

There are, therefore, many doctrines respecting the meaning
of the institution of the city. The most significant doctrines respecting the cities, which have appeared in the emergence of
what has become a globally extended European civilization, are
to be assorted and classified, roughly, as, predominantly, either
Classical or Romantic respecting their adducible, characteristic
principles of design. For implicitly obvious reasons, most emphatically, noting the exceptional achievements in physical economy per capita, reflected in the emergence of extended modern
European civilization, that aspect of European history provides
the best vantage-point from which to examine the functional

characteristics of the rise and fall of civilizations, and of the associated nature and natural functions of cities, in their respective entireties.

Notably, the Athens Acropolis, situated with respect to the ancient function and history of the city's port, is predominantly the indelible mark of a Classical conception of an ancient European city. The Acropolis, crafted over generations, reflects a single, unifying, coherent notion of its physical-geometric and related aesthetical principle of integrated design; it reflects this inward, and outward from its gateway, and from Erectheum to Parthenon. The heart of the city is, thus, the ancient city's reflection of its own soul, a legacy of Cyrenaica, of the Ionian city-state republics, of Solon's reform, and, thence, of the troubled Classical development, on which Alexander's doom of Babylon founded Hellenistic civilization as a whole. Its port, Piraeus, reflects the city's ancient, millennial roots in the maritime culture of the Peoples of the Sea, and also the special relationship of that city to the history and culture of ancient Egypt.

Cities, too, like nations, each have their place, like the figures of Raphael's **The School of Athens,** in the cognitive simultaneity of eternity.

The roots of civilization of historic times, from the preceding long periods of rises and ebbs in the development of transoceanic maritime cultures, are aptly reflected in the accounts given by, most notably, Plato.[75] Classical Greece, in its multi-millennial relationship to Egypt, expresses the connection of Atlantic maritime culture's extension, by way of the vicinity of the Atlas mountains, throughout the Mediterranean and its littoral.[76]

Notably, the distinctive feature of the medieval and modern

---

75. And in the rises and falls of the levels of the oceans and seas, according to the glacial cycles which have dominated the world, especially the Northern Hemisphere, for approximately two millions years to date.

76. Professor Barry Fell's contributions to deciphering Captain Rati's and navigator Maui's discovery of the Americas, matched against both the Dravidian language-group, maritime origins of Sumer, and Herodotus' report on the Dravidian origins of the ancient Yemen, Ethiopian, and Caananite maritime colonies, complement, rather than contradict, the Atlantic origins of ancient Egyptian and Greek cultures.

development of European civilization, is the cathedral, as it emerged from the time of Charlemagne. The emerging role of the cathedral, as marked by those established during the time of Charlemagne's reign, and the influence of the school of Chartres later, shows Europe in the West absorbing and transforming the relics of pagan Rome, and, in the best aspects of this, always preferring the Classical Greek to the pagans of Rome.

Notably, the medieval history of Europe is put behind us, with Filippo Brunelleschi's completion of the cupola of the Cathedral of Florence. From that time, in the shadow of that dome, the evolution of globally extended modern European civilization begins.

Such preceding and contrasting developments kept in view, brings our attention to the way in which the Fifteenth-Century emergence of modern European civilization, shaped the development of the city, and the city's evolving relationship to the countryside, in the Americas.

Look at the emergence and development of the city in what became the U.S.A. Plot three points in this development: the Massachusetts Bay Colony, Philadelphia, and the transfer of title to New Amsterdam, to New York. Trace the origins of American patriotism, from its beginnings among the Winthrops and Mathers of Massachusetts, through the leading role, as the city of patriots, which Philadelphia played, repeatedly, during the span from the days of Jonathan Logan and Benjamin Franklin, until the decline of that city in the aftermath of the assassination of President William McKinley, that by a terrorist assassin imported from Europe, a hateful killer deployed, under the control of Emma Goldman, from New York City's Henry Street Settlement House.

Circumstances of the mid-1980s, impelled me to focus my experience and early studies of the city to bear on the need for a unified, proper, functional definition of role of the modern city, as an idea, within the applications of my continuing work toward further development of the science of physical economy.

Notably, on this immediate sub-topic of our discussion, the subject of the comparative cultural impact of city and country, had fascinated me since a childhood spent chiefly in the city of

Rochester, New Hampshire, and an adolescence in the Essex County city of Lynn, Massachusetts, which latter had already become, functionally, if not politically, a part of greater Boston. Already, during the course of my adolescence, from such comparisons, I regarded the institution of the city as, in principle, a more efficient machine for the cultural development of the individual personality. Then, with the 1940s, there came my first experience with New York City, and its characteristic, readily felt contrast to the Boston of that time; during that time, came the war, and the war-time circumstances, in the U.S. and in Asia, in which my experiences and views were modified by experience of the people and places, of both the nation and the world at large. I propose that it will be of advantage to the reader, in addressing this topic of the city, to compare his or her experiences and reflections on such matters, with my own.

This is the appropriate place to bring a deeper aspect of this study into focus, the lessons to be learned from looking at U.S. cities of the future, from the standpoint of the technology needed to establish a permanent science-base on Mars.

During the mid-1980s, in the course of our Fusion Energy Foundation's international seminars on matters of physical-science research, a series of astrophysical topics, centered around a modern retrospective view of the work of Kepler, focussed our attention on specific, most radically significant topics of contemporary astrophysics. These included the topics of fast-rotating binary star-systems, and the Crab Nebula.[77] Thus, some among us took up the matter of how to construct the appropriate methods of observation of the spectrum of radiation which might be relevant to such investigations. Clearly, we would wish to situate very, very large array systems, for observations conducted at locations as far distant as possible from our electromagnetically so-noisy Sun. The most likely opportunity for such research, to be realized some decades ahead, would be the vicinity of Mars.

For such an undertaking, a permanent scientific base would

---

77. The principal source of so-called cosmic-ray radiation impinging on the Earth is traced from the otherwise extraordinarily anomalous Crab Nebula.

be needed, built into the immediate sub-surface of Mars. The general parameters of the technologies, already available, or on the immediate horizon, needed for that, were more or less immediately apparent. 1) As Werner von Braun had observed, back during the 1950s, we would not be such fools as to send single vessels alone on Earth-Mars missions; we would follow the example set by Columbus' first voyage to rediscover the Americas. 2) Manned flights, in flotillas, from Earth to Mars (and, return), must be along continuously powered, accelerated/decelerated trajectories; the technologies for that were either available, or on the horizon. 3) Present methods of reaching Earth orbits, were primitive, probably as much as ten times too costly; we must substitute the so-called Sänger project, instead.[78] However, to assemble flotillas of Earth-Mars round-trip flights on Earth, would be unreasonable. Krafft Ehricke's work on the feasibility of industries on the Moon, shows that they would better provide the bulk of the weight needed in both the flotillas and their necessary cargo. The suspected-to-be-significant caches of Helium 3, on the Moon, were viewed as a probable fuel for that and related space enterprises. That, and related matters, taken into account, the astrophysical research operations conducted from a Mars base, would require support for assigned personnel on the order of the Manhattan Project's Los Alamos city, or greater. This meant constructing a sub-surface base-habitation on Mars.

Science cities on Mars? Think, then, of employing the techniques and principles required for that, for a fresh approach to municipal zoning and related policy questions, here, back on Earth. This latter reflection was encouraged by the 1970s studies of the benefits to the U.S. economy from 1960s Federal invest-

---

78. This meant a rocket piggy-backed on a "scramjet" vehicle of up to Mach 8 capability, to establish and develop low-orbit stations, from which to move freight up to geostationary space-travel-station Earth orbit. This would reduce the physical-economic cost of bringing tonnage to the higher point by as much as a factor of ten. See Lyndon H. LaRouche, Jr. *The Woman on Mars*, national television broadcast on March 3, 1988, during the author's campaign for the Democratic Presidential nomination.

ments in connection with the Manned Moon Landing and related work: more than a dime returned to the U.S. economy for every Federal penny spent. The rich lode of treasure to be gained from space exploration, would not be found in mineral resources hauled back to Earth, but simply in the fact, that every physical principle and technology developed for space applications, would increase the productive powers of labor on Earth by many times every Federal penny spent. I proposed that we look, in that light, at the future of cities in the Sahara desert, the frozen tundra of Siberia, or anywhere else, on Earth. That prompted me to undertake the rethinking of the principles to be recognized as implicit in the function of the city, and of the city-country-side relationship.

The future potential of the institution of the city, requires a step up toward the goal of the essentially synthetic city: not one laid upon the surface, and dug slightly below that, as if by an ant-army of lusting real-estate speculators, but a machine for living, deeply rooted in the sub-surface, built from deep sub-surface, upwards, to, and slightly above the surface. Every future new city on Earth, should be built, or rebuilt, according to the principles forced to our attention by reflections upon the establishment of a science-city under the surface of Mars. The projection of the Mars-landing project, showed us that the needed technologies either existed, embryonically or otherwise, or were visible on the reachable horizon of but a half-century, more or less, ahead.

What was lacking, chiefly, was a renewal of the scientific optimism associated with the popular reaction to President John Kennedy's bold announcement of the manned Moon-landing commitment, a return to the best parts of the spirit extant prior to the mid-1960s' corrosive upsurge of the rock-drug-sex, cultural-paradigm down-shift. That is needed, more than ever before, planet-wide, today. Such great undertakings are not competently assessed in the bookkeeping department, certainly not on Wall Street, but rather in the benefits which could never be obtained without a great lunge forward, toward a destination beyond the rubble-strewn, present cognitive frontiers of the popular mind.

Then, think about the function of the institution of the city, in this spirit of scientific and cultural progress. The role of this conception in the ascending of mankind, to a higher conception of our species' functional relationship to nature, and to one another, becomes clear in that way.

From this vantage-point, certain enduring parameters are as appropriate to the cities of European civilization's past, as to the distant future. In those principled terms of reference, the institution of the city has an implied, and validatable quality of universality.

The evolution, or, better said, trashing of the institution of the U.S. city and countryside, in the name of suburbia, since the end of World War II, is to be ranked among the most unnecessary and disgusting works of Wall Street during this century. The world at large has been greatly polluted by the global influence of that same disgusting practice. Nothing in this syndrome supports the myth that Wall Street was ever motivated by actual economic prudence, or zeal for true efficiency.

For New York City, the pollution began with the growth of the physical-economic equivalent of toadstools in the potato field of nearby Long Island. This was known as Levittown.

Rather than refurbishing the relatively viable form of integrated residential, educational, industrial, commercial, and related structure, which had evolved in former New York, even often despite itself, the speculative sickness of ground-rent logic took over. New York City began to shed its industrial base in tax-revenues, its role as a great port and inland transportation center, the better quality of its "blue collar" employment opportunities, and its associated residential communities, too. While the viable economic functions of the city as a city, were looted in the process of recycling the deindustrialized decay, the nearby potato lands became a dump for those as if escaping from captivity in the City's tax-revenue base, who moved into the agricultural lands foolishly wasted in that accelerating emphasis upon the ecologically monstrous myth of new suburbia.

It was as if Wall Street and London, with their control over the policy-shaping of the post-Franklin Roosevelt U.S.A., were obsessed with the goal of uprooting everything, social, cultural, infrastructural, industrial, and agricultural, on which Roosevelt's leading role had depended, in both the recovery from the Depression, and in the war-time mobilization. That succubus, known as the rush into the "new suburbia," spreading across the nation, ruined the cities, the countryside, and the moral fabric of the nation. The resulting spectacle, in New York City today, is Mayor Rudolf Giuliani, standing amid the ruin of those past follies, cast for eternity in the presiding, monumental role of Lot's wife.

Look at the principled functions of the life of the extended family's household in the city. Consider a few crucial facts which illustrate, how the cultish spread of "new suburbia" has so lavishly looted the economy, intellect, morals, and physical conditions of life of the people of the U.S.A. Witness, what is perhaps worst of all: the spread of that ruin of a once-great republic, has brought the victims to the state of lunacy in which, this gruesome spectacle, is commonly called the surge of unbridled prosperity.

The fact which is most simply measured, is the factor of the relative access, from place of residence, to those other functions, within the community, on which physical and cognitive well-being depend. Access to securing employment, and to place of work. Access to educational and related activities, to health-care. The appropriateness of those means for satisfying such essential needs. The lapsed time between one's place at any functional point in that system, to other functionally significant points. The cognitive quality of social life within the community, and one's access to it. The cost of this access, expressed as a percentile of the family household's and individual's income. These are the typical markers, by means of which the quality of organization of urban life is estimated.

In that light, consider the commuter's nightmare. How many places of employment must the average member of the household occupy, during each week, each day, to sustain a physical standard of living, as compared to the circumstances prevailing five years, a decade, two decades, three decades earlier? What portion of the time awake, does that individual spend on such employment and the commuting-time associated with it? Quality and availability of educational facilities, measured in similar ways? And so on.

For a comparison, examine a somewhat parallel, similarly disastrous transition, which has affected the relevant bedroom areas associated with the recent twenty years' transformation of the land-use factors, in the region centered in the Frankfurt, Wiesbaden, and Mainz area, in Germany. Consider the monumental traffic congestion which erupts, as a ratio of traffic jams and their duration, to total population and highway capacity, as a result of changes akin to those pioneered in the post-Franklin Roosevelt U.S.A.'s slide into what has become the post-industrial pathology of "new suburbia."

Such problems were implicitly addressed, in my work comparing the required principles of design for a Mars science-base city, and the rational, technological, and related evolution of the institution of the city on Earth. The most significant factor in comparing those cases, was the factor of basic economic infrastructure: the hard infrastructure of power, water, sanitation, transport, parks and cultural facilities, and security, and the soft infrastructure of health, education systems, and security, of a rational design of new and rehabilitated cities. The cognitive aspects of the design of infrastructure are also crucial.

With that approach, as informed by contemplation of the requirements of establishing and maintaining a science city on Mars, virtually every part of Earth's surface becomes a habitable prospect for urban or agricultural and related development. The principles of design of urban amid rural areas, remain the same, in large degree. The physical space-allocations for the functionally required design of the quarters of the family household have not changed in nature, from the better urban areas of medieval European times. That is to say, what is required today, is what should have been considered functionally required then; the principal added emphasis must be on the functional requirements of cognitive privacy of each and all members of the household. Otherwise, on the latter topic, essentially it is the technology to be incorporated into those areas which has changed.

Our attention should be drawn to the vast tracts of this

planet's land-areas, which are functionally classifiable as poorly populated deserts, including the tundra of Siberia, and the jungles of Asia, Africa, and the Americas. This is a challenge to be faced in the interior of China. The same principles are applicable to South and Southeast Asia. Most of the continent of Africa and the Middle East, are to be included, as also the largest part of the land-area west of the proverbial twenty-inch rain-fall line, in the U.S. itself. The subsuming concept needed for this purpose, is the policy of making this entire planet a managed garden of human development. The adoption of that mission is, in itself, the most important aspect of the policy; but, the mission can not live on, without the nourishment of some significant degree of its actual implementation.

Typical of the problem to be addressed, is the challenge which had been represented, prior to 1983, by Egypt's cooperation with Sudan in shifting the over-concentration of population in the mega-cities such as Alexandria and Cairo, toward newly defined, irrigated agro-industrial complexes, each of the latter projected to house up to millions in urban industrial-oriented settings, within a large area otherwise devoted to agriculture. When we consider the incurred cost of providing adequate water-supplies for the Middle East and Saharan Africa in general, as against the benefits of having the streams of water and power needed to make a desert bloom with agro-industrial prosperity, water and power are the key bottlenecks to be mastered, to bring about a prosperous net result. Subsurface rivers (as opposed to wells of fossil water), are one source, in some areas; modern techniques of desalination and other water purification are crucial for such development. High-flux-density energy sources, are key to mastering both bottlenecks, that of power and water.

The building of new cities, set amid new farmlands and new forests, to reclaim arid regions and jungle deserts, forces us to think about the scale of new cities in a fresh way. How large, in area, in population, and in population-density, should a new city, so conceived, be? Are there not optimal sizes and densities, as determined by numerous factors, including the technology employed? Were it not better to speckle a new area of agro-industrial, urban-centered development, with blobs of rural farming and forested development, within which urban centers of optimum maximum scale were situated, than to increase the size of the urban core of such a complex? Were it not better to build several cities of optimum scale, as in the interior of China, or the Sahara, etc., than one in which the ratio of urban periphery to population-density of interior, were too cumbersome? Professor Nicolas Rashevsky would, doubtless, be amused by this question.

Such occupation with a new-cities policy, should condition the way we think about the rehabilitation of the old cities. Proper new definitions of regulatory measures, and related reshaping of taxation policies, at the Federal, state, and local levels, are to be developed for purposes of regional and city planning, on this account. We should aim toward the same standards of resulting effect, in rehabilitating old cities, that we would properly prescribe for new agro-industrial complexes. This must include a rigorous definition of policies respecting the development of a common infrastructural domain, including common transport, at sub-surface levels. The surface elements of the city may be viewed as plugged-in, in a modular way, to the substructure represented by the common infrastructural domain.

If we study the history of the urban communities of Europe, since Charlemagne, and even earlier in some instances, we should recognize how little, certain of the changes in the form of those structures has been, or need be, if we but add the requirement that they be readily adapted to even unforeseen specific new technologies centuries hence. The best way to accommodate to the inevitability of change, is to distinguish between those requirements which do not change in their nature, as distinct from the fact that many unforeseen specific changes will be made, from time to time, in the technologies inserted into durable structural forms of basic economic infrastructure, housing, park areas, and so on. Similarly, geographically optimal locations of urban centers and transport routes among them, have shown, like optimal choices of sites for ports and canals, a certain relative permanence on the scale of centuries and millennia.

Thus, accordingly, we should be able to foresee recommendable related kinds of objectives, for both new and rehabilitated areas, as far as a century or more ahead. On that basis, the checkerboarding of existing cities' areas, for progressive steps of rehabilitation, including building-in of the common infrastructural strata below, can be approached in an orderly, least disruptive way. Essentially, this is a matter of applying the lessons of new agro-urban complexes to the design for rehabilitation of the old.

In that process, the disease of the landscape, known as the inherently wasteful, and ecologically lunatic epidemic of new suburbia, must be quietly, but effectively weeded-out. This must be done for the sake of a healthier economy, and for the sake of healthier mental life among the inhabitants.

Since the disaster, known as the Presidencies of Teddy Roosevelt, Woodrow Wilson, and Calvin Coolidge, the latter great area of the U.S. has not seen the relevant development of the new eco-systems, agriculture, and new cities, which should have proliferated there over the course of the Twentieth Century, but, did not.

Thus, the prospect of new urban-rural developmental complexes, is posed to us today, as a leading policy-mission of the new-born century. All of this requires an acceleration in the development and application of relevant technologies, but those are in sight, if we have the political will to bring such development about.

The prospect of both new cities and matching rural productive development, such as that needed in large regions of North Africa and the Middle East, intersects the issue of rehabilitating the pre-existing urban areas of the world during the decades immediately ahead. This is an indispensable feature of the built-in design, of new accounting and forecasting methods. The cost of the future is an non-disposable cost of the successfully continued existence of the present.

Goals of Secondary Education

During the recent post-Kennedy decades, especially since the end of my namesake President Lyndon Johnson's term in office, the educational policies of the U.S.A. were shifted into the direction of a return to the oligarchical legacy, of cultivating the birth, growth, and maturation of children and adolescents according to rules traditional for the breeding, selective employment, and culling of flocks of human cattle. These latter are the rules implicit in the Code of the notorious Roman Emperor Diocletian, as continued practice under feudalism, and as that Code is to be seen reflected in the treatment of both the African-Americans and generality of poor whites, as Yahoos, in the southern U.S. slave-states.

Such relics of past decadence, became, and are the prevalent policies of primary and secondary education, currently in practice throughout virtually the entirety of today's Ritalin-ridden nation. The main thrust of that degeneration of secondary, and also much of higher education, and, soon, also public health policy, became suddenly visible in New York City, over the interval 1968–1975.[79] As usual, Wall Street, with its attached law-firms and private foundations, set and played the tune for decadence. Thus, did ignorance and depravity become apotheosized as today's popular opinion.

This must now be reversed. Yet, although we must use the precedents to be seen in the best among the educational practices of the pre-1968–75 post-war, and earlier periods, we must employ those precedents only as bench-marks on the landscape of past history, as we lay out a new national educational policy, which will come to represent the next step upward from the best our nation has done before.

Generally, our educational policies should echo those introduced to this continent by the Massachusetts Bay Colony's Winthrops and Mathers, and under Jonathan Logan's leadership in Pennsylvania. They should be a continuation of the Classical humanist programs, as set into motion by such figures as Germany's Gotthold Lessing and Moses Mendelssohn, and installed by their successors in Friedrich Schiller's and Wilhelm and Alex-

---

79. i.e., the 1975 municipal bankruptcy of New York City, so-called "Big Mac," which was the virtual death of the earlier successes of the Hill-Burton health policy in that city, and also, the beginning of the end for that system in the nation as a whole.

ander von Humboldt's Germany, as these policies were assimilated into the form of the reformed Philadelphia high school under the leadership of Benjamin Franklin's great-grandson and Alexander von Humboldt's associate, West Point's Alexander Dallas Bache. There is also the model of scientific education developed in France, the Ecole Polytechnique, for as long as it was operating, during the pre-Restoration period, despite Napoleon Bonaparte, under the common initiative and supervision of such great scientists as Lazare Carnot, Gaspard Monge, and A.M. Legendre.

Those models are to be known and appreciated by the educators and other relevant policy-shapers of today. Yet, a further step in educational policy is needed. Rebuilding this nation from the decadence into which it has been relegated, during the recent three decades and more, requires that we not only adopt the best precedents from the past, but add certain hard specifications, as to what shall be accomplished, and by what methods and means.

First of all, it must be made explicit, that the method and practice in public primary and secondary education shall be the standpoint of cognitive experience in reliving the act of discovery of validated universal principles from the past. A Classical humanist form of Classical-Greek-keyed public education, shall be prescribed, in which re-enactment of discoveries of principle, rather than textbook-cued, mass-testing drill-and-grill, that according to the standard set by standard examinations, shall be the standard for recruitment, selection, and assignment of teachers.

Second, it must be general policy, that classroom size for primary and secondary schools, shall be determined by the goal of having not more than fifteen to twenty pupils in a teaching classroom. This is to assure the possibility for the effective participation of all of the pupils in the process of sharing relevant cognitive experiences.

Thirdly, in accord with the requirements of a cognitive method of classroom practice, teachers shall be expected to spend an average of sixty percent of the working-day in preparing classes, and not more than forty in actual classroom teaching. This must be so, in recognition of the fact, that the teacher must teach the existing class, with its achievements and its problems, not some pre-homogenized standard classroom. The goals of the curriculum, are more or less constant from classroom to classroom; but, the lesson conducted in each classroom, for that day, must be pre-crafted to address the adduced achievements and difficulties represented by previous development of the entire class as an interacting group.

Fourthly, the programs for primary and secondary schools, secondary schools most emphatically, must emphasize the methods of "crucial experiments" for assisting the pupils to relive the discovery and validation of universal scientific and Classical principles.

The object assigned to the outcome of combined primary and secondary education, shall be to foster the development of the student's own private "School of Athens," within the mind of each pupil to graduate from secondary schools, as I have summarized that case earlier here.

The level of knowledge of science, art, and history, attained by the graduates, must correspond to the level of achievement represented by society up to that time. Thus, such graduates of secondary education, may go to their next step in life, as an integral part of what society and the nation has achieved, in its general cognitive and related development, up to that time. The object is practical, and also moral, in the sense the notion of a private "School of Athens" implies. The object is, that our secondary schools of the future, must graduate qualified individual citizens, who go on from there, as citizens, to conduct the pursuit of their chosen missions and professions.

That shall become the future, mandatory standard of cost accounting and forecasting, in these and related matters.

The Cost Accounting of Change

As I shall focus on other aspects of this same crucial matter in the following chapter of this report, on the subject of Budgetary & Cost Accounting Principles, the keystone of competence in future cost-accounting, budgetary, and forecasting practice must be the notion of non-linearity, as I have summarized such a distinction here, at an earlier point of the report. Here, I touch summarily on that matter from the standpoint of the process connecting paradox and cognition as such. I term this, "the cost accounting of change."

In itself, that term, so situated, expresses the following notions of function.

As the point has been outlined here thus far, the supply of a certain level of potential physical productivity of labor by the economy's labor-force, requires a corresponding development of the population in its family households and communities. This does correspond, more or less, to a specific bill of household and related consumption by the population in general; but, the quality of the social relations and circumstances is more or less decisive in determining the success or failure of what is otherwise a bill of consumption not inconsistent with the level of potential productivity considered.

The essential point is, that the nurturing of the cognitive potential of the members of the family household and community signifies a potential of the Riemannian form I have described here earlier. This cognitive potential, so nurtured, defines the anti-entropic effect inhering in the employment of a labor-force in a well-ordered economy, and its enterprises: *that the output of production, so ordered, will tend to ensure an increase of the total output over the incurred costs, including family and community consumption, of producing that output.* There is, thus, a specifically anti-entropic form of gain. However, to maintain that rate of gain, the content of the bill of consumption must be enhanced. That ongoing enhancement, represents an integral part of the function of maintaining the present rate of growth into the future.

The principled, functional determination of that gain, can not be understood from the standpoint of empiricism in general, nor those doctrines of the British East India Company's Haileybury School, which form the basis for what is foolishly described as "Classical economy" in universities and the practice of the IMF and U.S. Federal Reserve System, today. As I have emphasized, empiricism and the schools of political economy and social theory derived from it, presume that the chain of dot-like eco-

nomic and other perceived events, is ordered in some way which
is consistent with the assumption that the functional connection
among those dots is ordered in a way which is axiomatically
linear. Thus, human economic and social behavior generally, is
given an imputed form of expression, formally speaking, consistent with those notions of statistical thermodynamics set into
motion by Clausius, Grassman, Kelvin, Rayleigh, Boltzmann, et
al. That form is intrinsically entropic; theoretically, for them,
no gain such as the Eighteenth-Century Physiocrats and English
"Classical economists" promise us, were possible in a universe
which is consistent with the latter's so-called economic theory.
So, when reductionist physicists would profess to be also believ-
ers in "free trade," they must put aside their cap and gown, for
the dunce cap better suited to the occasion.

The explicit assumption on which all so-called "Classical
economics" is premised, is the assumption set forth by such
followers of the school of Sarpi and Conti as Bernard Mandeville,
François Quesnay, Adam Smith, and the British utilitarians. *The
assumption is, that in a universe consistent with Galileo's, and
with the derived doctrines of Thomas Hobbes. It is assumed
that the kind of so-called "freedom" of individual licentiousness,
as prescribed by Mandeville and Smith, and for the advantage
of the feudal landlord by Quesnay's laissez-faire, must result in
a net, in fact anti-entropic gain, in both economic and moral
benefits for the society as a whole!*

How is such a mystery-clouded system presumed to work
to such effect? Adam Smith anticipates the basis for his 1776
The Wealth of Nations, in his 1759 **Theory of the Moral Senti-
ments.** In this 1759 work, Smith speaks for Mandeville, Quesnay,
and others. The following excerpt makes the point. I have cited
that before, I repeat it here.

"The administration of the great system of the universe . . .
the care of the universal happiness of all rational and sensi-
ble beings, is the business of God and not of man. To man
is allotted a much humbler department, but one much more
suitable to the weakness of his powers, and to the narrowness of his comprehension; the care of his own happiness,

of that of his family, his friends, and his country. . . . But though we are . . . endowed with a very strong desire of these ends it has been intrusted to the slow and uncertain determinations of our reason to find out the proper means of bringing them about. Nature has directed us to the greater part of these by original and immediate instincts. *Hunger, thirst, the passion which unites the two sexes, the love of pleasure, and the dread of pain, prompt us to apply those means for their own sakes, and without any consideration of their tendency to those beneficent ends which the great Director of nature intended to produce by them.*" (italics added)

In summary, the entire doctrine of "free trade" depends upon nothing other than sheer, wild-eyed, hedonistic lunacy. It were useful to say, the doctrine of "freedom" of the followers of Mandeville, Smith, the Mont Pelerin Society's Lady Margaret Thatcher, et al., has no crucial point of difference with the same, Faustian, neo-manichean kind of lunacy, which we rightly associate with the doctrine of the "elite" introduced into western Europe by the Bogomils (Cathars). In some mysterious way, incomprehensible to the sane human mind, insist Mandeville, Quesnay, and Smith: as a simple matter of British notions of common sense, Satan contrives to deliver riches and power, as rewards, to the most consummately licentious degenerates our society might produce. And, all this is proof of the same Second Law of Thermodynamics which was derived, axiomatically, from the same general premises.

This frankly pro-satanic doctrine of Smith et al., is familiar to scholars of European history, including the theologians. The same basis is found in the axiomatic roots of all of the existentialist, and other similarly depraved and lunatic types. That Faustian argument, is that of Nietzsche, Martin Heidegger, and their present-day followers generally. Their argument, like that of their Nazi followers, is that man is essentially dionysiac (i.e., satanic), and that amorality, even immorality, is natural and healthy for mankind, if that course of action brings power to those who take that road. Hence, they, and like-minded others, profess man to be inherently, incurably evil by nature: and, who should object if he chooses to behave so? If Faustian man professes remorse on Sunday mornings, who should object if he is plainly evil during the remaining days of the week? Therefore, Faustian man takes pride in his chief distinction, that he and his like, unlike the poor Yahoo, have learned to be clever, and therefore, putatively, civilized, about such matters.

As I have stressed here, and in other published locations earlier, to understand the problems of statecraft, it is indispensable to grasp the point, that all the important fights respecting peoples of and among nations, are rooted in the issue of defining *human nature*. Is man made to be good, such that, therefore, each must be subject to the governing principle of promotion of the general welfare on that account? The Physiocrat, or other oligarch, whose practice is implicitly the treatment of most mankind as a landlord's human cattle, denies this principle, and, therefore, we should not be astonished to discover that, underneath all putatively clever disguises, the oligarch and his lackey— Don Juan and his Leperello—are essentially evil and irrational in their motives.

The lunatic followers of the "free trade" cults aside, there is a factor of *attrition* in the gains won through scientific and technological progress. Thus, continuing scientific and related progress is indispensable; there is no place in this universe in which mankind may stand still and survive as a species. The principle of scientific and cultural progress in a Riemannian form, expresses man's natural imperative. Progress or die! The physical-economic profitability of an economy never lies in a fixed level of technological and related progress; even standing still could not occur unless we continued to move ahead. Thus, for the science of physical economy, the functional value of labor lies in the rate of cognitive process being set into motion. This includes a relative improvement in the conditions of life of those who labor, and their family households. The essence of economic value lies thus in the *verb,* not the *noun.*

It is the current rate of cognitively defined progress which defines the current physical-economic values, and costs of labor and enterprise. It is the gains of this sort, which might be assuredly achieved, as a result of today's efforts, a generation ahead, which is the only meaningfully true measure of the rate of gain of society as a whole and of its individual enterprises. It is the action measurable as rate of change of rate of change, which defines what kind of a future the present is building, for a point a generation ahead. The action so represented is in the form of those verbs which take into account the intrinsic, Riemannian non-linearity of the cognitive processes of mind and the related non-linearity of the physical processes presented to the point of production. Such functional constructions must replace the application of linear statistical methods, and resulting projections, to a connecting of dots collected from the past. All meaningful determinations of values for cost accounting, are only those which measure the future in the kinds of terms I have indicated.

Thus, the rate of increase of the bill of consumption, is an incurred cost of the output of today's and yesterday's labor. Thus, also the rate of potential and realized Riemannian progress in science and technology, and the associated, incurred increase in capital intensity, is an integral, indispensable current cost of production. Failing to meet that requirement, must result in the decline of the physical economy and well-being of the nation, through the inhering frictional action of technological attrition.

The Oligarchical Factor

As I have summarized this consideration, in the immediately preceding section of this chapter, current accounting practice customarily fails to acknowledge the most prevalent source of the discrepancy between, on the one side, the proper definition of incurred costs of labor, as the preceding discussion of cognitive factors of cost indicates, and, on the other side, what have usually estimated, by most among recent generations among accountants and economists, as comparative sets of standard costs. The more significant of those customary underestimations, are products of political ideology, not a reflection of scientifically verifiable fact.

That presently widespread underestimation of actually in-curred cost, is, chiefly, a reflection of the manifest, increasingly savage hostility, by today's financier oligarchies, toward the so-

called lower eighty percent of U.S. family-income brackets. This
is a hostility which should be familiar to literate secondary and
university graduates, from study of the brutalized conditions of
most of the population under the rule of Mesopotamian empires,
the Roman Empire, European feudalism, and the advocacy of
chattel slavery by the Lockean ideologues of the Confederate
States of America. Most notably, this hostility is the same which
is embedded axiomatically in both the Code of the Roman Emperor Diocletian, and the feudal custom in western Europe (and
elsewhere). It is the same hostility expressed toward mankind
in general, by modern London's ruling, Venice-style financier
oligarchy, as typified by the British East India Company's repeatedly organized, genodical famines, deployed to regulate the population of the subjected people of the Indian subcontinent, during
the course of the Nineteenth and early Twentieth Centuries.

Such is the same bestiality shown by the followers of John
Locke, toward not only the slaves and poor whites of those
states briefly associated with unhappy memory of the Confederate States of America, but, today, by Wall Street and its radical
right-wing shock-troops, those operating, under the guidon of
"shareholder value," inside the leading circles of both the Republican and Democratic parties' "new center." The latter are typified by the same decadence expressed by the Mussolini-echoing
cult of "New Labor" in Prime Minister Tony Blair's United
Kingdom, the cult of little bread and pompously failed circuses.
Such is the bestial hostility toward humanity, the ideology of
so-called "shareholder value," as also expressed even among
some prominent Justices of the U.S. Supreme Court, and elsewhere, today.

That hostility toward the general population, should not
surprise us. Such oligarchies are established on the assumption
of a particular notion of the idea of property, under which the
mass of the population is ruled, bred, culled, and otherwise
administered, as either slaves or other forms of human cattle
forms of actual, or quasi-slavery dispensed under the authority
attributed, by the oligarchs, to what are for the followers of the
liberalism of John Locke today, the virtually interchangeable
names of slaveholder and shareholder values.

Consequently, the essential challenge confronting the oligarchy and its lackeys, is the question of how to induce submissiveness toward the oligarchy, a tiny minority in society, among the larger mass of the ruled subjects, the virtual or actual human cattle (chattels). The case of pagan Rome, is only typical of the oligarchical model on this account.

The fighting forces on which Rome's power to loot and subjugate other nations depended, were the ruling oligarchy's designated predators, the popular masses. The consequent, principal challenge to the ruling oligarchy, was how to induce both submissiveness of those masses toward the oligarchy, and yet also maintain, among those same masses, a wont and capability to fight, and enslave, or kill designated targets of Rome's ever-lustful ambitions. So, that legacy of ancient Rome, modern fascism, like London's Blair, follows the path of Mussolini and Hitler, as did France's Emperor Napoleon Bonaparte, and Lord Palmerston's French puppet, Napoleon III, earlier. For such degenerates, as for the maddened co-thinkers of Zbigniew Brzezinski and Caspar Weinberger today, as for Vice-President Al Gore, seeking wars, and loot abroad, is a way of inducing the looted masses of organized popular opinion to rally, like the followers of Napoleon, Mussolini, and Hitler, to enthusiasm for new prospective and actual wars abroad, and, at home, pathological mass phenomena akin to the "McCarthyism" of the 1946–1953 U.S.A., or the kindred domestic policies of nations under Mussolini and Hitler, in their time.

As in the U.S.A. today, the oligarchy's policy, is "dumb down the people," especially the young. This is being done, successfully so far, by aid of the schools and television screens of pre-adult generations, and others. The same oligarchical method, is exhibited, in the U.S.A. today, in the application of the same dumbing-down techniques to training and policy-directives for a new breed of law-enforcement shock-troops, the latter as in Mayor Rudolf Giuliani's New York. This is also to be seen in military policy, as in the conditioning of forces for such models as "Air-Land Battle 2000," as in the use of Nintendo-warfare methods used in "Desert Storm," and in the corrosive, "Big Brother" role of the major mass media generally.

A Pokemon tournament in Braintree, Massachusetts. Such entertainment is part and parcel of the oligarchical objective of creating a dumb, submissive population. (Photo: EIRNS/Cloret Richardson)

The decadence of the Roman people, and our own, is typical of what is to be recognized as vox populi *(popular opinion), a lesson which is crucial for understanding how the few, through the ages, have ruled, and ruined, the many.* It is the same policy to be witnessed in today's mass behavior in the sports stadia, and before the television screens, in the widespread, Nuremberg rally-like movements, in rock concerts, sports events, and otherwise, of large masses from among the U.S. population today.

In the history of the Mediterranean region, and elsewhere, until the revolutionary change which came with the Fifteenth-Century emergence of the modern sovereign nation-state in Europe, the fostering of the cognitive development of the lower classes, was, excepting such Classical figures as Socrates, Plato, and the Christian Apostles,[80] usually considered a source of grave threat to the "national security" of societies, such as ancient Babylon, pagan Rome, feudalism, and the Venetian financier-

---

80. Cf. Paul, *I Corinthians* 13, on *agapē*.

oligarchical, anti-republican, model. This is reflected in the systems of financier-oligarchical rule seen still in modern Netherlands and England, and in Wall Street's powerful influence inside
today's U.S.A.[81] In these forms of society, which were constituted
according to the so-called oligarchical model, the fear was, that
the cognitive development of the general population, would turn
the human cattle into insolent upstarts, who, like the framers
of the 1776 U.S. Declaration of Independence and 1789 U.S.
Federal Constitution, would constitute a threat to the continued
existence of financier-oligarchical forms of government, such as
those under that British monarchy which has reigned since the
accession of bloody tyrant William of Orange's one-time protégé,
Georg Ludwig of Hannover, as George I.

Therefore, the oligarchs always greatly prefer, in the masses
of people, the behavior of François Rabelais' famous "sheep of
Panurge."[82] They prefer this, in their subjects, and to a significant
degree, even among themselves, rather than the education of any
persons educated to be fully human beings.

On this account, gin served to intoxicate the otherwise
restive poor of Hogarth's and later England, into a stupor of
political impotence, under British Eighteenth-Century oligarchi-

---

81. In the history of European civilization, Lycurgus' Sparta typified
the oligarchical model, and Solon's reforms at Athens the contrary, republican model. From the lifetimes of Plato and Alexander the Great, "republican" signified the Greek Classical model, in opposition to the oligarchical
model of the empires of ancient Mesopotamia. Modern European republi-
canism, applies the Socratic notion of a universal principle, the obligation
to promote the general welfare of all of the population and its posterity,
as the only basis for legitimacy of government, as this is emphasized by
the U.S. Declaration of Independence and the Preamble of the U.S. Federal
Constitution. The British monarchy is an example of the opposing, oligarchical model of "rule of law," the model of Venice's financier oligarchy.

82. François Rabelais, *Pantagruel*, Book 3, Chapter 8: How Panurge,
in a foretaste of Vice-President Al Gore's campaign for the Democratic
Party's 2000 Presidential nomination, caused Ding Dong's sheep to drown
themselves at sea, together with the poor dumb Ding Dong who thought
he controlled them.

cal, so-called liberal rule.[83] Indeed, true to the Walpole tradition, the gin was therefore dispensed *as liberally as mass education in the U.S. today*. Similarly, the relatively novel measures introduced as law and other policy in today's U.S.A., have had the presently continuing, predominant intent, of destroying the family household; these novelties have succeeded in that, at least to a large, and increasing degree.

Such dementing measures, including the deliberate and massive destruction of families and their children, with substances such as Ritalin, and including the efforts, by George Soros, Secretary Madeleine Albright, and other accomplices, to legalize cocaine, marijuana, and kindred forms of "recreation," at sources such as Colombia, are the modern successors to the British monarchy's former reliance on gin, as a measure of mass social control of their "sheep of Panurge." "Spaced out" subjects are considered less an inconvenience to oligarchical rule, than sane plebeians, whose facing the reality of the world about them, might become troublesome to those in power. To that same malevolent purpose, we have today's U.S. mass media orchestrating the bleating of the present-day victims of popular entertainments, a kind of mass drugging in itself, as the expression of that contemporary "public opinion," the which is orchestrated liberally according to the doctrine of that notorious, and thoroughly disgusting American Tory, Walter Lippmann.

The statement, that the intention of the relevant financier-oligarchical establishment, is to degrade the moral and mental development of the overwhelming majority of the U.S.A., into the quasi-decorticated state of virtual human cattle, is no exaggeration. Look at the stratum of the U.S. population in the range of between thirty-five and fifty-five years of age today, especially the notorious U.S. pollster "Dick" Morris' so-called "suburban likely-to-vote," in particular.

---

83. Gin? What is in a name? Gineva, named for the old bogomil center at the head of the Rhône, Geneva, was introduced to England from the Netherlands, thus conveying the spirit of William of Orange into wider circulation under the reign of the newly founded British monarchy.

Observe those strata, especially those in the middle-management and higher echelons of professional and quasi-professionals, who are the increasingly infantile pace-setters among the upper twenty-percentile of U.S. family-income brackets today. These are the products of an induced cultural-paradigm downshift, which had already hit hard the middle- and higher-income families of the "White Collar" and "Organization Man" stereotypes of the 1950s post-war "new suburbia." The seeds of the corruption of the children of those of the family households of the generation of the young adults of the World War II veterans, became the ingrained, crippling emotional and intellectual disorders typical among their children, today's "new influentials" of the thirty-five to fifty-five age-brackets, sometimes referred to, paradigmatically, as "the new suburbia."

That cultural-paradigm downshift, including its Hollywood component, was crafted with that intent in mind, crafted by the existentialists, such as Frankfurt School types like Georg Lukacs, the Kordas, Heidegger, Horkheimer, Benjamin, Adorno, and Arendt, and H.G. Wells' and Bertrand Russell's Aldous and Julian Huxley, and the circles of MIT's and Michigan's Dr. Kurt Lewin, from as early as the 1920s and early 1930s. The professions of sociology and psychology, among others, were steered into service, as "Reesian shock-troops," for this purpose, under the coordination of the London Tavistock Clinic, the latter under Brigadier Dr. John Rawlings Rees and cronies such as Eric Trist and the infamous Dr. Sigmund Freud. This crew, under the banner of the Cybernetics cult and the circles of the Josiah Macy, Jr. Foundation of the 1940s and 1950s, played a central coordinating, intellectual role, inside the U.S. pro-oligarchical establishment, in making the perversion named for satanic Nietzsche's and Aleister Crowley's "Age of Aquarius," seem, to their dupes, a bright, if Orwellian "new age" of a Nietzschean transvaluation of values. The latter, the fanatically credulous, fad-ridden dupes, now appear to predominate, among those in the "Baby Boomer" age-range of between-thirty-five-to-fifty-five.

Just as the tyrants of pagan Rome and its empire ruled, by devices such as bread and circuses, so, more and more of the

U.S. population, is becoming duped, more and more, into a depraved state of mind approximating, like that of today's Presidential pre-candidates George W. Bush and Vice-President Al Gore, typifying candidates and party leaderships suited to the new, more brutal, political mass-media idols of collective cognitive imbecility.

There is a general principle which enables us to understand how such qualities of sheep-likeness are induced among the population of today's U.S.A., for example. Essentially, in order to have a labor-force trained to perform according to the oligarchy's needs, the labor-force must learn how to behave, as in Hitler's Germany, and thus acquire the police and other skills required of those newly prescribed functions, which the oligarchy's business now requires of it. However, the oligarchy, like its currently preferred clown-prince candidate, George W. Bush, does not wish to allow that education in routine skills, and other inculcation provided to that population, to bestir unduly the subjects' still-lurking cognitive faculties. Learn the formula you are expected to apply, but do not attempt to challenge the mind-set you are instructed to adopt! "Mass-testing for all; thinking for no one!" is the Orwellian policy of today's "New Age." Hence, the popularization of that Orwellian fad called the cult of "information," "Cybernetics." Hence, the preference for so-called "artificial intelligence," and disdain for actually human intelligence. Thus, we have today, the increasing ration of that variety of cognitively dull-witted human sheep, the appendages of, not the machine, but rather the digital flop, as typified by the often wild-eyed, bungling experts, such as those of Al Gore's financial backers at Long Term Capital Management (LTCM), in computer-assisted "mathematical modelling."

The result of such presently increasing virtual decortication of the generation now in the age-range of thirty-five to fifty-five, is the mass hysteria associated with gambling on Wall Street and other financial markets. These masses of foolish speculators, are truly the outstanding contemporary resurrection of Rabelais' drowned, dumb "sheep of Panurge." On that account, as I have remarked here earlier, some knowledgeable leading voices from Europe, in increasing numbers, rightly describe the collective behavior of the people of today's U.S.A.: "The inmates have taken over the asylum!"

Nonetheless, the situation is not yet hopeless. I emphasize the crucial point, again, now.

At this moment of writing, the entirety of the IMF-dominated present world financial and monetary system, is gripped by an increasing turbulence, marking, thus, the approaching eruption of the greatest, sudden, financial and monetary collapse in world history. Unless corrective action is taken along the lines I have prescribed for a "New Bretton Woods," one or more of a combination of three alternatives is now inevitable: 1) A chain-reaction deflationary collapse, which was then the principal immediate threat, up through the period between Spring-Summer 1997 and the Brazil crisis of February 1999; 2) A growing threat of a Weimar–1923-style hyperinflationary blow-out, the result of the "wall of money" tactics, adopted by the U.S.A. and others beginning October 1998–February 1999. That latter avalanche of fictitious monetary aggregate, was deployed in an increasingly frenzied effort to repeat, on a vastly expanded, world-wide scale, the blowout of 1923 Germany: resulting, now, in a presently, similarly hyperinflationary trend, in prices of petroleum and other real-community categories; 3) a threnody of mass-murderous social conflict and related catastrophes, building up toward the ignition of a virtual fire-storm of globally generalized warfare and related homicidal chaos.

With the offer of such alternatives, the Devil might greet the lost soul arriving in today's Hell.

The sudden, now-imminent collapse of the present world financial and monetary system, will define a point of decision, in which the "sheep of Panurge" may choose to destroy themselves, by leaping en masse into the realization of their present, bubble-headed financial-market delusions, or, hopefully, in the alternative, a situation, in such a crisis-setting, in which a reality-shock akin to the effect of the December 7, 1941 bombing of Pearl Harbor, transforms the behavior of most among the adult U.S. population, almost overnight. In such a latter alternative, when the existing financial and monetary systems are seen as hopelessly defunct, the only chance for a continuation of civilized life, will be the possibility, that the majority of the general population will arise, as this occurred under the leadership of President Franklin Roosevelt, to rally the power of the sovereign nation-state, to create a new monetary and financial system, and a return to the saner economic policies which dominated the U.S.A. and Europe prior to the disastrous, presently still-ongoing, cultural paradigm-downshift of the 1964–2000 interval.

Thus, humanity as a whole has come, again, to one of those times, like the brink of the collapse of imperial Mesopotamian oligarchical power, like the collapse of the self-doomed Roman culture into a prolonged Dark Age, like the New Dark Age of the mid-Fourteenth-Century, in which we either overturn the power of the presently ruling oligarchy, the present global financier oligarchy, or the entire planet will be plunged into a prolonged New Dark Age of death and chaos beyond the imagination of all but the rarest few living today.

In such a time of onrushing historic decision, we might choose to survive, instead of continuing our present, doomed ways. That is the hopeful prospect on which the early implementation of the accounting policies outlined here might be implemented, even soon.

Unless, and until that happy change occurs, neither the essential elements of the actual cost of maintaining and fostering the cognitive powers of the population, nor the true costs of maintaining even present levels of life-expectancy, will be taken into account, by either the accounting profession as a whole, nor by the ruling majorities in the leading political parties, nor in government. In official Wall Street and Washington's zeal to deliver timely payments to a worthless, self-doomed Caesar, less and less is paid to the universe's principal, and most powerful creditor, God. That is not a prudent practice for any civilization.

4. Budgetary and Cost-Accounting Principles

Today, the great irony of modern financial accounting, is that those so-called modern double-entry bookkeeping methods, which are, axiomatically, the standard of reference for practice today, are, quite literally, medieval practices, first developed by the same Thirteenth- and Fourteenth-Century Lombard bankers, whose accounting practices were directly responsible for that Fourteenth-Century "New Dark Age," the same dark age which wiped out half of the parishes of Europe, and which reduced the population by approximately the same amount.

Nonetheless, the financial houses of London, and especially those of Wall Street and the leading U.S. mass media, assure us, that their present, literally medieval policies, which have brought us presently to the brink of an analogous, global catastrophe, reflect the alleged wisdom of the historic experience, and "free trade" principles, of today's private banking.

Why should we wonder, therefore, that more and more leading European bankers, press, and political figures, even including some leading voices from around the City of London, find reason to say, quite justly, when looking at Wall Street and the so-called currently leading Presidential pre-candidates and their hyperventilating followers, that, to understand the U.S. today, you must understand that, there, "the lunatics have taken over the asylum"?

This spectacle should prompt us to suspect, that something is very, very wrong with what are, still, currently, the widely accepted principles of present-day accounting practice. Stripping away all of the mumbo-jumbo typical of most textbooks, classrooms, and conferences devoted to the subject of economics, current doctrines of economics are, usually, nothing but reflections of warmed-over accounting practices of the type known, and used by the Fourteenth-Century houses of Bardi and Peruzzi. These are essentially the same methods employed by Lombard agents such as the Bardi's notorious "Biche" and "Mouche"— the putatively original *gazzi ladri*—whose actions detonated the general financial, chain-reaction bankruptcy of Europe in their time.

There is another, presently most relevant irony in all this. The Fifteenth-Century recovery of Europe from the ruinous conditions of the preceding New Dark Age, was the Golden Renaissance's institution of principles of political-economy which, for a time, reversed the effects of Lombard banking and accounting methods. Ironically, it was a leading representative of one of the old Lombard banking houses, the great Cosimo di Medici, who played a leading role in the organizing and, also, the financing of that birth of the post-medieval, modern era, which appeared as the Fifteenth-Century, Golden Renaissance.[84] To sum up the point of the two ironies, modern political economy was born during the middle to late Fifteenth Century's Golden Renaissance. A system of accounting, and banking practices, based upon the simple-minded system of double-entry bookkeeping doctrine, is, in and of itself, contrary to all of the lessons in political-economy which experience should have taught us, to date, since the Fourteenth-Century, medieval New Dark Age.

Then, why are governments and others practicing Fourteenth-Century, New Dark Age, medieval bookkeeping methods, in the service of current, disastrous trends in economic policy-shaping, today? There lies the ontological paradox which should prompt us to consider changing the ways in which economic policies are currently made, especially during the recent thirty-odd years to date.

The kernel of the present crisis is, that central banking institutions, including the governments-sponsored International Monetary Fund, have been operating, since August 1971, under the influence of the "floating-exchange-rate" rules of the self-doomed, Fourteenth-Century Lombard bankers. This is typified, exactly, by the rise of the use of "junk bonds" and so-called "financial derivatives," especially since the immediate aftermath of Trilateral Jimmy Carter-appointed Federal Reserve Chairman Paul Volcker, in October 1979, especially since the ruinous introduction of the U.S. Garn-St Germain and Kemp-Roth legislation, in 1982. The rise of "globalization," which is a direct reflection of the situation in early Fourteenth-Century Europe, but repeated on a world scale today, is also an exact copy, in principle, of the policies which collapsed Europe into that New Dark Age.

The key to understanding such ironies, is the fact that the

---

84. The Medici had been associated earlier with the House of Bardi. The appearance of the double-entry method, created to control branch offices of such houses, is credited to something developed by the earlier Medici bankers during their association with the Bardi.

birth of political-economy, during the latter part of the Fifteenth
Century, was a direct product of a revolutionary change in history, since the rise of the power of Rome in the Mediterranean,
a surge to power which began about the same time that Roman
soldiers murdered the great Archimedes, in Syracuse. The revolutionary event, the Golden Renaissance, situated within the
shadow of Brunelleschi's cupola of the Cathedral of Cosimo di
Medici's Florence, was the virtual end of the failed medieval
system; it was the founding of the institution of the modern
sovereign nation-state, a state premised on the principle of the
general welfare.[85]

The key to understanding this revolutionary establishment
of the modern sovereign nation-state, is that it came as a product
of a millennium and a half of Christian adoption of the Classical-
Greek standard of culture. As, I have stressed earlier in this
report, the unprecedented rate of increase of the potential relative
population-density of mankind, under the impact of modern
European civilization, has been entirely the benefit of that revolutionary change, a result of the adoption of the principle underscored in the opening paragraphs of the 1776 U.S. Declaration
of Independence and the Preamble of the 1789 Federal Constitution: the only legitimate basis for government, is government's
efficient dedication to the promotion of the general welfare, both
for all of the living, and for their posterity. It was the impact,
and radiated influence of that revolutionary change in the definition of the state, which has been the unique, indispensable premise of all the notable relative successes in practice of political-
economy ever since.

This establishment of that sovereign form of nation-state,
was the fruit of a long struggle against the Romantic tradition
of Rome and European feudalism, a struggle associated with
such heroic work as the defense of reason, against irrationalism,

---

85. Another account of the same essential point, is that of one of
the greatest legal minds of the past century, Professor of international
law Friedrich August Freiherr von der Heydte, as documented in his **Die
Geburtsstunde des souveränen Staates** (Regensburg: Druck und Verlag Josef
Habbel, 1952).

by Abelard of Paris, and Dante Alighieri's **De Monarchia,** an effort leading into Nicholas of Cusa's great work on that subject of law of nation-states, **Concordancia catholica.** These were works in direct opposition to the Romantic principles expressed by the "zero growth" doctrine axiomatically embedded in the Code of Diocletian. The issue between the two, opposing systems of thought, the oligarchical tradition of pagan Rome and the republican Classical Greek tradition of the Christian Apostles, is key to understanding the revolutionary character of the change. The issue was what I have already developed here, in outline: a fundamental, axiomatically uncompromisable opposition between two contrary conceptions of the nature of man.

Contrast that modern sovereign nation-state with the oligarchical state of ancient Rome and European feudalism thereafter. Herein lies the solution to the present world financial crisis. Here is the standpoint from which to recognize the principle of folly embedded in accounting systems and economic dogmas in the Lombard bankers' tradition. Here is the standpoint, from which to understand the urgency, as posed by the presently looming threat of a new, global dark age, of subjecting modern accounting practice to the standpoint consistent with the founding of the modern sovereign nation-state.

There are the customary, so-called "factual" ways in which the issue, so located, could be argued, differently than I do here; but, those other ways are, at their best, only plausible, merely academic in character, not scientifically conclusive. To understand a problem of such a profoundly paradoxical character, a paradox of this depth and historical magnitude, we must establish the relevant, validatable universal principle at stake, and draw our conclusions on the basis of the validation of that principle, rather than what are worth, relatively, little more than debater's points.

To that point, let us now summarize the immediately relevant argument made, cumulatively, thus far in this report. Let us define the issue, respecting the two opposing views of human nature, as the respective, absolute incompatibility of the *oligarchical* and *cognitive* standpoints.

The oligarch's practice implicitly defines his subjects as to be

Adam Smith, the East India Company's propagandist for free trade, epitomized the view of mankind as a beast, which underlies the oligarchical method of "cost-accounting" today. (Photo: Library of Congress, Prints and Photographs Division)

treated, appropriately, as human cattle, as Wall Street's current policies of practice respecting HMOs, Social Security, population control, and so forth, do. Thus, that financier views those victims as if they were merely beasts, and his conduct toward such targets, reflects an implicitly adopted, beastly nature of his own. This is the pervasive axiomatic feature of the Code of Diocletian, for example. This is the axiomatic characteristic of Quesnay's doctrine of *laissez-faire*, for example, and of the related "free trade" dogma of Lord Shelburne's lackey Adam Smith. To treat man as a beast, or a lackey, is to be a beast to mankind, to a victim who may respond, from time to time, like his master's lackey, like those poor Yahoos, the Lockean Confederacy's poor whites, fighting, and willing to die, like hordes of medieval flagellants, like the pathetic hordes of Rome's *vox populi,* to destroy civilization, all in a bestial way.

That signifies that the oligarch is self-obliged to view the management of human cattle, as he does those other cattle whom he, similarly, uses, milks, breeds, and culls, according to his anticipated profit and pleasure. He wishes to limit the freedom of action, including breeding, of human chattels, to confine the chattel's behavior to those dimensions of action which prohibit the chattels from acting independently of their assigned roles as human cattle. He desires to inculcate in them a propensity for predetermined, fixed ranges of behavior, as the Code of Diocletian does.

They may be trained to pass standard qualifying examinations in universities, but not to actually think. Were the human cattle to show the insolence to introduce unauthorized forms of principled changes in man's relations to nature, the oligarch would slaughter them as unsuitable cattle. Cognitive impulses exhibited among the chattels, would constitute a threat to the existing oligarchical system. Since the oligarchs themselves are men or women, like their victims, the oligarch must also define the limits of freedom for action of his own behavior similarly: even his status, as among the privileged relative few, must not upset his own prescribed system of relations to nature and to his human cattle.

Were the oligarch to regard human beings as categorically defined by cognitive qualities of individual and pair-wise behavior, he would cease to be an oligarch. When any among us evokes the innate nature, the unique power of the human species, the cognitive potential for discovering and applying validatable new universal principles, the principle of change, comes into play. In that case, the use of Lombard styles in double-entry bookkeeping, immediately go out the window respecting the shaping of economic policies and their forecast consequences. Instead of projecting a fanciful future from the misunderstood past, as the foolish, failed Lombard bankers did, the point of reference must shift axiomatically: any present decision, *or lack of decision,* must be judged by its knowable future outcome, as cognitive reason permits us to know this.

Accounting then shifts *axiomatically,* to emphasize non-linear methods of forecasting the consequences of both axiomatic changes in behavior, or the effects of a lack of such change. Such an axiomatic shift immediately obliges a corresponding shift, to emphasis upon the non-linearity of shaping present choices of performance, to the standpoint of non-linear causal (functional) connections of looking from a relevant point in the future, backward to the present. Thus, the mind of the competent policy-shaper, must dwell in the realm of the simultaneity of eternity, in the domain of Plato's philosopher-king.

Under the ruinous conditions in which our nation, and the world at large, find themselves, after nearly thirty foolish years of a floating-exchange-rate monetary system, the only hope for mankind is a science-driver, crash-program approach to effecting general, physical-economic recovery of our ruined economies. Under such an urgently required approach, we may continue to use presently institutionalized methods of financial accounting for the simplest routinely administrative aspects of business and related practice, but we should not place much belief in such medieval traditions. Under the required forced-draft conditions, of successive non-linear changes, all accounting practice pertaining to functional assessment of cost and forecasting, must proceed on an entirely different basis, a non-linear basis. Let the accountants keep their books. Policy-making must focus on the verbs, not the mere nouns.

The problem has not been merely, that we continue to use medieval methods, those of double-entry bookkeeping, for accounting. The problem is not that such methods are used, still; the problem is, that such archaic administrative practices are worshipped as a fetish, as a guide to misjudging real-world performance of real-life, physical economies. It is implicitly anal fetishism respecting the financial accountant's so-called "bottom line," which has been the great folly of recent economic policies.

Economics and the new cost accounting must be practiced, not as a branch of bookkeeping, but as a branch of physical science. John von Neumann's and Norbert Wiener's childish play with "connect the dots" is to be expunged from the system.

The transformations expressed in the relation between man and physical processes at the point of production, are intrinsically non-linear processes, whose characteristics must be examined from the standpoint of the recognizable principles involved, and measured according to the same state of mind as the scientist and machine-tool specialist crafting and conducting a "crucial" experimental test of physical principle. This approach to the point of production considered in the small, must be the benchmark for understanding the larger process in which these typical qualities of transformations occur.

Getting a revolutionary model of aircraft, or a space exploration into operation, should be recognized, as in former, better times, as a product of that approach I have just illustrated. Those scientists, engineers, machine-tool specialists, and so on, who should set the standard of competence by their work at the frontiers of technology, so, should be adopted as a mark of excellence to be emulated at all levels of design of products and production processes. There is nothing incomprehensibly mysterious about the proper meaning of "non-linearity;" it is practically and clearly expressed by such examples from the frontiers of technology. The point is to cause that same standard to become operative in forecasting the results of changes in designs of productive processes, at all levels in the society. By increasing the relative emphasis on science-driver crash-program strategies and tactics on the frontier of scientific and related physical-economic practice, we school the nation, and the world, to think in ways which correspond to the universally intrinsic non-linearity of reality.

This means, to increase significantly, and increasingly, the ratios of the total labor-force represented by the science and machine-tool-development categories of employment. It means that, in this way, we must escape from the recent three decades of folly, of descent into the virtual serfdom of a cheap-labor, "outsourcing" and "benchmarking" enshackled economy. It means to move upward, at an accelerating rate, to the higher standard of employment and quality of production, to an economy driven chiefly by scientific crash-program efforts, always pushing back the physical-scientific frontiers of existing human knowledge and practice.

Capital, Real and Fictitious

The essential difference between a sovereign nation-state and a financier-rentier-dominated form of feudal, or pro-feudalist—e.g., financier-oligarchical—society, is expressed, typically, as the difference between *national banking* and *central banking*. In the latter, it is assumed that some primeval hoard of money, which squinty-eyed ideologues of that persuasion insist, must never exceed the amount of specie in banks; in other cases, such as today's merchant banking circles, or the current management of the private-banker-controlled U.S. Federal Reserve System, it is specified, that some like-spirited, other expression of the inhering wisdom and munificence of the merchant-banker usurers, must reign. As specified by U.S. Treasury Secretary and patriot Alexander Hamilton, in any actually sovereign nation-state republic, as under the U.S. Federal Constitution, only the national state itself has the ultimate authority to create money, that against the sovereign credit of the nation-state itself.

Notably, one of the best, if relatively short-lived features of the post-war Bretton Woods system launched by President Franklin Roosevelt, was the notion of using a gold-reserve system, in tandem with relative fixed parities among currencies, to establish the conditions under which the economies of the U.S.A. and Europe could come to prosper through large-scale extensions of credit at low borrowing costs. This provision, facilitated by the U.S. Marshall Plan, and Germany's matching Kreditanstalt für Wiederaufbau, enabled us to build up war-ruined Europe to the advantage of maintaining a large and growing market for U.S. goods, thus effecting the U.S. growth of prosperity during the span of the first two decades following the end of the war.

It should be remembered, in studying the roots of the gold-reserve function under the original Bretton Woods system, that the first step in that direction had been taken by that same President Roosevelt early in his Presidency, in clearing away the post-1931 vestiges of the ruinous, oligarchical, British-dominated, gold standard system.

The 1945–1971 U.S. dollar was not based on gold specie, but on a current balance in trade and financial-credit accounts, in which the pledge of gold bullion reserve at a fixed price supplemented payments of U.S. current-account obligations which were made chiefly in U.S. commodity exports. The principle was, that gold bullion is a produced commodity, which has a natural price of production like any other produced commodity; thus, a stable exchange-rate could be managed in terms of, chiefly, trade-balances plus marginal pledges of gold bullion transfer.

The same approach must be revived in response to the presently onrushing disintegration of the world's present financial and monetary system, if the world is sane. The 1945–1958 precedents under the old Bretton Woods system, must be returned, otherwise a global chain-reaction plunge into a decades-long new dark age is now imminently inevitable for virtually the entirety of the planet.

Many important things could be said on this subject of two opposing types of money-systems. On this occasion, the leading points to be made, are two.

First, that without the emergence of the sovereign nation-state during the late Fifteenth Century, the level of world population and standard of living would never have risen significantly above those of the period of European feudalism. The corollary of that is, that the return to a globalized "free trade" system, would necessarily cause a collapse of the world's population and conditions of life to approximately those, or worse, of Europe's Fourteenth Century. It is the measures of state-directed large-scale, long-term investments in basic economic infrastructure, and in protectionist measures designed to promote state-protected programs of technological progress and other improvements of the real incomes (as distinct from merely nominal, money incomes) of all of the population, which made possible every general improvement in the human condition which has occurred during the recent half-millennium.

It is precisely, the intentional, and vicious elimination of such protectionist measures, peculiar to the modern sovereign nation-state institution, which have brought the world as a whole to the now-catastrophic, rapidly worsening, global financial and physical-economic state of affairs today.

The placing of the world under the control of private banking interests, would quickly doom civilization for perhaps decades to come.

Second, it is the use of the sovereign nation-state's monopoly on the creation of credit, which is the key monetary and credit mechanism by means of which sustained high rates of increase of the potential relative population-density of nations is accomplished. Under the contrary, so-called "free trade" policies, growth in one nation, or one sector of a population, can be sustained, and that only temporarily, by looting other populations and natural resources. The British Empire and Commonwealth are prime examples of this implication of "free trade." Under what is recognized as Adam Smith's so-called "free trade" doctrine, England's policy toward itself was almost savagely protectionist; "free trade" was enforced only to the purpose of looting other nations.

Now, examine these matters from the standpoint of the preceding discussions here. How does the nation-state's sovereign monopoly on the issuance of money as credit, bear upon the most appropriate methods of using the future to invest in the improvement of the present?

In the world, there are always resources and labor, which are idle, or idled. The money presently in circulation, or in money deposits, may be often insufficient to effect the utilization of available reserve margins of labor and other resources for production. The prudent state, in such circumstances, will adopt the intention to muster such idle resources, chiefly to the net effect of accelerating technological progress in some categories which will yield the greatest future net benefit, per capita and per square kilometer, to the nation or humanity in general.

The additional employment of the labor-force required for this purpose, must be paid, of course. More precisely, the family households of that portion of the labor-force must be supported. There exist machinery, materials, and so forth, which might be newly produced and purchased from existing or expanded capacities, to effect the desired net increase in the employed amount and percentile of the entire labor force available. If the

Franklin Delano Roosevelt's programs of employing otherwise-idle labor in major infrastructure projects demonstrated a competent grasp of how governments should utilize credit for the general welfare of the population. (Photo: National Archives)

relevant wage and capital goods can be mustered, then effecting that investment in growth, becomes predominantly a matter of combined will and money. The unrivalled degree of success of Germany's Kreditanstalt für Wiederaufbau, in utilizing Marshall Plan credit, typifies the effectiveness of such methods.

In short, to such ends, money can be issued against the sovereign credit of the nation-state. In a crisis such as the presently onrushing one, one emphasizes the drastically reorganized credit of the nation-state and its associated banking system. This summarizes the general idea of the business, in net effect. Some of the special features to be considered for such action, should be mentioned here.

In the case of Franklin Roosevelt's "New Deal," much of the initial emphasis was on employing otherwise idled portions of the labor-force for maintenance and development of basic economic infrastructure. Looking backward from World War II, to the anti-unemployment measures of the 1930s, the most conspicuous implication of the Roosevelt employment-creation measures of the 1930s, was that we would not have been able to mobilize for that war as we did, but for the included role of major infrastructure programs, such as the Tennessee Valley Authority, the net benefits of the PWA and WPA generally, and the Rural Electrification effort.

Roosevelt's first challenge, was to overcome the ruinous effects of the dilly-dallying under President Herbert Hoover's Andrew Mellon-dominated administration. The 1929 crash occurred just under four years prior to Roosevelt's March 1933 inauguration. The worst of the 1929–1933 period under Hoover hit in tandem with the September 1931 crisis of the British pound sterling. The accumulated damage of the 1929–1933, pre-Roosevelt interval, and earlier effects such as the agricultural crisis and collapse of the railway boom during the mid-1920s, bequeathed to the incoming President a greatly damaged nation, an acute and worsening, social crisis, and a wrecked economy.

Entire communities around the nation were dying as communities. The most urgent thing, then, as will be the case when the onrushing financial collapse soon hits hard into the present upper twenty-percentile of family-income brackets, was, and will be the collapse of local economy and its tax-revenue throughout large chunks of the nation. The first priority was to get members of the labor-force back to work, by any means possible, to ensure the stability of those localities. The quickest remedy available to the combined governmental resources at the Federal, state, and local level, was, and will be, to get people employed again, as many and as quickly as possible, as we will face that same problem, with great force, as the presently onrushing global financial crisis hits the planet, soon. The generally available possibility for such urgently wanted, quick remedial action, was in the area of repair and development of basic economic infrastructure.

Otherwise, as we might show by study of the effects upon the U.S. economy, by the accelerating investment in basic economic infrastructure, until the late 1960s, and in the spectacular contributions to the increased wealth of the national economy from the Kennedy Manned Moon Landing effort, infrastructure-building and maintenance are not only among the most appropriate areas for direct economic action by various levels of government, they, in and of themselves, especially in emergency circumstances, are great physical-economic as well as financial stimulants to the recovery and growth of local and national economy.

Looking at Twentieth-Century history of the U.S. economy, there were three outstanding factors behind the highest rates of economic recovery and net growth during that century. The first, was, despite President Teddy Roosevelt's efforts to ruin the power of entrepreneurial forces of industry, the impact of what had been launched as the Edison-centered electrification, especially the role of electric power delivered to the individual workplace, which has been one of the greatest stimulants for the growth in national wealth and the productive powers and income of labor during the past hundred years. The second, was the U.S. 1914–1917 mobilization for backing the British monarchy's orchestration of World War I. This was the model immediately referenced by President Franklin Roosevelt for a more expanded version of such a military build-up, beginning about 1936, for oncoming World War II. The third was the combined effect of the two leading crash programs in technology of the past fifty years, nuclear power and space exploration.

There is a precedent for those three factors, in 1792–1794 France. One of the world's greatest scientific and military minds of that period, France's Lazare Carnot, taking command of French forces generally considered to be virtually pre-doomed to defeat by combined invading armies, not only succeeded in crushing all of the invading armies, over the interval 1792–1794, but, together with his collaborator Gaspard Monge, launched a science-driven military revolution in methods of warfare, mobilizing every branch of physical science, and launching the greatest scientific institution of that period, the Monge-directed Ecole Polytechnique. Another case, is that of the crash-program achievements of so-called "Gulag science" under Josef Stalin;

*A successful pathway to economic development for the generations
ahead, will require long-term investment in more and more energy-dense
technologies, per capita and per square kilometer. Nuclear power is
typical of the first generation of this kind of technology. (Photo: North
Anna Power Station, Richmond, Virginia)*

that is a notable case, but of special features, and complexities,
to be discussed in a different location.

War is otherwise terribly wasteful, and protracted warfare,
such as that conducted by the U.S. in Indo-China, is inherently
ruinous. However, one must look at the lessons from crash-
science-driver military programs with a cool mind's eye. The
military expenditure is unquestionably wasteful, by and large;
but, we must not delude ourselves that crash programs mustered
for wars are also wasteful in and of themselves.

The working point is, that a nation at war can be mobilized
to do what it should have done anyway, but finds the will to
undertake such beneficial efforts only when the passions and
circumstances of warfare arouse the passions of the nation's
institutions and population. Would that those passions had been
aroused to muster the same kind of "crash program" for ordinary

economic and related circumstances. Cool the mind's eye, so, and think about that in that more clear-headed way.

The practical side of the paradox I have just summarized so, is the role of the individual citizen's sense of personal identity, as I have reviewed this point earlier. It is usually only when a people are aware they face a situation in which the possibility of being able to live depends upon willingness to pay the price of death for that, that the typical modern individual person rises above the customary narrowness, lack of foresightedness, and general pettiness of his passions, and develops a sense of highly motivated concern for problems which seem to affect someone else, especially in such distant places as the next town or neighborhood. Ordinarily, as today, the mind of the typical citizen is extremely small in the breadth, depth, and forward reach of its active concerns. How often does one recall hearing onself, or someone else say words to the effect, "If we could do that under wartime conditions, why can't we do it now?" For many veterans of World War II, "the war" was, thus, the big moment in their lives thereafter.

Nonetheless, the world is now being confronted by an onrushing financial catastrophe, and accompanying related catastrophes, whose effects will be as bad as those of any war, and may even include some major wars and kindred expressions of mass homicide. Under such conditions, if leadership is visible which can play the part which President Franklin Roosevelt contributed, the onrush of the looming crisis will awaken many sleeping souls from their customary, entertainment-ridden torpor. Under such circumstances, the kinds of emergency mobilizations, including science-driver forms of crash programs, are not unlikely prospects for the near future. Under such circumstances, these measures can no longer be passed off as "pie in the sky;" they are the only cookable edible to be found in the oven.

The trick of the matter in such cases, is to define a destination to be reached in the future, to find the connection to that from a starting-point in the present, and to move forward with determination, measuring everything in terms of the progress toward that destination which now governs one's choices of action. When that logic is applied to use of the sovereign nation-state's potential authority to create and deploy its sovereign credit for such missions, wonderful things may result, including happy recoveries from even such financial catastrophes as those which loom immediately before us all today.

As a matter of caution, also note the following.

The issue of credit, whether as credit as such, or credit in the form of loan of money, is a form of *financial capital,* as distinct from *physical* capital. If that credit is taken for making a purchase of goods or services invested into an operation, the capital can be viewed as a capitalization in the ordinary sense. However, there is another kind of activity also sometimes treated as capital, *fictitious capital.* Consider the following example, which be sufficient to make the relevant working point.

Suppose you are a landlord in possession of a rental property. For how much would you sell another party the right to take that entire annual rent payment? Or, for the more general case of this type: what is the going price paid for buying up the right to collect some ongoing financial income-stream. In the typical cases of this general type, the price of sale of an income stream will be some multiple of the anticipated actual, or merely speculated monthly or annual amount of that income. The price of the sale of that income-stream now goes on the account of the buyer as a financial asset, an asset listed at many times the current rate of actual payments on the account that income-stream. A financial capital gain on the holding of a stock, or even a side-bet on a market index of some kind, is also market-able (among some people) as an income-stream, even for a stock, for example, which may have paid no dividend recently!

Fictitious financial capital of this type is to an economy what cancer is to a living body. It should be simply outlawed, for the sake of the general welfare.

Thus, when we speak of capital, even financial capital, under the headings addressed here, we should recognize that we are restricting the use of such terms among us, to those of the type indicated, or otherwise implied by the summary description supplied here. The notions associated with financial capital, should be associated, thereafter, with what functions as physical capital, as advanced expenditures which are used-up in the unfolding of a process leading to an intended physical-economic event or condition to be reached at some time in the future. Accordingly, we should think of capital so defined, as typically at the least, as something which, speaking functionally, the present borrows from the future. We now turn to an exemplary case of such relationships, under the rubric of basic economic infrastructure.

Basic Economic Infrastructure

We turn now, briefly, to interpolate certain general, qualifying observations on what is to follow. These remarks include definitions, bearing upon indispensable elements of cost, which would be required, to be put before any audience considering non-linear approaches to world and national economic development. However, it is urgent to address, at least implicitly, the dangerous delusions which have crept into popular, professional, and official opinion through the corrupting influence of current lust for wildly exuberant forms, and scope of "privatization."

The term, "basic economic infrastructure," may be fairly restated as, "activities which, by their nature, ought to be chiefly functions relegated to the economic functions of government." Sometimes, they are quite rightly farmed out to private entrepreneurs, as state-regulated public utilities. These are distinct from military arsenals, which might fall, sometimes, to functions of national, or private enterprises, and, in other cases should not.[86]

---

86. I personally, prefer a state-run basic arsenal capability, complemented by private production, to either an entirely state-run industry, or an essentially privatized endeavor. The responsibilities of the state, to assure itself that what is necessary must be done, require the existence of a state-controlled arsenal system for any well-run government, through which military contracts may be assigned to qualified existing entrepreneurships. The way in which the original, March 1983 SDI proposal was turned into, predominantly, a farce, at the mercy of the cupidities of today's species of shareholder value, is a case in point. In any case, the control of the quality of the deployed product should be among the duties and authorities of assigned professional senior military officers who have a keen interest in the outcome.

The analogy for the function of "hard" infrastructure generally, is modern agriculture, in which, often, previously most unsuitable land-areas are transformed into fertile tracts under water management and kindred arrangements.

Infrastructure falls under two broad categories. The first, which might be distinguished as "hard" infrastructure, emphasizes the development and maintenance of rural, urban, and other areas as such; the second, which may be distinguished as "soft" infrastructure, emphasizes social and related systems, needed for the protection and development of the health, cognitive, governmental, and related requirements of the entire population, or large categories of that population. In other words, "infrastructure" signifies, broadly, things which must be done on behalf of entire regions, or sectors of the population, whether or not any simply entrepreneurial profit should, or might be decently extractable from such activities.

"Hard infrastructure" includes the development and maintenance of the needed functional quality of sea and land areas, and now includes the similar, expanding responsibilities within the Earth's atmosphere, and into the Solar system beyond. It prepares and maintains such areas, providing conditions suited to the level of existing and prospective cognitive potentials of the population and its activities. Power, water management, area land management, transportation, and sanitation, are typical. All such development and maintenance have in common, the provision of the environmental conditions needed to support the living conditions and activities of the population in general. "Hard" urban infrastructure, is a leading sub-classification of such activities.

As I have also emphasized earlier, here and in other published locations, the growing awareness, among the scientifically literate, that space exploration is an urgent mission, not merely an option, has impelled some among us to think of life on Earth itself in a new way. More among us, especially in government, should. This means a new way of defining what the term "infrastructure" ought to signify. For related reasons, the continued progress of science and technology requires space-exploration, as an integral part of the science-driver activities on which we shall depend, increasingly, for maintaining the growth of per-capita physical productivity on Earth itself. As the example given earlier, illustrates this point, space-exploration requires massive development of a supporting infrastructure for this activity in space, and also back here on the surface.

There is also something which is far more urgent than that, if in the longer term.

In the longer term, human life on Earth is threatened by many causes which have their basis in the Solar system (and beyond), rather than merely processes controlled within the bounds of the Earth-ball itself. The repeating cycle of glaciation, and the catastrophic flooding attending the recurring melts, are the results of cycles inhering in the Solar system, not local conditions internal to the Earth. Meteorite bombardments, can suddenly destroy any existing human life on large portions of the planet. The Sun has cycles which also pose dangers to our planet, including long-range ones. These and other recurring or potential catastrophes, are generated within the Solar system (or beyond), and are not controllable within the bounds of the Earth's surface. Some of these potentially catastrophic, Solar-system events, such as the presently oncoming new Ice Age, are approximately pre-calculable, the next one due to be seriously felt a few thousand years ahead; that cycle is not "environmental," but a product of the long cycles in the Solar system itself. Some other catastrophes are more distant. We must think ahead, to discover how we can better understand, and control the relevant mechanisms.

The probable date of certain known threats from other factors, have yet to be forecasted as needed. Our science has much to learn in the intervening times, discoveries needed to prepare to overcome such variously known or possible threats.

In any case, reaching outward in astrophysics, ever-deeper into microphysics, and assault upon the mysteries of the physical basis or correlatives for living and cognitive processes, are the key indicators of the scientific and technological progress on which the successful continuation of human life on Earth depends.

These considerations intrude into the policy-shaping thinking among the literate and sane. We think thus of the challenge of Earth-forming the Earth itself: making deserts and tundras habitable, for example. We think of Earth-forming the travel from Earth's surface into geostationary orbit, of industrialization of the Moon, of virtually regular traffic between Earth- and Mars-orbit. We think of managing increasing portions of the Solar system, all as part of building the necessary supporting infrastructure for mankind's life here on Earth.

Science, the father of technological progress, makes two general types of direct contributions to the economy on Earth. First, as I have addressed this earlier in this report, it is assigned to rid us of false, even dangerous, but popularized axiomatic assumptions. Otherwise, it pushes back the frontiers, as in astrophysics, microphysics, the science of living processes as such, and, as prompted by the challenge of mastering senile dementia generally, uncovering the physical-process substrate needed to support cognitive activity. By no accident, space exploration brings all of these frontiers into a common task-oriented mission-focus.

Therefore, should there be a sane future for mankind, at this juncture, science so viewed, will become increasingly situated in relationship to space-exploration and its needed supporting infrastructure. It is from this phase of activity, that the sources of new technologies will pour onto the Earth's surface, and increasingly so. Thus, the division of labor in production as a whole, will reflect increasingly larger portions of total employment in science and science-driven machine-tool and related design; the thinking of everyone on Earth will tend, more and more, to view the world around us in those terms of reference, will meet the problems to be addressed, here on Earth, more and more, in those terms of reference.

In summary of the foregoing point. Respecting "hard" infrastructure, we must think of it as subsumed under the general notion of "terra-forming our planet," of making this planet as we find it, a more suitable habitat for human life as we are able to foresee the future requirements of human life from standpoints more or less accessible to us today. Or, to restate that same point, imagine that we are to adopt a future goal of "terra-forming" some object, such as the moon Titan. What would we wish to build into Titan's transformed atmosphere, etc., to make that moon a suitable habitat? Take those criteria, and look at Earth itself from that standpoint: think of a principle governing the development and maintenance of "hard" infrastructure on Earth, as a policy of "terra-forming" the Earth, in this, or a similar sense.

Such is the general nature of the emerging, broader definition of infrastructure today.

On Earth itself, we shall need, constantly, more and more energy-density, and also energy-flux density, per capita and per square kilometer of the Earth's surface. We shall consume more water, similarly, and must have the reprocessing capabilities to make this manageable. We must increase the tonnage of movement per mile/kilometer second. We must improve the conditions of life by increasing urban population-density, but must also increase living area and privacy at the same time. We must build environments adapted to the nature of human beings, for such included purposes as a pleasant walk, of perhaps an hour or so, in a conveniently neighboring park-area. Yet, in all this, we must not deprive the inhabitant of his or her necessary sense of place. We need a leisurely walk in the urban park, but ready, rapid access to a distant seashore and mountainside. And so on. We need the increased per capita productivity which makes the fulfillment of such requirements generally available.

We must develop the infrastructure needed for realizing the goals of rising productivity, that in a way which coheres with the development of the Classical-humanist character of the person and social relations.

The proper object of economy, is the production of a certain quality of individual human personality, and social relations to match. We increase productivity, not out of greed, but because we are human. We must improve living on this planet, and the portions of the Solar system in which we shall deploy during the foreseeable century or so to come, as a region we must bring, more and more, into conformity with the principle of promoting mankind's general welfare.

In the meantime, production is the fruit of the infrastructural development of the land-area and its inhabitants. Infra-

structure is, immediately, the responsibility of the sovereign nation-state, the only agency which, by its nature and design, could
provide the basis for the levels of productivity which we require
for the coming century and more of life on and near Earth.
Beyond that, the development of the infrastructure of both the
planet and nearby regions of space, is the common goal and
responsibility of the cooperating sovereign nation-states of this
planet. It is, for all aspects of human physical-economic activity,
the successor to the notion of the development of wild or wasted
land-areas for a future rich harvest from agriculture.

To define the national and multi-national goals, as project-
goals, for the nation's and nations' infrastructural undertakings
of the coming half-century, and longer, we must proceed from
a commitment to continually revised, broad, but well-grounded
estimates of the requirements of production and life will be,
for no less than a half-century ahead. This supplies a needed
perspective to shape the nation's and nations' periodically updated sense of the principal economic responsibilities of sovereign nation-state government, that over the generations ahead.

The necessary changes in cost, which must be allowed to
accommodate such needed improvements, represent part of the
need for a continually rising capital-intensity in all aspects of
economy, public and private. We must therefore increase the
productive powers of labor accordingly.

Capital Factors

The, unfortunately, widely popularized notions of state-
versus-"free enterprise," among today's "free trade" fanatics,
such as the Mont Pelerin Society's ideologues, represent more
of an infantile fantasy, than a debatable form of rational opinion.
As a reading of the writing of Friedrich von Hayek attests, his
views on the subject of "freedom" are recognizably a product
of the same Conservative Revolution which, among its variants,
supplied us the syphilitic rantings of Friedrich Nietzsche, gave
the world the utopian imperial fantasies of such representatives
of the lower feudal aristocracy's family Romantic traditions, as
the Emperor Napoleon Bonaparte, and unleashed upon history

dictators such as Mussolini and Hitler. *Conservative Revolution-aire* von Hayek's perverted notion of "freedom," is that of a real-life "Miniver Cheevy," of an unreconstructed fanatic, dreaming of returning to a past which never existed, but which he and his lot seek in a fantastic utopia, seeking there the kind of "freedom" otherwise desired by a would-be slave-master of the lost Confederacy. His notion of freedom is, in practice, one of freedom from the influence of such institutions as the U.S. Declaration of Independence and Preamble of the Federal Constitution.

In short: "This is my money, and I should be allowed perfectly licentious liberty to do more or less as I please, wherever and whenever I choose, with all of that money, gained in whatever manner I happened to prefer, with virtually no interference from government." Feudal ideologue François Quesnay said as much; von Hayek, for all his fantasies, is certainly not to be classed as an original thinker. If anyone wished to suggest that I have exaggerated in making that point, he or she has neither read von Hayek's eulogies to Mandeville, nor gathered any relevant knowledge of related developments within modern European history.

Like the morbid rantings of England's John Ruskin on the subject of the kind of pre-Raphaelite utopia, in practice, von Hayek yearned for, the kind of neo-feudalist utopia which he, and such followers as Bernard Shaw, the Webbs, H.G. Wells, and Bertrand Russell, espoused over the course of approximately the last century and a half to date, are, intrinsically, as Wells and Russell insisted, anti-capitalist conceptions. It is ironically suitable, that his most celebrated political dupe, former Prime Minister Margaret Thatcher, the green-grocer's daughter, proceeded with unblemished imbecility on all of the practical sides of a modern form of agriculture and industry, and in evidence of that, we have today the resulting, hideous ruin of the United Kingdom's economy, under her ministry, to show for it.

Not only were von Hayek's ideological effusions objectionable; they have, to this day, no correspondence to a successfully functioning modern capitalist economy. That is what is so terribly dangerous about his followers; mentally, they are not in the real world, but they insist, all the more strenuously, in bringing the world into conformity with their utopian delusions, in a Marat-Sade world, in which the inmates have taken over the asylum. He must be, for some among his foolish admirers, an apostle of "freedom;" in fact, any effort actually to impose his ideology, can have only one kind of practical outcome: fascism.

In fact, the principle of true "freedom" is that implicit in **Genesis** 1:26–30, as I have defined cognition and its implications, once again, in this report. It is from that vantage-point, that the essential function, and legitimacy of private entrepreneurship is defined, both historically, and otherwise. The principle of a modern entrepreneurial form of society, is the same expressed as the principle of scientific progress: the principle that those innovations which yield revolutionary progress in the general welfare, are the fruit of overturning previously established mind-sets.

The model of the American entrepreneur, is supplied by the cases of persons such as Thomas Edison, and such as those followers of Philadelphia's Alexander Dallas Bache who enabled Edison to succeed globally, over the enraged objections of the **New York Times,** and of the London and Wall Street rentier-oligarchy generally. But for entrepreneurs such as Thomas Edison, the world would not have had the electric light-bulb and a host of other improvements in the life and productivity of national economies which he, explicitly, set into motion, not only in the U.S.A., but from New York, from Germany, and along Mendeleyev's trans-Siberian railroad. Indeed the model of the modern capitalist industrial entrepreneur is the Benjamin Franklin who launched the industrialization of mid-Eighteenth-Century England, and sent Scotsman James Watt to France, to learn from scientists such as Lavoisier, how to develop a steam-engine. After all, the Alexander Dallas Bache whose organization made Thomas Edison possible, was the great-grandson of the same Benjamin Franklin who supervised the crafting of our Declaration of Independence and Constitution.

Indeed, the direct origin of the U.S. model of law governing entrepreneurship was in the England of Henry VII and such followers as Thomas Gresham, composer John Bull, and playwrights of statecraft as Christopher Marlowe, and William

Shakespeare. This model grew out of the awarding of monopolies (i.e. royal patents) for a term, to authors of a useful invention and their backers, the model upon which the U.S. Patent Office used to operate, before the craziness, such as trying to patent *my genome,* which set in a quarter-century or so ago. The notion of the granting of such corporate and related privileges of ownership, was prompted by the overturning of those medieval craft-guild-monopolies derived, as by-blows, from the Roman Code of Diocletian. That change was a product of the same principle known by such rubrics as the principle of the commonwealth, or general welfare, as introduced into government under France's King Louis XI and under the ensuing establishment of the new form of monarchy, in Henry VII's England.

The legitimate, and necessary function of the private entrepreneurship, is to promote the development and sale of useful inventions, i.e., new technologies, which will be of benefit to the general welfare. By awarding that specific form of state-created private monopoly, the state created the preconditions for the investment of financial capital into the development and proliferation of useful inventions.

This is, of course, in contradiction to the recent decades' trends in behavior among what are, today, predominantly, Wall Street-controlled corporate parasites. The difference is demonstrated in U.S. history, by the fight between patriots such as Jay Cooke and the Wall Street crowd. It was demonstrated in the war which entrepreneurship more or less lost, with the inauguration of Wall Street's own "trust-busting" predator, Teddy Roosevelt, as U.S. President. It was a war expressed by the role of Wall Street's Martin van Buren, in installing his virtual puppet, Andrew Jackson, as President, and guiding Jackson to ruin the credit of the U.S., by disbanding the Second Bank of the United States, and installing the outright scam, Wall Street's Land Bank scheme, which, modelled after the John Law-style financial bubbles of early Eighteenth-Century England and France, virtually bankrupted the U.S. in the inevitably resulting Panic of 1837. It was the issue in which Aaron Burr's killing of Alexander Hamilton had been situated. Aaron Burr, an agent of the head of the British Foreign office, Jeremy Bentham, had established a swindle known as the Bank of Manhattan, using fraudulent pretexts; Hamilton opposed that swindle, but Burr's killing of Hamilton killed the political opposition, and thus enabled the Burr-Bentham looting of upstate New York to succeed. That latter battle continues today.

The same lessons are to be adduced from tracing the post-1876 history of the industrial development of Germany, as that is illustrated by the close collaboration between the backers of Edison and Henry Ford, successors of Philadelphia's Alexander Dallas Bache, who worked with the Rathenau and Siemens family to replicate the successes of the Lincoln-Carey-led American industrial revolution in Germany, Russia, Japan, and elsewhere. In studying the history of modern corporate and related forms of ownership, one must always recognize the crucial distinction between the power to create new dimensions of useful wealth, and the power, such as that of the contemporary junk-bond bandits, to conduct legalized theft.

The relationship among the functions of the republic, of a sovereign nation-state, private entrepreneurship, and economic forecasting, is best illustrated by the role of the building of the transcontinental railroads, which provided the key basis, in infrastructure-building, for the U.S.'s rapid rise to world supremacy in agro-industrial nation-state economy, the model admired and copied in Germany, Russia, Japan, and elsewhere, over the 1861–1876 period of the Lincoln-Carey economic revolution. The writings of Benjamin Franklin followers such as Alexander Hamilton, the Careys, and the German-American Friedrich List, show us a fully conscious, deliberate conception of the way this result of the 1861–1876 enterprise would benefit the nation.

What I have done in my discoveries and related work in this field, is to render more explicit, more coherent, the conceptions of those, beginning with the founder of modern economic science, Gottfried Leibniz, who have preceded me in this field. I say, with those predecessors, the included function of the state is to foster and protect the true entrepreneur, and to protect both them, and the general welfare, from the kinds of predators presently typified by the Wall Street bandits, the financial houses and their associated law firms, which have reigned and ruined in the

U.S.A., virtually unchallenged since about the time President John F. Kennedy was assassinated.

The essence of economic forecasting, and related policy-shaping, is to foresee the probable advantage to the general welfare, by the government's regulatory measures, and development of infrastructure, to the effect of fostering the indispensable function of scientific-progress-oriented entrepreneurship. Government must provide the basic economic, hard and social infrastructure; increasingly capital-intensive entrepreneurship must realize the potential in the opportunities which only government's regulatory role can provide. Then, if one understands the relationship between the fostering of cognitive development and the effects of scientific progress, effective and reasonably reliable, long-range economic forecasting becomes feasible.

What Are Productive Costs?

Thus far, we have developed the notion, step by step, that productive costs are everything which is essential to ensure the regeneration of the existing productive powers of tomorrow's labor on a higher, more advanced, net level, superior to that today. This includes not only the physical well-being of the entire population and its posterity, but also the fostering of those circumstances of life, in the family household, and beyond, which are essential to raising the level of the cognitive development of the population as a whole.

Consequently, we argued, the action of production, the *verb* of the economy, is twofoldly non-linear. The cognitive development of the individual mind, by means of which the act of production is controlled, is intrinsically non-linear. The physical processes of production and design of product, express physical transformations, transformations which are physically non-linear. Productivity is therefore expressed as the interaction of these two combined types of non-linear transformations. Hence, I have stipulated, economic processes can be described by science only as the kind of multiply-connected manifold known as the LaRouche-Riemann model. Exactly how the practical man is to understand the principle of non-linearity itself, I shall clarify here soon. In the interim, we must first clarify some crucial points respecting the proper approach to determination of cost and price.

The implicit recognition of that fact, provided the basis for the emergence of the modern form of sovereign nation-state economy, and for the inherently protectionist economic policies of any sane form of practiced national economy. The following notable, consequent points of policy must be emphasized at this point.

Stated most simply, the price must usually exceed the properly determined cost of production and distribution. This must reflect costs which the private enterprise does not always recognize as its included responsibility, such as the future level of education, health, and so forth of the population as a whole, and the maintenance and ongoing improvement of the quality of "hard" infrastructure, which is an integral cost of the environment on which the particular private enterprise depends absolutely.

For example, the production of the labor-force to appear approximately a quarter-century from now, is a cost which must be paid, without compensating income, over that intervening period. The improvement of the cognitive and related development of those entrants, must be considered part of the currently incurred cost of production.

In a similar way, the capital outlays which must be paid, by government, or others, today, to produce the improvements which today's private enterprises, and society generally will enjoy and use years ahead, are currently incurred costs of all currently produced wealth.

Accordingly, the largest portion of the incurred costs reflected in the individual private enterprise are paid directly, not by that enterprise itself, but by government or other institutions apart from that enterprise. How, then, shall those incurred costs be paid?

In part, the answer is: through taxation. Yet, there are also other ways this has been managed by sound government in the past. The general names for those alternatives, are *protectionist* and other *regulatory* measures. These latter are the kinds of measures which, as matters of general policy, should be made by the consent of the governed, and therefore should be applied generally only through the actions and mediation of government. These are measures of precisely that type which the U.S. government, seized by some economic-suicidal passion, has been uprooting and destroying, since the fateful decision of mid-August 1971, a rape of reason itself, unleashed with full force by the Trilateral Commission and the Carter Administration, the which that body created and controlled throughout those years. Now, that rampage of economic lunacy has come near to all the way, to the measures of so-called "globalization" which have carried the entire planet presently to the brink of a global new dark age, and to the immediate, accompanying obliteration of the institutions of the sovereign nation-state. We are racing back to barbarism, barely pausing to linger amid a reversion to feudalism, all the way back, it often appears, to perhaps Sodom and Gomorrah. The inmates have, indeed, taken over the asylum!

The function of protectionism, is to set prices at *indicative, "fair trade"* levels, which allow for covering the calculably incurred cost *to the entire national economy,* of providing a type of good produced through private entrepreneurship. This is done by three mechanisms. The first, is protective tariffs, bearing on imports and exports. The second is internal, governmentally established and enforced regulation, most emphatically in the domain of essential categories of basic economic infrastructure, such as power, water management, public transportation, and so on. The third is the protectionist and regulatory impact of taxation policies, such as the investment-tax-credit policy adopted by the administration of President John F. Kennedy, or the shaping of the graduated income-tax, as a way of acknowledging the preferential chartacter of the expressed national interest, in the general welfare of family households and private enterprises.

The included purpose of these three kinds of measures, is to cause the burden of cost to fall where it must.

Thus, the combination of such approaches to fair trade, tariffs, regulation, banking, and taxation, the power which should be granted only to government, is shaped in application.

The effect of such measures, is to present each individual enterprise, public undertaking, and family household, with an honest reflection of the totality of actually incurred costs of maintaining the general welfare and progress of the nation as a whole. This implies, of course, the elementary responsibility of government to know what it is doing by such measures, and also of the consequences of the failure to enact such means, properly and efficiently.

The result of such exercises in reasonable forethought, is what memory of France's Fifth Republic under Charles de Gaulle calls to mind as "indicative planning," an enterprise which rescued France from looming ruin at that time, and which served France very well over the course of the two decades and longer following.

Since the future condition of a nation will be shaped by the capital factors inhering in today's choices of such policies, if we are sane people, we give considerable forethought to such decisions, rather than letting them simply happen irrationally, in some helter-skelter fashion. This obliges the nation, and its government, to adopt a mission-orientation, as typified by the brilliant success, for as long as it was continued, of the Kennedy Manned Moon Landing mission.

Thus, and only thus, can the true costs of anything be competently defined. The comprehension of the implications of such a national mission, as an orientation of policy-shaping for a decade or so ahead, provides the basis for determining, with fair approximation, the direction of evolution of true costs over a considerable period ahead. That determination, in turn, serves as a guide to corresponding elements of the policy-shaping activities of the corresponding elements of a responsible form of government.

Freedom is never to be used as a synonym for anarchy, for a Romantic or outrightly existentialist I-do-it-because-I-feel-like-doing-it kind of the mass lunacy popularized among much of what became today's thirty-five-to-fifty-five generation. Freedom is cognition; freedom is the provision of the circumstances in which the individual powers of cognition, and their expression, are fostered in their development, to flourish for the sake of the happiness of each and all of the people.

Planetary and Economic Orbits

How can the future state of a national economy be forecasted over the longer range of capital cycles? For an insight into that, it were best to compare the implications of such forecasting with the most important of the modern discoveries in astrophysics, which is to say the successive contributions of Johannes Kepler and Carl Gauss. One common, usually overlooked feature of the Kepler-Gauss connection, is crucial for the subject-matter of this report.

The point to be made, thus, is clearly set forth, for astrophysics, in the relevant contributions of Kepler and Gauss, but, with their currently characteristic regard for honesty, most of the relevant textbooks and institutions prefer to pretend that discovery of Kepler, as validated by Gauss, never existed.

Kepler demonstrated, as a central feature of his founding of the first comprehensive approach to a mathematical physics, that the axiomatic structure of the Solar system as a whole, predetermined the locations and characteristics of the orbits of the planetary bodies associated with that Sun. This is in contrast, and opposition to the notion of individual orbits as determined by some universal principle of "action at a distance." It is a stunning irony, that in that work, Kepler specified a necessary such orbit, of determinable harmonic-orbitable characteristics, assignable to a missing planet lying between Mars and Jupiter. Kepler insisted that such a planet must have existed, but indicated the grounds on which its disruption had been virtually inevitable. Approximately two centuries later, Gauss, in showing that the motions of a briefly observed body corresponded to a planet-like orbit of that body, also determined that that body's orbital pathway coincided with the characteristics of the missing planet.

Kepler was right: the circles of Newton and his devotees, were wrong. The mistake of the Newtonians was not in a calculation; it was a fundamental error respecting the way the universe a whole is, in the language of Plato's *Timaeus, composed.* The same point, respecting lawfulness, is to be applied to long-range economic forecasting. This same matter provides the most direct means by which the practical man can come to understand the applicable significance of the term *non-linear,* as applied to physical-economic processes.

To sum up the immediately relevant features of Kepler's argument, we have now the following.

Return to the discussion of anti-Euclidean geometry, in the second chapter of this report. Situate the specific kind of anti-Euclidean geometry required for economic science, in respect to my elaboration of the axiomatic implications of a LaRouche-Riemann model.

Kepler's determination of the way in which available planetary orbits are ordered within the Solar system as a whole, was derived from defining the axiomatic characteristics of the subject-matter of his experimental approach. Therein lies the secret for his success, where the astronomy of Claudius Ptolemy, Copernicus, and Tycho Brahe had essentially failed. For Kepler, the laws of motion were determined by the physical-space-time geometry of the Solar system, a geometry which is expressed by a set of axioms, in the sense that Leibniz defined a principle of universal least action, and of monadology, and in which Gauss and Riemann, following Leibniz in this, successively defined the anti-Euclidean geometries of multiply-connected manifolds.

The connection to be made is clarified by studying and thinking about the way in which Kepler writes, and rewrites his several principal works. His method is not that of the textbook, but rather of the Socratic dialogue. It is the method, as Albert Einstein reflected on his affinities to both Riemann and Kepler later, of anti-Euclidean geometry, of letting paradoxical evidence lead one to successively new discoveries of validatable universal principles.

If, in economic matters, we look at forecasting from the standpoint of a science of physical-economy, rather than financial accounting, and, if we understand that the consequences of human decision-making are predetermined, axiomatically, by the combination of known and implied axiomatic assumptions which rule our behavior, the result is to define the available trajectory of the consequences of our decision-making accordingly. Thus, with one important exception to this, we define the orbital trajectory of an unfolding economic process as Kepler conceived of defining, experimentally, the lawful determination of a set of planetary orbits. The difference is, we can change the axioms, as Kepler's solar system could not.

That, of course, is what the preceding chapters and pages of this report have been, from the beginning, all about. By smoking out what may have been the hidden axiomatic assumptions of our decision-making, we are able to see the way in which those assumptions, like Hamlet's, are leading us to bring about our own doom, even contrary to any other willful desire which may seize us. In allowing those assumptions to rule our wills, we thus choose a fate from which we will not be able to escape. Such is the first level of long-range forecasting.

However, as the greatest Classical tragedians have done, we are capable of rising above the grip of a fixed set of axiomatic assumptions, if we but first recognize them to exist in that way. We then foresee the tragedy which must unfold from adhering to such follies. Aha! But, to see this, is to prompt the will to free ourselves from it! That is true long-range forecasting, in economics, in cost-accounting, and anything else which the cognitive powers of the individual human mind may care to see.

5. A Global 'Monroe Doctrine'

From before its beginning, the fundamental interest of the United States, its true "manifest destiny," has been, as Lafayette and others recognized, to be a temple of liberty and beacon of hope for all mankind. The same point was restated, although in a negative way, in a written communication to President James Monroe, by then Secretary of State John Quincy Adams. In this memorandum, Adams warned the President the United States must flatly reject the British Foreign Office's proposal of a treaty agreement, respecting the Americas, between London and Washington. His argument was, that between the financier-oligarchy represented by the British monarchy and the republic of these

United States, no community of principle could exist, for as long as the United Kingdom remained the form of state it was.

During the same general period, Adams broke openly with the incurably corrupted Federalist party, to emerge as a key figure in a great collaboration among Mathew Carey, Henry C. Carey, and, in the course of time, the Abraham Lincoln who would lose a string of elections, to supersede a pack of virtual or outright traitors, van Buren, Polk, Pierce, and Buchanan, to become our greatest President since George Washington. The victory of the U.S. over the British puppet called the Confederacy, and the emergence of the U.S. as the world's leading national economy, over the 1861–1876 interval, gave more substantial meaning, throughout this planet, to the role of the U.S. as a leader among nations, in building up what would become, hopefully, the establishing of control over the world by a community of republican principle among perfectly sovereign nation-states.

The time for realization of that latter goal, is now become somewhat overripe.

We are presently gripped by the maelstrom-phase of the greatest threat to civilization since the Roman Empire. The present world financial and monetary system, is irrevocably doomed, to early obliteration, in one way or another.

To find a quick alternative to that prospective hecatomb, we require a sudden, brief meeting among a group of leading and other nations representing the majority of humanity today. The leading nations include a western and other parts of Europe centered on the still-barely viable economy of Germany, Russia, China, India, Japan, and the United States. The purpose of such a meeting must be to put hands together on the sword, both to avow the present world financial and monetary system to be irremediably bankrupt, and to instantly launch a new world monetary system, premised upon the proven best features of the pre-1959 Bretton Woods system. This time, the system must be restored as President Franklin Roosevelt had intended, with the former victims of colonialism equal partners in directing the system.

Otherwise, without such agreement, the effort will not be a viable one. Hence, all geopoliticians, as typified by Sir Caspar

Weinberger, Zbigniew Brzezinski, and their like, together with their bloody machinations, must be securely retired to places from which they could do no more harm. We must have the relevant hands together, on the sword, or none of us shall escape the ruin now coming down upon the world.

The assembly of those to put their hands to that sword, will have no time to waste, when the moment for action strikes. Like the sudden Washington, D.C. meeting of March 1, 1968, called by President Lyndon Johnson, the gathering must be sudden, and the fateful decision prompt; but this time, it must also be the right one.

Once that fateful deed is done, we must proceed to build the road we have thus chosen to travel.

This means to cancel extant agreements to all forms of "globalization." It means to return to absolute defense of the principle of the perfectly sovereign nation-state. It means the adoption, as overriding emergency agreement, of a return to protectionist quality of monetary and trade and tariff agreements, akin to those in place during the pre-1959 period, but to the acknowledged mutual advantage of the partners to this new community of principle.

It also means a mission-orientation, which means, in turn, the resumption of the high-technology export function by states which had formerly represented that capability, to the benefit of states whose general welfare demands large and growing infusions of access to the relevant most modern technologies, that they might thus develop their basic economic infrastructure, and accelerate the growth of the productive powers of labor of all their people. This must be a mission of not less than a generation in projected duration, a mission facilitated by low-cost long-term credit, to ensure the needed flow of advanced technology into the nations which urgently need this form of cooperation.

This means an end to the kinds of cheap-labor and dumping policies which have ruined the world under the conditions of "free trade" and "globalization." It means that the pressure to export cheap products, produced by cheap labor, shall be brought to a halt, and that quality products produced by labor-forces whose productive powers are being increased through capital improvements, will become the new, long-term basis for world trade.

That signifies, inside the U.S. economy itself, a massive retooling of agriculture, industry, and basic economic infrastructure, to reflect the new world realities being brought into being. It means a revolution in education, suited to the export-role which the U.S., in particular, must play in world trade during the coming generation. It means a return to forced-draft technological progress, and high rates of real-capital formation per capita.

Past performance of nations, operating under the influence of such kinds of policies, assures us that if we learn now from such precedents, we shall come to do very well—all of us participating in such an emerging new community of principle.

APPENDIX

Ad Hoc Committee for A New Bretton Woods

The following call, to form an Ad Hoc Committee for a New Bretton Woods global financial system in support of the proposals of Lyndon H. LaRouche, Jr., was initiated on April 7, 2000.

THE GOVERNMENTS OF THE G–7 nations, have repeatedly demonstrated their unwillingness and inability to prevent the threatened collapse of the global financial system, through a prompt and thorough reorganization of the system. This renders it urgently necessary that all those who recognize the devastating consequences of a systemic financial crisis, raise their voices.

We, the signators, refer to Lyndon LaRouche as the economist, worldwide, who has analyzed the causes of the systemic crisis in greatest depth, and over the longest time, and who, at the same time, has elaborated a comprehensive package of measures to be taken to overcome it: the anti-crisis program for a New Bretton Woods.

We, the signators, take note of the recent initiative of members of the European Parliament, which states:

THE EUROPEAN PARLIAMENT:

- WHEREAS the 1944 agreement of Bretton Woods mechanisms contributed to the realization of monetary stability and to postwar economic reconstruction;

- WHEREAS a divergence was created between the real economy and the financial economy after the decoupling of the dollar from the gold reserve system;

- WHEREAS financial crises have exploded in different parts of the world since 1997;

- WHEREAS the international monetary and financial institutions have malfunctioned, failing to carry out their tasks;

- WHEREAS it has been ascertained that the "speculative bubble" has had devastating effects for the economies of the developing countries, transforming completely the structures of the world economy, and reaching the level of at least $300 trillion, compared to a world GDP of about $40 trillion;

INVITES THE EUROPEAN COMMISSION:

a) To propose the convocation of a new Conference, similar to the one at Bretton Woods, with the purpose of creating a new international monetary system, capable of gradually eliminating the mechanisms which led to the "speculative bubble";

b) To evaluate the possibility of anchoring the currency values to a real reference point, and to exert more effective control over exchange rates;

c) To propose the creation of new credit lines oriented to develop investments in the real economy and to define infrastructure projects of continental dimensions.

The most dangerous absurdity of the present situation is underlined by the fact that the so-called "New Economy" is being celebrated by the White House in the USA and by government leaders of the European Union, as a great success, at the very same moment that the financial bubble, blown up with this myth, is bursting! Far from advancing growth and development of the world economy, so-called "globalization" has in reality shown itself to be a form of unbridled predator capitalism, which has exacerbated the divergence between financial titles and real economy on the one hand, and rich and poor, on the other, in an intolerable manner—both on the national and the international plane.

Considering the increasingly accelerating systemic crisis, we, the signators, have decided to constitute the Ad Hoc Committee for a New Bretton Woods.

(What follows is a selection of signers of the above statement. Affiliations are for identification purposes only.)

UNITED STATES

FORMER U.S. CONGRESSMEN

Sen. Eugene McCarthy, former Presidential candidate, Minnesota
Rep. Clair A. Callan, Nebraska
Rep. Father Robert J. Cornell, Wisconsin
Rep. Mervyn Dymally, former Chair, Congressional Black Caucus, California
Rep. Walter Fauntroy, President, National Black Leadership Roundtable, Washington, D.C.
Rep. Cornelius Gallagher, New Jersey

STATE LEGISLATORS

Endorsed by the entire Alabama House of Representatives, as well as by the following individually:

Rep. William Clark, Pritchard, Alabama
Rep. Johnny Ford, Tuskegee, Alabama
Rep. Andrew Hayden, Uniontown, Alabama
Rep. Tommy Houston, Birmingham, Alabama
Rep. Thomas Jackson, Thomasville, Alabama
Rep. John J. Letson, Moulton, Alabama
Rep. Bryant Melton, Tuscaloosa, Alabama
Rep. Demetrius Newton, House Speaker Pro-Tem, Birmingham, Alabama
Rep. George Perdue, Birmingham, Alabama
Rep. John Rogers, Birmingham, Alabama
Rep. James Thomas, Selma, Alabama
Rep. Gerald Willis, Piedmont, Alabama
Rep. Dennis Williams, Wilmington, Delaware
Rep. Michael Kahakina, Honolulu, Hawaii
Rep. Howard Kenner, Chicago, Illinois

Rep. Coy Pugh, Chicago, Illinois
Sen. Walter Blevins, Jr., Senate President Pro-Tem, West Liberty,
  Kentucky
Sen. Dan Seum, Louisville, Kentucky
Rep. Perry Clark, Louisville, Kentucky
Rep. Charles Hoffman, Georgetown, Kentucky
Rep. Art Morrell, New Orleans, Louisiana
Del. Clarence Davis, Baltimore, Maryland
Rep. Ed Vaughn, Detroit, Michigan
Rep. Earle Banks, Jackson, Mississippi
Rep. Erik Fleming, Jackson, Mississippi
Rep. Melinda Curls, Kansas City, Missouri
Rep. Charles Quincy Troupe, St. Louis, Missouri
Sen. Joe Neal, Chair, Nevada Legislative Black Caucus, Las Vegas,
  Nevada
Rep. Derek Owen, Hopkinton, New Hampshire
Rep. David A. Welch, Kingston, New Hampshire
Sen. Carlos Cisneros, Questa, New Mexico
Rep. Ray Begaye, Shiprock, New Mexico
Rep. Fred Luna, Los Lunas, New Mexico
Rep. Roger Madalena, Jemez Pueblo, New Mexico
Sen. Luther Jordan, Wilmington, North Carolina
Rep. Howard Hunter, Conway, North Carolina
Rep. Vernon Sykes, Akron, Ohio
Sen. Vincent Hughes, Philadelphia, Pennsylvania
Rep. Harold James, Philadelphia, Pennsylvania
Rep. William Robinson, Pittsburgh, Pennsylvania
Sen. Maggie Wallace Glover, Florence, South Carolina
Rep. Walter Lloyd, Watersboro, South Carolina
Sen. Jerry Shoener, Rapid City, South Dakota
Sen. John Ford, Memphis, Tennessee
Rep. Jerry Kreitzer, Rutland, Vermont

CIVIL RIGHTS AND HUMAN RIGHTS LEADERS

Rev. Nimrod Reynolds, Nat'l. Sec., Southern Christian Leadership
  Conference (SCLC), Anniston, Alabama
Amelia Boynton Robinson, Civil Rights activist, Tuskegee Institute,
  Alabama
Hunter Huang, Chair, National Association for China's
  Reunification, Washington, D.C.

Cesar Flores, Project Coordinator, State Economic Opportunities
Division, Hawaii

Bernard Broussard, Co-Founder, Louisiana Human Relations
Council, Franklin, Louisiana

TRADE UNION LEADERS

James Barnett, President, NW Alabama CBTU (Coalition of Black
Trade Unions); Chair, Martin Luther King Annual March,
Florence, Alabama

Bill Dickens, President, United Container and Rail Haulers of
America, Baltimore, Maryland

Melvin Muhammad, former State Chair, NAPE/AFSCME (Nebraska
Association of Public Employees), Omaha, Nebraska

Carlton Horner, former National Organizing Director, United Auto
Workers (UAW), Broken Arrow, Oklahoma

RELIGIOUS LEADERS

M.R. Thomas J. Gumbleton, Roman Catholic Auxiliary Bishop of
Detroit, Michigan

M.R. Juergen Bless, German Evangelical Lutheran Bishop, California

The Rev. J.E. Bridges, President, Eastside Ministers Union of
Southern California, Los Angeles, California

The Rev. Antanas V. Bitinas, M.S., Th.D., Pontifical Lithuanian
University of Rome (Italy), Connecticut

The Rev. Richard T. McSorley, S.J., Director, Center for Peace
Studies, Georgetown University, Washington, D.C.

Minister Abdul Alim Muhammad, Minister of Health and Human
Services and National Spokesman for the Nation of Islam,
Washington, D.C.

The Rev. Carl Washington, President, Baltimore Baptist Ministers
Conference, Baltimore, Maryland

Syed Ahsani, Texas Chair, American Muslim Association, Arlington,
Texas

The Rev. Martha Knight, Director, Social Action Committee, State
AME Conference, Virginia

CANADA

Benoit Laprise, Member, National Assembly of Quebec

Claude Pinard, Member, National Assembly of Quebec

Chor-Bishop Elias El Hayek, Montreal

Bishop Raynauld Rouleau, Roman Catholic Diocese of Churchill-Hudson Bay

Gilles Grondin, President, Campaign Quebec-Vie, Montreal

EUROPE

ARMENIA

Haik Babookhanian, Member of Parliament, Yerevan

Hrant Khachatrian, Member of Parliament, Yerevan

AUSTRIA

Prof. Dr. Hans R. Klecatsky, former Minister of Justice of the Republic of Austria; University Professor, Innsbruck

Prof. Dipl.-Ing. Jakob Christian Neyer, Deputy, State Parliament, Vorarlberg, Egg

Dr. Hans Koechler, President, International Progress Organization, Vienna

BOSNIA-HERCEGOVINA

Rusmir Mahmutcehajic, International Forum Bosnia, Sarajevo

Prof. Dr.Sc. Fahrudin Sebic, Faculty of Economics, University of Sarajevo

Prof. Dragoljub Stojanov, Faculty of Economics, University of Sarajevo

CROATIA

Antun Abramovic, Professor of History and Sociology; former Member of Parliament (1990–92)

Prof. Dr. Antonije Djukic, University of Dubrovnik

Niko Gunjina, Hrvatska Udruga Sindikata (HUS—Croatian Federation of Trade Unions), Zagreb

Prof. Dr. Branko Horvat, Institute for Advanced Studies, Zagreb

Faris Nanic, General Secretary, SDA Party, Zagreb

Ilija Rkman, Board Member, Croatian Christian Democratic Union (HKDU), Zagreb

Branko Stancic, President, Senate of HKDU (Croatian Christian Democratic Union), Rijeka

Dr. Marko Veselica, President, HKDU, Zagreb

CZECH REPUBLIC

KSCM (Communist Party of Bohemia and Moravia) Parliamentary Group in National Chamber of Deputies

Josef Dolejsi, Ph.D., Kladno
Stanislav Fischer, Ph.D., Member of Parliament
Prof. Dr. Jiri Vackar, Czech Technical University; Czech Christian
   Academy, Prague
Dr. Bedrich Vymetalik, Attorney-at-Law, Frydek-Mistek
Marcel Winter, Director of WMC (Winter Management and
   Consulting), Prague

DENMARK

Prof. Dr. Charles Akinde, former State Legislator in Ondo State,
   Nigeria, Brondby Strand
Joseph Bangurambona, former Burundi Ambassador in Kenya,
   Hedehuene
Fritz Hermann, President, United Farm Organization (LFO), Karup
Leon Ngarukiye, former Director of Cabinet, Ministry of Foreign
   Affairs of Rwanda
Laurent Niyongeko, former CEO for Development Bank of Burundi,
   Copenhagen
Erling Svendsen, President, Danish Grain Producers Association,
   Hvelsoe

ENGLAND

Dr. Mostafa Al Barzagan, *Al Arab International,* London

FRANCE

Andre Gerin, Deputy, National Assembly; Mayor, Venissieux
   (Department of Rhone)
Jean Royer, former Deputy, National Assembly, Mayor, Tours
Jean-Jacques Bilcaz, Mayor, St. Pierre d'Allevard
Louis Dejean, Mayor, Corbreuse
Etienne de Ravinel, Mayor, Nossoncourt
Marcel Georges, Mayor, Bonnecourt
Noubar Kechichian, Deputy Mayor, Valence

GEORGIA

Prof. Vakhtang Goguadze, former Speaker, Georgian Parliament;
   Member, International Coordinating Bureau, Peoples Patriotic
   Forces of CIS, Tbilisi
Dr. Teimuraz Dokvadze, Expert in Computer Sciences
Dr. Vladimir Kilasonya, Economist, Tbilisi

GERMANY

Robert Becker, Publisher, Eschau

Prof. Peter Graebner, President, House of Environment, Construction and Traffic, Dresden

Prof. Wilhelm Hankel, Economist; former State Secretary in the Finance Ministry

Dr. Bruno Huegel, Academic Director, Eichstaett University

Gisela Krieg, Chancellor, Technische Fachhochschule (THF), Berlin

Helmut Knebel, Member of State Parliament of Lower Saxony, Salzgitter

Dr. Hermann Schneider, Professor of Physics, Heidelberg

Prof. Dr. Ing. P. Guenther Werner, Technology Advisor, Kerpen

HOLLAND

Y. Zhang, Chinese Christian Democratic Union, Almelo

HUNGARY

Andor Mandoki, Chair, Expert Committee, Christian Democratic People's Party, Budapest

Istvan Morvay, former State Secretary, Interior Ministry

Prof. Imre Pozsgay, St. Laszlo Academy, Budapest

ITALY

Rosario Alessandrello, Industrial Manager, Milan

Giuseppe Bidese, Industrialist; Board Member, Financial Committee, Association of Middle-Sized Industry of Vicenza

Sergio Bindi, Journalist; Spokesman, Partito Democratico Cristiano, Rome

Aldo Brandirali, City Council Member (Forza Italia), Milan

Paolo Caoduro, former President, Immobiliare Fierae, Vicenza

Dr. Quintino de Notariis, Nuclear Physicist; President, ASPE (Association of European Political Studies) of Alleanza Nazionale, Termoli

Pietro Giubilo, former Mayor, Rome; National Council Member, CCD Party (Centro Cristiano Democratico), Rome

Sergio Sabelli, State's Attorney, Rome

Alberto Servidio, former President, Cassa del Mezzogiorno, Rome

Roberto Tengg, Industrialist; Vice President, Italian Federation of Wood Traders, Cremona

LUXEMBURG

Bernard Zamaron, Centre Robert Schumann pour l'Europe (Robert Schumann Center for Europe)

POLAND

Sen. Jozef Fraczek, Chair, Senate Committee on Agriculture
Janina Kraus, Member of Parliament (Sejm) (KPN-OP)
(Confederation for the Independent Poland-Patriotic Camp),
Warsaw
Prof. Aleksander Legatowicz, Economics Professor and former
Member of Parliament
Jerzy Oledzki, former Vice Minister of Education (1992–93)
Prof. Aleksander Krzyminski, former Vice Minister of Foreign
Affairs (after 1990)
Prof. Pawel Bozyk, SGH (Warsaw School of Economics), Warsaw
Bishop Antoni Dydycz, Drohiczyn
Dr. Marek Gruchelski, Economist, Advisor of the Trade Union
Solidarity for individual farmers, Warsaw

RUSSIA

A.A. Chudin, Scientist, Institute of Management, Moscow
C.V. Gulyajev, Scientist, Institute of Management, Moscow
A.G. Makarov, Scientist, Institute of General Physics, Moscow
Prof. Stanislav Menschikov, Central Mathematical Economics
Institute (CEMI), Russian Academy of Sciences, Moscow
Prof. Grigorii G. Pirogov, Senior Scientist, Institute for Comparative
Political Studies, Russian Academy of Sciences, Moscow
A.A. Samochin, Scientist, Institute of General Physics, Russian
Academy of Sciences, Moscow
Prof. A. Shelepin, Institute of Physics (FIAN), Russian Academy of
Sciences, Moscow
Prof. Nodar A. Simoniya, Deputy Director, Institute for World
Economy and International Relations (IMEMO), Russian
Academy of Sciences, Moscow

SCOTLAND

Alan Clayton, Convener, Council Liaison Committee, Scottish
National Party Argyll and Bute
Prof. John Erickson, Professor of Defense Studies, Edinburgh
University

SLOVAKIA

Prof. Dr. Michal Drobny, Member of Parliament, Bratislava
Laszlo Hoka, Member of Parliament, Bratislava
Prof. Dr. Augustin Marian Huska, Member of Parliament, Bratislava

SPAIN

Kuan Chu, Chair, Chinese Christian Democratic Union, Madrid
Gen. (ret.) Emilio Garcia Conde Cenal, former Chief of the Spanish
    Air Force, Four-Star General, Madrid
Rosa Maria Romero, Economist, Spain

UKRAINE

Ljudmyla Bzuglaja, Member of Parliament
Natalia Lymar, Member of Parliament, Kiev
Volodymyr Marchenko, Member of Parliament, Kiev
Petro Romanchuk, Member of Parliament, Kiev
Mykhailo Sadovchuk, Member of Parliament, Kiev
Natalia Vitrenko, former Presidential candidate; Member of
    Parliament, Kiev
Prof. Dr. Viktor Fedosov, Chief, Department of Finance, Kiev
    Economic University
Svitlana Kurkartseva, General Director, Joint Ukrainian-Russian
    Ventures "Stankomplekt," Kiev
Prof. Dr. Viktor S. Naidyonov, Scientific Consultant, Dikom
    Investment Company, Kiev
Mykola D. Rudenko, Writer, dissident, and human rights activist;
    author, "The Energy of Progress: Essays on Physical Economy";
    Honorary Chair, Sergei Podolinsky Science and Technology
    Center, Kiev
Prof. Dr. Petro O. Stepanenko, Doctor of Economic Sciences, Kiev
    Economic University
Dr. Volodymyr Shevchuk, Economist, Trade Economic University,
    Kiev
Prof. Dr. Vasyl Stolyarov, Institute of Finances, Kiev
Dr. Borys Svetlov, Dean, Faculty of Studies, Kiev
Prof. Dr. Mykola M. Yermashenko, Section Chief for Finance and
    Credit, Staff of the Ukrainian National Security and Defense
    Council, Kiev

IBERO-AMERICA

ELECTED/GOVERNMENT OFFICIALS

Jose Lopez Portillo, former President of Mexico
Julio C. Gonzalez, former Secretary of State, Argentina
German Winox Berraondo, former Trustee, National Development
    Bank, Argentina

Dr. Anuart Jarma, former Deputy Secretary for Budget and Treasury, Argentina

Hector Claudio Salvi, former Governor, Province of Santa Fe, Argentina

Franciso Dontaf, Deputy, Brasilia State Parliament, Brazil

Jorge Carrillo, former Minister of Labor, Colombia

Sen. Amylkar David Acosta, Member of Congress, Colombia

Rep. Dr. Humberto Carrillo Torres, Member of Congress, Colombia

Pastor Garcia Marin, Mayor, Santa Rosa, Bolivar, Colombia

Elsa Valbuena Otiz, Member, City Council of Bogota, Colombia

Cong. Rafael Mendez, Member, Chamber of Deputies, Congress of the Dominican Republic

Dr. Jorge Yeara Nasser, former Ambassador of the Dominican Republic; President, Domimican-Arab Association, Santo Domingo, Dominican Republic

Aldo Bugarin, former State Legislator, Jalisco, Mexico

Prof. Alfredo Gomez Gomez, former Member, Chamber of Deputies, Congress of Mexico, Jalisco, Mexico

Antonio Chavez M., former Member, Chamber of Deputies, Congress of Mexico; Sec. Gen., Local 252, Union of Workers of the Bottling Industry of Coca Cola, Guanajuato, Mexico

Lic. Juan Jaime Hernandez, former Member, Chamber of Deputies, Congress of Mexico, Jalisco, Mexico

Rep. Roger Caceres Velasquez, Member of Congress, Peru

AFRICA

Sam Aluko, Professor of Economics; former Chair, National Economics Intelligence Committee of Nigeria (1994–1999)

Lawrence Fejokwu, Editor-in-Chief, *Nusa International,* Lagos, Nigeria

Jean Gahururu, Economist, on behalf of the RDR (Rally for the Return of Refugees and Democracy in Rwanda)

P.R. Malavi, Speaker/Legislator, Provincial Legislature, Northern Province, South Africa

MIDDLE EAST and ASIA

Mark Faber, Investment Advisor, Hong Kong, SAR, PRC

K.R. Ganesh, former Indian Union Minister of Finance, New Delhi, India

Meilono Soewondu, Member of Parliament, Republic of Indonesia

Nasser Motameeh, former Deputy Minister of Foreign Affairs, Iran, Burbank, California

Akira Nambara, former Executive Director, Bank of Japan (central bank), Tokyo

Dr. Masaki Shiratori, former Japanese Executive Director for the World Bank, Tokyo, Japan

Laith Shubeilat, former Member of Parliament, Jordan

Dr. Gongpil Choi, Chief Economist, Korea Institute of Finance, Seoul, Korea

Dr. Wonchang Jang, Senior Economist, Korea Institute of Finance, Seoul, Korea

Dr. Yunjong Wang, Director, International Macroeconomics and Finance, Korea Institute for International Economic Policy (KIEP), Seoul, Korea

Professor Khurshid Ahmad, Chair, Institute of Policy Studies; former Federal Minister; Deputy Chair, Planning Commission, Government of Pakistan; Chair, Senate Standing Committee on Finance and Economy, Islamabad, Pakistan

Dr. Ahmed Al-Kedidi, Professor, University of Qatar

Dr. Mete Gundogan, Turkish Virtue Party, Economic Advisor to former Prime Minister Necmettin Erbakan, Turkey

AUSTRALIA

ELECTED OFFICIALS

The Hon. Jim Cairns, former Deputy Prime Minister (1974–75); former Treasurer (1974–75); former Minister for Overseas Trade (1972–74)

The Hon. Clyde Cameron, former Federal Minister for Labour (1972–74) and Minister for Works in Whitlam Government

The Hon. R.C. Katter, Federal Member of Parliament for the Electorate of Kennedy

Tom Helm, Member, Legislative Council (Western Australia State Parliament), Mining & Pastoral Region

Robert Mitchell, Shadow Minister for Mines and Energy; Member of Queensland State Parliament for the Electorate of Charters Towers

TRADE UNION LEADERS

Adrian Bennett, Secretary, Municipal Employees Union (MEU), W.A.; Chair, Curtin Labor Alliance, W.A.; Federal Member of Parliament for Swan, 1969–75

Les Crofton, Secretary, Rail, Tram and Bus Union (RTBU),
    Queensland
W.J. Game, State Secretary, Engineering & Electrical Division,
    Communications, Electrical & Plumbing Union (CEPU), W.A.
Ken Griggs, Branch Secretary, United Firefighters Union of Australia
    (Australian Government Branch)
Anthony Papaconstuntinos, former Deputy National Secretary,
    Maritime Union of Australia

About the Author

LYNDON H. LAROUCHE, JR. emerged, over the course of the 1970s and 1980s, to rank among the most controversial international political figures of his time. This controversy, which also features such related issues as his efforts to destroy the international drug traffic and his initiating role in formulating what President Ronald Reagan announced on March 23, 1983 as the "Strategic Defense Initiative (SDI)," is principally rooted not just in domestic U.S. issues, but also in global political-economic considerations.

The recent, fresh demonstration of his exceptional qualifications as a long-range economic forecaster, has placed LaRouche at the center of the presently erupting global systemic crisis of the world's economy. Thus, the relevant resumé is that which helps to situate his career in terms of his actual and prospective role in dealing with that present global crisis.

LaRouche as an Economist

Both Lyndon LaRouche's standing as an internationally known economist, and his exceptional successes as a long-range forecaster, are the outgrowths of his original discoveries of physical principle, dating from a project conducted during the 1948–1952 interval. These discoveries arose out of his opposition to Bertrand Russell devotee Professor Norbert Wiener's efforts, as in the latter's 1948 *Cybernetics*, to apply so-called "information theory" to communication of ideas. As part of that same project, he also opposed Russell devotee John von Neumann's efforts to degrade real economic processes to solutions for systems of simultaneous linear inequalities.

The outcome of this project was LaRouche's introduction of axiomatically non-linear notions of individual human cognition, explicitly, to that science of physical economy which had been first established by the relevant 1671–1716 work of Gottfried Leibniz. His own work located the determining, nonlinear factor in increase of society's potential relative population-density in the relations exemplified by the role of the machine-tool principle in linking proof-of-principle experiments to the development of advanced designs of both products and productive processes.

In his subsequent search for a metrical standard for this treatment of the functional role of cognition, he adopted the Leibniz-Gauss-Riemann standpoint, as represented by Bernhard Riemann's 1852 habilitation dissertation. Hence, the employment of Riemannian conceptions to LaRouche's own discoveries became known as the LaRouche-Riemann Method.

His work is best known through his success in two long-range forecasts. The first of these was developed during 1959–1960, forecasting, that, if the axiomatic policy-shaping assumptions of the Truman and Eisenhower Presidencies persisted, the second half of the 1960s would experience a series of international financial-monetary crises, leading toward a breakdown in the existing Bretton Woods agreements: This occurred during the interval from the British sterling devaluation of November 1967 through the breakdown of the Bretton Woods agreements, on Aug. 15–16, 1971.

The second was premised upon the implications of the 1971 breakdown. He forecast, that, if the dominant powers resorted to a combination of increasingly rapacious, monetarist forms of austerity measures, the result would be, not a new cyclical crisis, but, rather, a systemic crisis, a "general breakdown crisis" of the global system. Since the October 1987 U.S. stock market crisis, and the strategic, economic, financial, and monetary decisions of the 1989–1992 interval, the existing global financial-monetary system has become locked into the presently erupting series of seismic-like shocks expressing such a global systemic, or "general breakdown crisis.

A Figure of Political Controversy

His work and activities as an economist have always inter-sected a continuing commitment, since military-service experi-ence in postwar India, to what has been often termed "a just new world economic order": the urgency of affording what have been sometimes termed "Third World nations," their full rights to perfect national sovereignty, and to access to the improvement of their educational systems and economies through employment of the most advanced science and technology. On this account, he has continued the same quarrel with the policies of the British Empire and Commonwealth which U.S. President Franklin Roo-sevelt had, on these same issues, with Britain's wartime Prime Minister, Winston Churchill.

To similar effect, he opposed the economic and related policy-matrices of the administrations of Presidents Truman and Eisenhower, and Nixon, Carter, Reagan, and Bush (most nota-bly). Today, inside U.S. domestic and foreign-economic policy, his commitment is typified by intractable opposition to the rele-vant policies of Henry A. Kissinger, of Robert Bartley's *Wall Street Journal,* and also the neo-malthusian doctrinaires gener-ally. On these issues of both U.S. domestic and foreign policies, he is aligned with the tradition of what used to be known as the "American System of political-economy," as that patriotic, anti-British tradition is typified by the policies of Benjamin Franklin, and such adversaries of the dogmas of British East India Company apologist Adam Smith as U.S. Treasury Secretary Alexander Hamilton, Philadelphia's Mathew and Henry Carey, Friedrich List, and President Abraham Lincoln. He has always supported the kinds of "dirigist" policies associated with that American System tradition, and that tradition's emphasis upon fostering investment in scientific and technological progress, and development of basic economic infrastructure, against the "free trade" and related dogmas of the Haileybury and positivist schools.

Since his studies of the 1948–1952 interval, he has always situated the deep political basis for the opposition between the two modern camps in economic policy in the struggle of those forces which find their self-interest in national economy, such as farmers, industrial entrepreneurs, and operatives, against those oligarchical financier interests which loot the national economy through mechanisms of financial and analogous forms of usury.

In a related matter, he has located the historically exceptional importance of the American Revolution and Federal Constitution in the fact, that although the ideas of the American Revolution were products of the European tradition of the Fifteenth-Century Renaissance, North America provided the relevant strategic distance from a Europe still dominated by those combinations of feudal landed aristocracy and feudal financier oligarchy which were typified by the Castlereagh-Metternich alliance at the Vienna Congress. Thus, the nation-states of Europe emerged chiefly as quasi-republican, parliamentary reforms within nations still ruled from the top by feudal oligarchies, such as the United Kingdom, rather than true republics, such as the 1789 U.S. Federal Republic.

On this account, as soon as LaRouche began to achieve some degree of political influence, first inside the U.S.A., and then abroad, he came into increasingly embittered political conflict with the financier-oligarchical strata and their lackeys, both inside the U.S.A. and internationally. In the U.S.A., these are the combination of oligarchical families formerly associated with the New England opium-traders, Manhattan bankers in the tradition of Aaron Burr, Martin van Buren, August Belmont, and J.P. Morgan, and those who cling to the tradition of Southern slave-holding.

Additionally, since 1964–1972, he has been a leading organizer of the opposition to the 1964–1972 cultural paradigm shift. On this account, he has become a leading target of bitter enmity from ideologues of such sundry New Age cults as the "rock-drug-sex counterculture, post-industrial utopianisms" generally, and "neo-malthusian" forms of anti-scientific, "environmentalist" fads.

As a result of that, he has been the target of sundry known efforts to eliminate him, even physically, by sundry official and private agencies inside the U.S.A. and abroad. This pattern is typified by a 1973 plot directed by the U.S. Federal Bureau of Investigation, as admitted in official documents subsequently released, and by a 1983–1988 U.S. official operation run under the cover of Executive Order 12333.

Campaigns for Public Office

He has campaigned repeatedly for the office of U.S. President, beginning 1976: six times for the Democratic Party's Presidential nomination. He was a candidate for that party's nomination for the year 2000. In each of the 1976, 1980, and 1984 campaigns, the leading motive was the same: the virtual inevitability of a long-term, downward slide into a global, systemic financial and monetary crisis, unless certain specific types of changes in economic, financial, monetary, and social policies were introduced. In 1988, the theme of the campaign was the imminent collapse of the Soviet system, and prospective early reunification of Germany, beginning in Eastern Europe as early as 1989. In 1992, the theme was the fact that a financial-monetary "mudslide" was already in progress, leading toward a threatened general financial-monetary collapse sometime during the course of the decade. In 1996, that the outbreak of a general, global financial-monetary systemic crisis was imminent. The premises offered for this perspective were always the same, the long-term prospect for a breakdown crisis, already forecast in the setting of the 1971 breakdown of the Bretton Woods agreements.

During each of those campaigns, the proposed remedy was always the same: a fundamental reform of the planet's economic, financial, and monetary systems, emphasizing: a) a return to the best features of the 1950s Bretton Woods system; b) the general replacement of central banking by the kind of national banking which U.S. Treasury Secretary Hamilton attributed to the U.S. Federal Constitution's implications; c) a just new world economic order as a new quality of partnership among sovereign nation-states; d) emphasis on both large-scale development of basic economic infrastructure, adequate food supplies, and fostering of growth of per-capita productivity through investment in scientific and technological progress.

During the 1976–1984 campaigns, a leading included feature, were proposals for measures of scientific and technological cooperation between the U.S.A. and U.S.S.R., to realize what Dr. Edward Teller described, in late 1982, as "the common aims of mankind." Exemplary of such proposals was the original, 1979 version of the "SDI," featured as a leading plank of the 1980 campaign for the Democratic nomination. In 1988, SDI was superseded by a program of "food for peace," premised upon the cascading economic crisis expected for Eastern Europe and the Soviet Union, beginning 1989. For 2000, the campaign just ended was intended chiefly to foster the early establishment of a "New Bretton Woods" agreement, centered around cooperation between the Presidents of the U.S.A. and China. The campaign was geared to foster the realization of that objective by the incumbent U.S. President, William Clinton. The aim was to establish a new form of global financial and monetary stability, one consistent with the principles of a just new world economic order, one established in time to prevent the presently ongoing process of financial, monetary, and economic collapse from plunging the planet, very soon, into a planetary New Dark Age.

Science and Classical Art

The central feature of all his activities, is emphasis upon those sovereign cognitive powers of the individual human mind whose functions are merely typified by validated discoveries of physical principle. Since his original discoveries of the 1948–1952 interval, he has always emphasized that the processes responsible for discovery of physical principles are identical in nature with those responsible for the composition of metaphor in great compositions in Classical forms of poetry, music, tragedy, and plastic arts. This view he acquired in rejecting Immanuel Kant's Romantic dogma for aesthetics. Accordingly, he rejects the empiricist, Cartesian, and positivist notions of both "objective science," and the separation of science from art. He treats science and art as intrinsically subjective, rather than objective, as the subjective generation of objectively validatable new principles of science, new ideas spawned as resolutions of metaphor.

These were leading considerations in his co-founding of the scientific association, the Fusion Energy Foundation, during the mid-1970s, and his support for his wife Helga Zepp LaRouche's founding of the international Club of Life and international Schiller Institute, during the 1980s. During the 1980s, he launched a project for clarifying certain crucial principles of Classical musical composition and performance, out of which one important book has been produced. He is currently working with some among his collaborators in developing improved approaches to education, based, inclusively, upon pedagogical models adduced variously from the scientific work of Classical Greek culture, Leonardo da Vinci, Johannes Kepler, Gottfried Leibniz, Carl Gauss, and Bernhard Riemann. The principle underlying this effort, is that the student must know, rather than merely learn the subject-matter, this by reenacting the original act of discovery of a principle in such a fashion that the student reexperiences the mental processes employed by the original discoverer of that principle. This is his definition of the Classical Humanist method in education.

Born: 8 September 1922, Rochester, New Hampshire, U.S.A.

Parents: Lyndon Hermyle LaRouche, Sr., native-born citizen, internationally known technological consultant to Footwear Manufacturers; Jessie Weir LaRouche, native-born citizen.

Married: December 1977, Helga Zepp LaRouche, native and citizen of Germany, specialist in Nicholas of Cusa, Friedrich Schiller; founder and director of the Schiller Institute; political figure of Germany.

Son: Daniel Vincent LaRouche, born August 1956; data-processing specialist.

Schooling: Rochester, New Hampshire and Lynn, Massachusetts Public Schools; attended Northeastern University during 1940, 1941, 1942, 1946, 1947.

Military: AUS, 1944–1946. Overseas service in India, Burma.

Professional: Management Consultant, Economist 1947–1948, 1952–1972. Founder: (1974) *Executive Intelligence Review* weekly; Co-Founder: (1975) Fusion Energy Foundation; Member: Schiller Institute.

Books: *So, You Wish To Learn All About Economics?* (1984, 1995) *The Science of Christian Economy* (1991) and many others.

Political: Candidate for U.S. Presidential nomination of Democratic Party: 1980, 1984, 1988, 1992, 1996, 2000. U.S. Presidential Candidate, U.S. Labor Party, 1976. Candidate, U.S. Representative, Virginia, 1990.

Conviction: Convicted and sentenced on conspiracy charges, December 1988 (imprisoned 1989–1994), in a political show-trial which was described (1989) by Germany law specialist Professor Friedrich A. Freiherr von der Heydte as comparable to the scandal of the case of France's Captain Alfred Dreyfus: "Everything we have been able to find out about the trial against Lyndon H. LaRouche, has been yet another painful reminder that the exploitation of the judicial system for the achievement of political ends, is unfortunately a method used repeatedly today in the West as well as the East." Testifying Sept. 2, 1994 before a Commission investigating the same case, former U.S. Attorney General Ramsey Clark described the case as representing "a broader range of deliberate cunning and systematic misconduct over a longer period of time utilizing the power of the Federal government than any other prosecution by the U.S. Government in my time or to my knowledge."

Sponsors

The publisher would like to thank the following people, whose generosity in contributing to the broad circulation of these works by Lyndon H. LaRouche, Jr., has made publication of this book possible.

Donald Adams
Anna Ahlers
Lewis J. Alary
Marjorie Alberda
Lt. Com. John P. Anamosa
Edward A. Anderson
Joe Andreis
Letitia Angelone
Gabriel Arroyo
John Bailey
Julius D. Baker
Wayne Baker
Purificacion Barron
Normand Belanger
Leah Anne Bettag &
   Jonathan Cody DeFranco
John E. Bigelow
Gene Borders
Genevieve Bork & Family
Ronald A. Bowden
Earle Briggs
Othel Brodie
Thelma Brown
Vivian Browner
Frederick A. Bucher

The Citizens of Camden, N.J.
Lillie M. Carley
John W. Cartwright
Raphael Cervera
Eva Cheesman
Huiling Chen
Charles Chresfield
Beatrice Clark
Donald & Judy Clark
Virginia Cobb
Eugenie Cory
Noel S. Cowling
Douglas T. Crawford
Perry Crawford III
Lester and Mary Louise
   Dahlberg
Anthony & Susan DeFranco
Sharon Del Principe
Michael DiMarco
Dan Dickson
Bert B. Dieter
Elmer Dobbs
Michael Dobson
Harold L. Domerude
Rodney N. Dotson MD

251

Edward J. & Julie Drouse
Dennis Dymszo
Lt. Col. (ret) Eugene E. Egan
Mary Eicher
Herman Eilers
Dorothy Elliott
Wilma Eyster
Muriel Fairchild
Richard Folks
Bernice A. Fountain
Bill Franchuk
Norma Jeanne Fredrickson
Mary Frueholz
Beryl Furner
Louise Gentry
Julia Gerland
George Gessler
Carl W. Gettig
Robert Glennon
Mildred Golden
David Goulart
David Greenspan
Betty J. Gregory
Craig Gregory
Grace Gugliotti
Valere Hache
Anne Hanse
Howland Hanson
Edgar Harder
Dalas Harris
Clara A. Harter
James Harwood
David A. Hayter
Mary Hazelbaker
Charles J. Hill
Clovis Hinton
Robert Hoare
Ken Holland

Edward J. Hondel
Charlotte Hopfstock
Mildred Houser
Marie Hughes
Lucetta Hunt
Winifred Ingram
Carol Jaklitsch
Albert Jensen
Alan D. Johns
Evelyn Johnston
John Paul Jones
Virgil A. Jordon
Edward Joshie
J. William Kaeser
Harold Kannel
Dr. William & Carol Keane
Jimmy & Martha Kibbe
Virginia M. Kimball
Alvah King
Harry Knights
Mike Kostic
Martin W. Kron
James Kummerer
Jack LaPoint
George & Josie Laurence
Robert E. Lauten
Rodney Leeb
Barbara Lett-Simmons
Charles Lieberman
Elizabeth Lindberg
Estelle Lorenz
Dorothy Love
Mildred Lynch
Grace Maltzman
Luigi Marietti
Helen G. Marois
James A. Mas
Jean Maurice Masse

Paul T. McCartney
Loretta D. McGann
Euchlich McKenna
Richard McMeekin
Allison W. Merriam, Jr.
Dale Merrick
Glen Miller
Robert L. Miller
Wanda Miller
Georgia Milner
Michael Mirand
Louise Mitchell
Fred Mocking
Julia Moore
Eddie Moore
Kevin Morgus
Laura Morland
Ray Lynn Mull
Helen Murray
Nebraska-South Dakota
   LaRouche Democrats
Joann B. Neville
Martha F. Nichols
Lawrence J. Nixon
Trela Noe
Norma Norvell
Ned & Judith Nuerge
Lillian O'Daniel
Thomas P. O'Leary
Brian O'Neill
Elizabeth & E. Allan Orem
Nellie Osband
Sigurd Overgaard
Dorothy Patras
William E. Perry
Paul H. Piña
Robert Poczulp
John Polish

Everett W. Poulter, Sr.
Lloyd Quick
Bob Rapp
Dominique Reca
Redwood Falls Chapter FDR-
   PAC
Elsie L. Reed
Olala Reinheimer
Ruby Robinson
Cora Rogers
Marty Rowland
Herman A. Rudolph
Jim Ryan
Steve Salem
William E. Samland
John Sauber
Ralph Saul
Christine Stamps Sayre
Anna Schow
Donald Schwarzkopf
Eugene Shannon
Gerte & Seamour Shavin
Don Sheffield
Roy Sheumaker
John K. Shrader DVM
Leonard & Alberta Sigurdsen
Thomas L. Simpson
Carolyn Smith
R.F. Smith
Vincent Smith
Michael W. Sperry
Josephine Stauer
Fred A. Steiner
Leo Stewart
James Straub
David Sullivan
Maryann Sullivan
Joseph J. Szela

Gerda Talesnik
Olive Thornton
Dan Tipton
Nancy Tooke
Gerald & Barbara Tuttle
Peter Umana
Richard Van Bergen
Robert H. Van Hee
Lorenzo Vasquez
John Veldman
Paul Wagner, Jr.
Merikay Warnke
Pete Warren
Marion Weber
Ty G. Weiler

Albert Welker
Edith West
John R. Wheeler
Peggy Wienholz
Irene Willette
Bill Willibey
Velna Willoughby
James Winey
Bernice Wolter
Claire Wright
Jane B. Yanulis
Ruth Young
David Yakel
Kevin & Muriel Zondervan